Contents

Tables and Figures

Tables

Figures

Box

Foreword

Health care reform appears finally to be close at hand in the United States. It has become increasingly clear to all concerned—physicians and other health care workers, patients, purchasers of health care, and those who actually pay for it—that the status quo is unacceptable. Americans have come to recognize that they are paying too much for a health care system that guarantees neither security nor access to services.

Yet all of us will express the firm belief that when the health care system is changed we must be able to retain those features that we hold most dear, whether that is autonomy for physicians, choice of provider for patients, or the opportunity for drug manufacturers or insurance companies to make a profit. All this is to take place in a system that provides high quality, reasonably priced health care for all.

What is apparent is that we are addressing for the first time the possibility of a fundamental restructuring of the health care system in the United States. The Medicare and Medicaid programs of the 1960s should be seen only as "add-ons," and although the prospective payment system for hospitals introduced in the 1980s provided a new approach to reimbursement, in many ways it was more of a technical fix to the system. What we are now considering is a change in the fundamental relationship between those who purchase health care and those who provide it. And it is in that context that we benefit greatly by the detailed review of several nations' health plans in this second edition of *Health of Nations*.

What is so intriguing about the detailed analysis in this book is that it reveals the substantial similarity among seemingly dissimilar systems, what the author refers to as "limited convergence." We learn that not only are the fundamental issues of access and quality preserved across international borders but also that nations can learn and have learned from one another, both from their successes and from their failures. The seeming paradox is that innovation appears to be bringing us closer together.

I commend Laurene Graig for this prodigious work and the Wyatt Company for sponsoring it. Those of us in the U.S. Congress who are engaged in the monumental struggle to improve our health care system will be the beneficiaries of this detailed analysis. We need to understand better the experiences of other health care systems as we move forward; we also need to understand the fundamental societal issues that influence the development of solutions to problems such as health care. This will help us in our efforts to craft a health care system that will serve all Americans for years to come.

Senator John D. Rockefeller IV

Preface

Health care reform is not an abstract policy issue of interest to only a handful of experts. Rather, it touches all Americans, from the worker with health insurance to the worker without it, from the unemployed uninsured person to the person covered by a government insurance program. The 1992 elections—both congressional and presidential—erased any doubt that health care was near the top of the list of voters' concerns.

The research that ultimately culminated in the first edition of this book began in late 1989 when the rumblings of health care reform had not yet reached a crescendo. At the time, the Wyatt Company—an independent worldwide human resources consulting firm—sought to provide a comprehensive review of international health care systems that might serve as models for reform of the U.S. system.

This second edition of *Health of Nations* is especially timely as the United States moves toward implementation of one of the most important social policy changes in the nation's history under the direction of First Lady Hillary Rodham Clinton. Many health care reform proposals now under consideration have borrowed ideas from other nations. It is therefore important to understand how these foreign systems work. What is the role of government, employers, and individuals in these other systems? What are the particular political, economic, and social factors that shaped the development of health systems in other nations, and what distinguishes them from our own? How are these nations responding to the exploding costs of high-technology medicine, aging populations, and an unlimited demand for finite health care resources? What lessons for the United States can be learned from their experiences?

The five nations profiled here—Canada, Germany, the Netherlands, Japan, and Great Britain—dedicate far fewer financial resources to health care, both on a per-person basis and as a percentage of national income, than does the United States. Equally important, these nations insure larger portions of their populations than does the United States. The ability of other nations to achieve a higher level of coverage at lower overall cost certainly merits U.S. attention. Indeed, while health care reformers in the United States will undoubtedly arrive at a uniquely American approach to the health care dilemma, it would be wise to benefit from the lessons learned by other nations.

The research for this book was conducted by Wyatt's centralized Research and Information Center in Washington, D.C., which includes more than 100 highly qualified professionals with expertise in economic analysis and modeling, survey research, legislative and regulatory affairs, systems development, and benefits and compensation programs. Analysts devoted specifically to health care and public policy issues have developed health care databases and modeling capabilities to provide analyses for businesses and organizations concerned about health care reform.

Just as no nation's health care system came into being fully formed, health care systems are constantly changing and evolving. Trying to capture the essence of a particular system is consequently somewhat akin to trying to hit a moving target. This second edition of *Health of Nations* represents an attempt to hit that target.

I would like to express my appreciation to the many people who assisted in the review and preparation of this book. These individuals include senior analysts and consultants in the Wyatt Company's two Research and Information Centers, as well as senior consultants and managers in Wyatt's worldwide offices who provided reference materials and advice.

Special thanks are due to Sylvester J. Schieber, vice president of the Wyatt Company and director of Wyatt's Research and Information Center in Washington, D.C., for giving me the freedom and support to pursue this important project. Senior health care analyst Roland D. McDevitt provided comments on, and assistance with, the entire draft.

I would also like to thank Sheryl Smolkin, director of Wyatt's Canadian Research and Information Center, and her staff; Kirsten Johnston and the Group Health Care Practice in Toronto; Alfred E.

Ghodes, manager of Wyatt's Munich office; Bryan Joseph, actuary in Wyatt's London office; and Eiji Mizutani, manager of Wyatt's Tokyo office. Special thanks are also due to Daniel B. Holmes, manager of Wyatt's Boston office; Barbara J. Kalfin, health care consultant in Wyatt's Boston office; and Roger S. Taylor, former national leader of Wyatt's Health Care Practice. Finally, Marjorie Kulash, who directs legislative research for Wyatt, gave me valuable counsel and support.

I also owe a debt to all those people who assisted in the preparation of the manuscript. These include Tanya B. Weiss and Susan E. Prahinski, who edited the study. The word processing and graphics production was a team effort by Judith L. Lahocki, Patrice Y. Brown, Jacqueline L. Peranio, and Barbara A. Nelson.

Frank H. de Man, Attaché for Health and Environment of the Embassy of the Netherlands, kindly read through the chapter on the Dutch health care system and gave me valuable comments and suggestions.

I also received great support and assistance from Congressional Quarterly Books, particularly Debbie Hardin who did a tremendous job editing the text, Jeanne Ferris, and Nancy Lammers.

This list would not be complete without acknowledging the help of my husband Ian, whose loving support and confidence in my work have been unwavering.

All these individuals and many more unnamed assisted in the preparation of this book. However, the content of the book, and any errors therein, are solely the responsibility of the author.

Laurene A. Graig

C H A P T E R 1

In Search of New Directions for U.S. Health Care: An International Perspective

Introduction

The troubling state of health care in the United States has drawn policymakers, business leaders, and health experts to search for viable ways to reform a system that, by most accounts, is in the throes of an unprecedented crisis. The search for solutions has become global in scope, as the United States looks beyond its borders to examine how other industrialized nations provide and finance health care. Such lessons from abroad are made possible by cross-national comparisons and analyses of the extensive comparative data and information available.

America's interest in other nations' health care systems has been spurred by growing discontent over the seemingly inverse relationship between health care expenditures and the access to necessary services in the U.S. health care system. The United States spends more on health care than any of the other twenty-four industrialized nations belonging to the Organization for Economic Cooperation and Development (OECD). But the United States trails many OECD nations according to such health care indicators as infant mortality and life expectancy. Moreover, there are between thirty-five and forty million uninsured Americans and many millions more who are underinsured.

The crisis in health care has been particularly troubling for businesses. U.S. employers, who pick up a large portion of the nation's health care tab, are becoming increasingly concerned about the deleterious effect of health care costs on their profits. Some business leaders have called for relief from the government in the form of nationwide health care reform, contending that they operate at a financial disadvantage when competing with companies from nations with national health insurance programs. At the end of the 1980s, employer efforts to shift some health care costs to their employees resulted in numerous nationwide strikes as workers fought to preserve their health care benefits—even if that meant sacrificing wage increases.

Escalating U.S. health care costs are linked inextricably to the particular system of health care organization, delivery, and financing that has evolved in the United States. The United States is caught in the paradox of committing ever more financial resources to health care while leaving large numbers of the population uninsured or underinsured. The United States is beginning to look to other nations for possible cures for what ails the U.S. system.

The need to look elsewhere for answers seems inconsistent with the claim by some experts that the U.S. system of health care is the best in the world and could serve as a guide for other nations. However, despite its leadership in many unique and highly technological procedures, the current state of health care in the United States does not support this position. In fact, in the words of one U.S. health policy expert, "It would be, quite frankly, ridiculous for an American to suggest that we have achieved a satisfactory system that our European friends would be wise to emulate" (Enthoven 1990, 57).

An international perspective is important because the experiences of other nations that provide comprehensive coverage for their populations at lower costs than the United States can serve as models for reform of the U.S. health care system. It is quite unlikely that the United States will completely restructure its health care system along the lines of a European or Canadian system. Those involved in the health care reform debate are interested, instead, in specific features of other systems that could be adapted for use in the U.S. system—not unlike the way American companies have become more efficient in part by adapting Japanese manufacturing and quality-management techniques. Adaptation is clearly the key, for it is not possible to import one nation's health care system into another. As Robert Evans, a noted Canadian health economist, points out:

> Nations do not borrow other nations' institutions. The Canadian system may be 'better' than the American. . . . Even if it is better, I am not trying to sell it to you. You cannot have it. It would not 'fit' because you do not see the world, or the individual, or the state, as we do. . . . *The point is that by examining other people's experience you can extend your range of perceptions of what is possible.* . . . [emphasis added] (Evans 1986, 26).

Industrialized nations use various methods to provide health care services to their populations. The complex array of mechanisms involved in the organization, delivery, and financing of health care reflects the cultural, economic, and political characteristics particular to each society. But, while health care systems differ from country to country, industrialized nations share such common concerns as the "difficult financial and ethical questions concerning reconciliation of needs and costs, the rationing of care, and choices between therapy and death," as defined by noted health economist George Schieber (OECD 1987, 11).

The challenges currently facing the American health care system certainly are not unique; health care systems around the world are buckling under the pressures of aging populations, exploding medical cost increases, and reliance on expensive high-tech solutions and procedures. Nations are focusing consequently on strategies to contain or to manage the rate of increase in health care costs. Industrialized nations all battle to balance the three shared concerns in modern health care: cost, access, and quality.

Health Care Paradigms

Industrialized countries have chosen different approaches to addressing their shared concerns. Different methods have been devised to simplify the comparative analysis of international health care systems. One way is to group health care systems according to the following three models:

1. The *national health service model,* characterized by universal coverage, national general tax financing, and national ownership and/or control of the factors of production;
2. The *social insurance model,* characterized by compulsory universal coverage generally within the framework of Social Security, and financed by employer and individual contributions through nonprofit insurance funds, and public and/or private ownership of factors of production; and
3. The *private insurance model,* characterized by employer-based or individual purchase of private health insurance coverage financed by individual and/or employer contributions and private ownership of the factors of production (OECD 1987, 24).

Some examples of nations that have taken these approaches to meeting the health care needs of their populations include the United Kingdom (national health service model), Germany (social insurance model), and the United States (private insurance model). Few health care systems fit neatly within the parameters of a single model, however. The U.S. health care system, for example, is patterned most closely after the private insurance model, but certain aspects of the social insurance model are included in the protection provided to the elderly through Social Security and Medicare programs. Thus, the U.S. system is characterized as "an uneasy equilibrium between private and public control and financing" (Anderson 1989, 118). Such a combination of health care models is at work in the health sectors in many other countries as well. In Japan employers play a large role in financing the compulsory national health system, while private insurance exists side by side with the National Health Service in the United Kingdom (OECD 1987).

Conflicts over the appropriate balance of private-sector and government involvement in the health care system have been at the center of health care reform debates in many nations, but the three models detailed previously do not fully reflect the concept of the "public-private mix" of health care. Clearly, no model can be "wholly analytically satisfying" (OECD 1987, 24), although such models serve as important starting points for comparing health care systems around the world. But they would be *more* analytically satisfying if they reflected the balance of public- and private-sector forces or if they reflected such changes as the shift in focus from expanding health coverage to cost control that has occurred in many nations.

Health Services Continuum

A broader framework than the three models is needed for a close look at the relationships between political, economic, and cultural factors that shape health care systems, and for a fuller understanding of the uneasy equilibrium that exists between the public and private sectors. A useful approach to classifying health care systems has been devised by Odin Anderson, a leading health-policy scholar with extensive experience in cross-national studies. Anderson locates the health care systems of various nations along a "health services continuum" (Figure 1-1) whose boundaries of the continuum are set by the level of centralization of decision making, particularly over funding for such programs as health care. According to Anderson,

> the degree to which a state centralizes financing and planning and the relative size of its public sector determine its position in the continuum, as does the extent to which it intervenes in the operations of the economy itself (Anderson 1989, 21).

Figure 1-1 The Market-Minimized/Market-Maximized Continuum

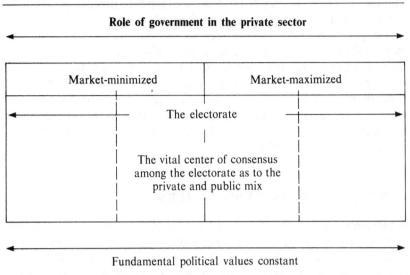

Role of government in the private sector

Market-minimized	Market-maximized
The electorate	
The vital center of consensus among the electorate as to the private and public mix	

Fundamental political values constant

Source: Reprinted from Odin W. Anderson, *Health Care: Can There Be Equity? The United States, Sweden and England,* p. 27. Copyright © 1972 by John Wiley & Sons, Inc. New York. Reprinted by permission of John Wiley & Sons, Inc.

Anderson places the United Kingdom's health care system at one extreme—the "market-minimized" pole of the continuum—because its National Health Service is completely government-financed and operated. The United States occupies a position at the opposite extreme— the "market-maximized" end of the continuum. Of course, this is not to deny that there is significant government involvement in the U.S. health care system—particularly with the Medicare and Medicaid programs— but, compared to other nations, health care services in the United States "have been cut loose in an open field in a way that no other country has conceived of or dared to try" (Anderson 1989, 118).

Anderson's notion of a continuum underscores the importance of the overall political process and the decision-making roles played by the public and private sectors regarding the development of health care systems. As Anderson notes, "the philosophy of government's counterbalancing private-sector interest groups affects the structure, financing and equity of the health services" (Anderson 1989, 8). Such public sector-private sector relationships shape the debate over health care reform as well.

These relationships are extremely important in any effort to apply the health care experiences of other nations to the reform of the U.S.

system. The relevance of any lessons from other nations is severely limited by the boundaries of the U.S. public policy process, particularly the "comparative incapacity of American government" to take decisive action (Morone 1990, 133). In the United States, federal, state, and local governments all compete for a slice of the power pie—and for a slice of the revenues available for social programs such as health care. This fragmentation stands in contrast to other nations, particularly those in Western Europe, where there is much more centralized control over domestic policy. The effect of fragmentation in the United States has been that political stalemate has become the rule rather than the exception (Morone 1990).

Convergence among Health Systems

Anderson's idea of the health services continuum takes into account such important differences between health care systems as control over funding and the mix of public and private roles and responsibilities. A country's health care policies are shaped largely by its location on the continuum. Yet this continuum is not static; certain developments change the continuum, thereby narrowing the gaps between systems.

Swedish health economist Bengt Jonsson argues that health care systems—particularly European and American systems—are evolving in ways that are bringing them closer together. In particular, the primarily public-sector systems are incorporating private-sector elements; the privately based systems are experimenting with greater public regulation. Thus, the role of government planning is becoming increasingly important in private systems, while free-market principles are being adopted by public systems (Jonsson 1990) (see Figure 1-2).

One example of convergence among health care systems can be seen in such U.S. inventions as Health Maintenance Organizations (HMOs) and Diagnosis-Related Groups (DRGs—used to set prices centrally for hospital reimbursement under Medicare). HMOs were encouraged by the U.S. government in the 1970s to allow for a certain degree of control over the American free market health care system, using an approach known as "managed care." Such arrangements were also consistent with the market ideology that prevailed during the 1980s. The DRG system was developed as a means of predetermining hospital prices in an effort to control costs.

These American innovations have captured the attention of health care experts in other nations, particularly in Europe. Rather than grafting a planning or controlling mechanism onto a free-market system like that of the United States, competitive mechanisms were introduced

Figure 1-2 The Shrinking Continuum

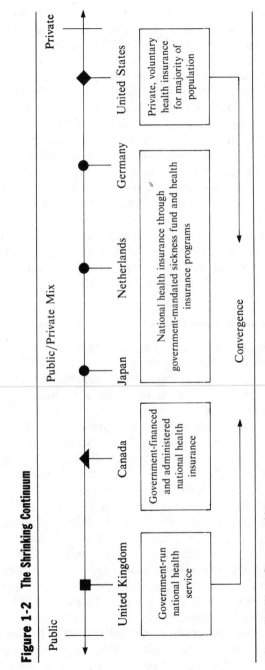

Source: The Wyatt Company, 1991.

into the European tradition of comprehensive coverage through planned health care systems. It will be very interesting to see the outcomes of such experiments, and to see whether HMOs will work in environments very different from the United States (Jonsson 1990).

The convergence of health care systems is being given impetus on the one hand by growing European disillusionment with the tight monetary controls used to limit expenditures, and on the other by increasing American willingness (in light of the failure of the free market system to provide affordable health care for all) to reconsider a historic avoidance of government regulation (Reinhardt 1990). While convergence seems rational in this context, health economists Evans and Barer point out an inherent paradox: "the serious weaknesses of the American system are rooted in its decentralized structure; the advantages of European systems are rooted in their centralized funding control" (1990, 84). Thus a compromise position must be crafted that would preserve the best elements of existing systems using "selective adaptation" of processes and techniques that have been successful in other health care systems (Kirkman-Liff 1989, 469).

Shrinking Continuum, Shrinking World

Application of Jonsson's convergence theory to Anderson's health services continuum would suggest that the continuum itself will constrict as health care systems move toward a common point. This is not to say that there will be one standard model of health care dictating the design of policies and practices around the world. Each system will certainly keep its own particular characteristics because health care systems are, above all, reflections of the society in which they have evolved. It is possible, however, that the differences between systems will become less significant. Nations could learn valuable lessons from one another as their health care systems change and evolve along parallel tracks. For example, the United Kingdom is implementing market mechanisms (based on Stanford University Professor Alain Enthoven's managed competition concepts, which combine managed care and market competition) to increase efficiency and encourage competition in the National Health Service, while the United States is examining ways to increase regulation over costs and quality in the predominately private U.S. health system (Jonsson 1990).

Such a view of the shrinking continuum is not surprising given the remarkable changes occurring around the world. The dismantling of communist regimes and the introduction of free-market practices throughout Eastern Europe and the former Soviet Union are certainly the most vivid illustrations of the dramatic changes sweeping the globe.

But restructuring is occurring elsewhere as well. In Scandinavia, for example, Sweden passed its biggest tax-reform program in a century, and is reassessing the basic tenets of the welfare state while considering further steps to put the country on track toward a more market-driven economy.

The forces of change at work in Western Europe can be seen not only in the reunification of Germany, but also in the twelve-nation European Community's ambitious plan to create a single European market. The program—dubbed Europe 1992—aims to remove barriers preventing goods, services, people, and capital from flowing freely across national borders within Western Europe. In the United States, the emphasis on personal gain that was the hallmark of the 1980s has seemingly given way to an approach that pays attention to issues of social justice. Health care reform was a key campaign issue in the 1992 elections at both the state and national levels. Yet, the financial resources needed to support a broadening of such social programs as health care are seriously constrained by a burgeoning federal budget deficit and sluggish economic growth.

For the first time since the two world wars, the emergence of a truly global economy is also changing the rules of the game. Eastern European nations will gradually be drawn into the global trading arena as they start to form links with major economic powers such as the United States, Japan, and Western Europe. Money now flows around the world without regard to national boundaries. The elimination of trade barriers, as envisaged by the program of European unification and the North American Free Trade Agreement, are certain to increase even further the growing interdependence among nations. Such interdependence is aided by advances in communications and high technology.

The gradual evolution of a more interdependent world has important implications for the health care systems of industrialized countries. Many nations, for example, are realizing the potential benefits that could be enjoyed from working together on approaches to such shared health-related problems as Acquired Immune Deficiency Syndrome (AIDS), drug addiction, and aging populations (Davis 1990). On another level, nations are increasingly exchanging health care strategies to address shared concerns: Canada is looking to the U.S. experience with HMOs, while the United States examines the Canadian experience with universal access and overall health care cost control. In the same way, as already mentioned, the proposed far-reaching changes to the National Health Service of the United Kingdom—namely the introduction of greater competition among health care providers—would involve adaptation of certain aspects of the U.S. free-market health care system. The experience of other nations with different avenues of health care reform could provide the United States with beneficial lessons as it struggles to define its own particular health policy and planning alternatives.

The convergence of health care systems seems to be consistent with, and a reflection of, the dramatic tide of change sweeping the world. This convergence is not without its limits, however. Existing differences between health care systems will not disappear, just as a truly borderless world will probably never emerge.

Limits to Convergence

Philosophy is perhaps the most striking difference separating the U.S. health care system from those of other countries. The United States places greater emphasis on individual responsibility, free choice, and pluralism, while the overriding goal for other nations is access to health care for the entire population. The greater involvement of the government in health care financing and delivery in Western Europe is more easily understood within this context (Jonsson 1990). The difference in philosophies is difficult to surmount and can distort perceptions of other systems. As health economist Uwe Reinhardt notes:

> American critics of European health care frequently decry it as two-class medicine—so-called socialized medicine for the poor and private medicine for the rich. Conversely, European critics of American health care frequently depict it as leaning toward Social Darwinism (Reinhardt 1990, 110).

Thus we return to the point made earlier that while no one expects— in the near future—that the United States will jettison its health care system in favor of a European model or that the Europeans will unconditionally embrace a free-market system, aspects of other systems could potentially be molded and shaped to conform to U.S. political, economic, and cultural realities. Health care reform need not involve radical change; the goal really should be to "identify and design politically feasible incremental changes . . . that have a reasonably good chance of making things better" (Enthoven 1990, 58). As the health care systems of industrialized countries evolve and converge, each country stands to gain from the experience of others going through similar changes.

While radical change is not expected, even incremental change is difficult within the context of the U.S. health care system. It is clear that any attempt to change the status quo in the United States will be hampered by lack of federal or regional control over health care costs, as well as the power wielded by U.S. health care providers. Given this environment, it would seem that any convergence toward other systems on the part of the United States would occur in a "pluralistic, fragmented way—toward broader coverage and tougher cost controls that bear down on providers" (Meyer 1990, 118).

Parameters of the Study

This book is not designed to compare and contrast different systems in an effort to determine which system is the best. As one health policy analyst points out, there is no best system, no right or wrong system, only different systems (Iglehart 1990). Policies that are successful in one nation will not necessarily work in the U.S. health care system. Instead, the book is aimed at learning from diversity. It is often noted that the world is one large laboratory of ongoing health care experiments available for observation by the United States. Mutual exchange of ideas and practices is central to U.S. efforts to reshape its ailing health care system.

The shrinking-continuum/limited-convergence theory will serve as the framework for this book. Anderson and Jonsson have taken a macro-oriented approach to a *comparative* analysis of health care systems. This study will be more micro-oriented; the health care systems of six nations will be examined in depth. The nations selected are situated along various points of the continuum, yet as democracies they all have a common basis of public policy formulation that allows for the participation of various interest groups. Successfully balancing these various interests is critical to health care reform efforts in all nations.

In an attempt to examine health care from a truly global perspective—in geographical, cultural, political, and economic terms—examples will be drawn from North America (the United States and Canada), Asia (Japan), and Europe (Germany, the Netherlands, and the United Kingdom). These systems were selected for analyses due to the availability of information and because they will serve as good reference points for comparison to the United States, either due to differences or similarities. Indeed, while Americans may feel closer in terms of common heritage and culture to Canada or the United Kingdom, numerous analysts contend that the United States has more to learn from the public-private mix of the health care systems in Germany and Japan than from the high level of government involvement characteristic of the Canadian and British health systems (Henke 1990; Jonsson 1990; Iglehart 1989).

This study will reveal a broad array of alternative systems of health care organization, delivery, and financing that exist around the world and that represent potential ideas for reform of the U.S. health care system. The study is intended to provide a sound basis for understanding how other industrialized nations organize and finance their health care systems, and thereby enhance awareness of the "range of what is possible" (Evans 1986, 26). At the same time, this book could be used to contribute additional substance to the debate currently raging over the future shape of the U.S. health care system.

U.S. Health Care Crisis: Moving Toward a National Solution?

Introduction

Few issues have so galvanized American business leaders, policymakers, and workers as the state of health care in the United States. The nation's health care dilemma, which promises to remain at the top of the public policy agenda throughout the 1990s, is of such magnitude that the term "crisis" is generally used to describe its current state. Such fundamental problems exist in the organization, delivery, and financing of health care throughout the United States that one poll found that only 10 percent of Americans surveyed were satisfied with their health care system (Blendon, Leitman, Morrison, and Donelan 1990). Moreover, a survey of almost 2,000 senior executives across a broad range of industries revealed that the rising cost of health care is the leading issue challenging companies today (see Figure 2-1) (Wyatt Company 1990). The state of health care remains one of this country's most serious social problems.

Increasing discontent with the health care status quo has brought a broad array of reform proposals, ranging from building on the current system to replacing it with a universal, tax-financed health system similar to Canada's. Many of the proposals envisioning broad-based change, which would have once been derided as "socialized medicine" or faulted for being too expensive, are now being seriously considered. Some of these proposals are being supported by an unlikely set of backers: organized labor, business leaders, and members of the medical profession. The precise direction health care reform should take still eludes consensus, however.

Figure 2-1   Percentage of Executives Rating Problems As Very Important

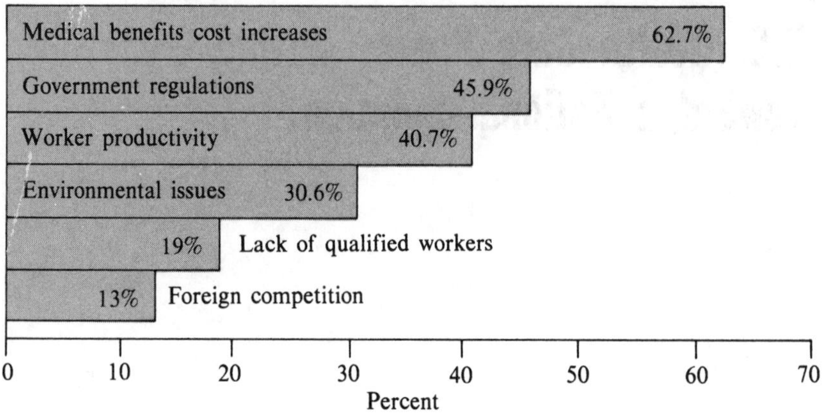

Problem	Percent
Medical benefits cost increases	62.7%
Government regulations	45.9%
Worker productivity	40.7%
Environmental issues	30.6%
Lack of qualified workers	19%
Foreign competition	13%

Percent (scale 0 to 70)

Source: The Wyatt Company, *Management USA: Leading a Changing Work Force,* 1990.

Business leaders are at the center of the controversy because the U.S. health care system is built on a network of employer-sponsored, private health insurance plans. Business assumed the role of health insurance sponsor during the World War II era when employers competed for scarce workers by offering attractive employee benefit packages (Starr 1982). Since then, government tax incentives have encouraged businesses to provide benefits because employer-sponsored health insurance premiums are treated as a tax-deduction for the employer. At the same time, health benefits are not included in an employee's taxable income.

In 1990, U.S. businesses paid $186.2 billion in health care costs— nearly one-third of the nation's total health care bill (Levit and Cowan 1991). The deepening crisis in health care sends shock waves through the business sector in five major ways. First, health care costs are perceived as absorbing larger and larger amounts of corporate profits. Second, some executives contend health care costs represent an increasing burden on U.S. companies competing with foreign companies that do not have to include the price of health care in their products. Third, the attempt to shift some of the burden to employees has resulted in labor unrest; it is expected that disputes over health benefits will be a continuing flashpoint of industrial relations throughout the 1990s. Fourth, the problem of large numbers of uninsured people in this country has become corporate America's problem because the cost of care provided to the uninsured—"uncompensated care"—is shifted to the insured through increased insurance premiums. Fifth, new regulations issued by the Financial Accounting Standards Board (FASB) require companies to carry the financial liability for postretirement medical care benefits, further increasing the call for relief from future health care costs.

The crisis in the U.S. health care system should have all Americans concerned and involved. As employees, employers, and taxpayers, we all have a stake in health care reform. We all pay for health care—directly through the purchase of our own individual health insurance plans; indirectly as consumers of goods carrying higher price tags; as employees paying higher deductibles and co-payments, or receiving lower wage increases; and as taxpayers contributing to such government programs as Medicare and Medicaid (see Figure 2-2). Therefore, it is in our combined interest to chart a safe course out of the health care morass.

This chapter is devoted to an overview of the state of health care in the United States. The changes in U.S. health care over the years are discussed from the perspective of whether or not they indicate a convergence on the part of the United States toward health care systems of other countries.

Facing the Challenges of Modern Health Care

The perception of a deepening crisis in the U.S. health care system derives from the interrelated problems of rising costs, declining access, and the need to provide quality health care. The debate over strategies to address these three problems has evolved into a potent public policy issue with significant political, economic, and ethical ramifications. While most industrialized countries share these concerns, the problems in the United States are more acute. The absence of a universal health insurance system for all Americans distinguishes the United States from Canada and Western European nations, whose systems guarantee the entire population access to health care at minimal, or no, *direct* cost to the patient. The following sections describe some of the particular characteristics of the U.S. health care system—what one analyst terms the "manifestation of American exceptionalism"—that set the health care system of the United States apart from that of other industrialized countries (Rodwin 1987).

Health Care Costs

The United States dedicates greater financial resources to health care than any other industrialized country, having broken the $2 billion-a-day barrier in health care spending in 1991. Expenditures totaled $738

Figure 2-2 The Nation's Health Dollar: 1990

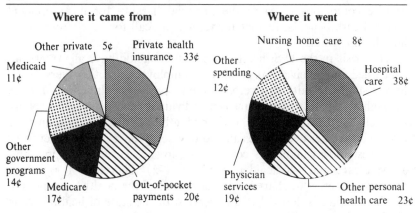

Where it came from

Other private 5¢   Private health
Medicaid   insurance 33¢
11¢

Other
government
programs
14¢   Medicare   Out-of-pocket
        17¢   payments 20¢

Where it went

Nursing home care 8¢

Other
spending
12¢

Hospital
care 38¢

Physician
services
19¢   Other personal
           health care 23¢

Source: Levit, Katharine R., Helen Lazenby, Cathy A. Cowan, and Suzanne Letsch. 1991. "National Health Expenditures, 1990." *Health Care Financing Review* 13, 1:(29-54). HCFA Publication no. 03321. Office of Research and Demonstrations. Health Care Financing Administration. Washington, D.C.: U.S. Government Printing Office, October, 1991.

Notes: Other private includes industrial in-plant health services, nonpatient revenues, and privately financed construction. Other personal health care includes dental, other professional services, home health care, drugs and other nondurable medical products, and vision products and other durable medical products. Other spending covers program administration and the net cost of private health insurance, government public health, and research and construction.

billion that year and topped $800 billion in 1992. According to estimates from the U.S. Department of Commerce, health care spending will pass the $1 trillion mark in 1994 (Pear 1993).

Health care spending has increased faster than overall economic growth over the past three decades. U.S. expenditures on health care absorb a larger portion of the national income each year, as measured by the Gross National Product (GNP). Health expenditures have increased from 5.3 percent of GNP in 1960 to more than 14 percent of GNP in 1992. Analysts predict health care expenditures could reach 26 percent of GNP by the year 2030 (Sonnefeld, Waldo, Lemieux, and McKusick 1991). Health economist Uwe Reinhardt points out that at this rate of spending "we will have it all, an entire economy devoted to health care, by the middle of the twenty-first century" (Morone 1990, 130).

These figures can be put into perspective by comparing them with expenditures of other industrialized countries. Cross-national differences in health expenditures, figured on a per capita basis (shown in Figure 2-3), are significant. In 1990, the latest year for which such statistics are available, U.S. per-person health care costs totaled $2,566—more than double the OECD average. The United States

Figure 2-3   Per Capita Health Spending in U.S. Dollars, 1990

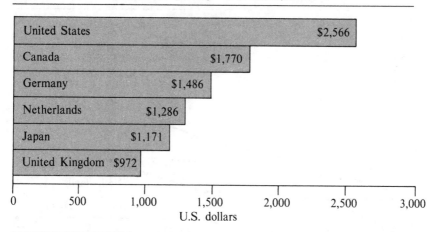

Source: Schieber, George, Jean-Pierre Poullier, and Leslie M. Greenwald. "U.S. Health Expenditure Performance: An International Comparison and Data Update." *Health Care Financing Review* 13, 4:(1-15). HCFA Publication no. 03331. Office of Research and Demonstrations. Health Care Financing Administration. Washington, D.C.: U.S. Government Printing Office, September 1992.

outspent Canada by 45 percent, Germany by 73 percent, and Japan by 119 percent (Schieber, Poullier, and Greenwald 1992).

In terms of gross domestic product (GDP),[1] a broad-based measure of a nation's economic activity used most often in international comparisons, the United States dedicated 12.1 percent to health care in 1990, again surpassing all other industrialized nations (Figure 2-4).

The United States stands apart from other industrialized nations not only in the total expenditures for health care, but in the public-private mix of those expenditures. Approximately three-quarters of the cost of health care in most OECD countries is funded by central or local government. In 1990 the public share of health spending was 73 percent in Canada and Germany; 72 percent in the Netherlands; and 84 percent in the United Kingdom. In 1990 the public share of U.S. health expenditures, on the other hand, was 42 percent (Schieber, Poullier, and Greenwald 1992).

---

[1] GDP is a measure of the total economic output produced *within* a country, by all residents, whether citizens or foreigners. In contrast, GNP (Gross National Product) is a measure of the total output produced by the country's citizens, regardless of where the production takes place.

Figure 2-4   Total Health Expenditures As a Percentage of Gross Domestic Product (in percent)

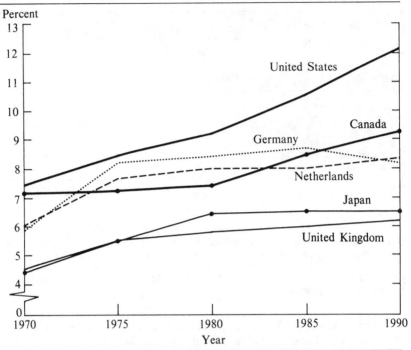

Source: Schieber, George, Jean-Pierre Poullier, and Leslie M. Greenwald. "U.S. Health Expenditure Performance: An International Comparison and Data Update." *Health Care Financing Review* 13, 4:(1-15). HCFA Pub. no. 03331. Office of Research and Demonstrations. Health Care Financing Administration. Washington, D.C.: U.S. Government Printing Office, September 1992.

While health expenditure levels of most industrialized countries grew rapidly throughout the 1960s and early 1970s, most countries managed—through various cost-control policies—to hold down health expenditures in the 1980s. An examination of health care expenditures over the period of 1980 to 1990 reveals that U.S. health care expenditures increased more sharply than in other nations. In Germany, for example, health care expenditures as a percentage of GDP actually decreased from 8.4 percent of GDP in 1980 to 8.1 percent of GDP in 1990. In contrast, U.S. health care expenditures increased from 9.2 percent of GDP in 1980 to 12.1 percent of GDP in 1990 (Schieber, Poullier, and Greenwald 1992).

Control over health care expenditures in other countries occurred as a direct result of specific health care interventions employed by those countries, as the following chapters will show. Such developments have critical implications for the future of U.S. health policy, for they "clearly do not support the claims of those critics of universal public insurance systems who consider the expansion of coverage to be a major source of expenditure growth" (Pfaff 1990, 21).

Declining Access

Contraction of coverage is one of the many anomalies of the U.S. health care system. The high level of U.S. expenditures for health care has not been sufficient to purchase a safety net for all Americans. The uninsured are estimated to number between 35 and 40 million, and this does not include the millions more who are underinsured—those who are without adequate coverage for a major illness. According to calculations based on the March 1992 *Current Population Survey,* 36.3 million Americans lacked health insurance coverage in 1991, up from 33.6 million in 1988 (Foley 1993).

One might assume that the uninsured in the United States do not have coverage because they are unemployed. In reality, however, more than half (56.4 percent) of the uninsured are working adults. One half of all uninsured workers are either self-employed or work in companies with less than twenty-five workers (Foley 1993). Many of the uninsured have fallen through the cracks in the system: They are not poor enough to qualify for Medicaid and they are too young to qualify for Medicare, yet they lack sufficient funds to pay for the high costs of private health insurance coverage.

Many consider it inconceivable that one of the world's wealthiest nations has allowed such large numbers of its people—approximately 17 percent of the nonelderly population—to be without health care coverage. These numbers become even more shocking when compared with the experience of other Western nations: Canada, Germany, Japan, the Netherlands, and the United Kingdom provide health care services for their entire populations either through national health insurance or a national health service.

Maintaining Quality

The large U.S. expenditures on health care have not necessarily bought better services. Widely used measures of health reveal that the quality of care is not any higher in the United States than in nations that devote far fewer financial resources to health care. For example, U.S. rates of infant mortality are among the highest of all industrialized countries.

Among the twenty-four nations of the OECD, the United States ranks seventeenth in male life expectancy at birth and sixteenth in female life expectancy at birth (Schieber, Poullier, and Greenwald 1991). It is important to note, however, that measures such as infant mortality and life expectancy are influenced by factors beyond the scope of the health care system. These include lifestyle factors such as nutrition and whether one smokes or drinks, environmental factors such as pollution, and socio-economic factors such as crime and poverty.

Another issue related to health care quality is the impact of soaring malpractice premiums on the practice of "defensive medicine"—the use of tests and procedures that may not be medically necessary but are conducted to protect physicians from potential legal action by patients. It is estimated that between 15 and 30 percent of all tests and procedures performed in the United States are not medically necessary (Relman 1991). These unnecessary tests and procedures add billions of dollars to the nation's health care bill but do not necessarily improve the quality of care provided. The high rate of malpractice claims in the United States reflects further disenchantment—real or perceived—with the quality of U.S. health care.

The Center of the Crisis: Escalating Costs

Of the three concerns just outlined—cost, access, and quality—alarms have sounded loudest over the continued rise in health care costs. No one has discovered a magic formula to determine the appropriate ratio of health care expenditures to GNP, so it is impossible to say how much is too much. But U.S. health care expenditures continue to grow at twice the rate of the national economy and the rapidly escalating share of the nation's revenues spent on health care clearly is on a collision course with the reality of limited resources. The more money spent on health care, the less money available for investment in such areas as education, infrastructure, research and development, and other investments critical to future economic growth. Indeed, some analysts argue that this is the true competitive cost of U.S. health care—the investment lost to other areas necessary for economic growth (Reinhardt 1989).

A number of factors are responsible for the health care cost explosion in the United States. Consider the 10.3 percent average annual increase in personal health care expenditures from 1980 to 1990.[2] Almost half of

---

[2] Personal health care expenditures (PHCE) includes all expenditures for health services received by individuals, as well as health products bought in retail stores. PHCE represented 87.9 percent of all health care expenditures in 1990.

that increase was due to general economy-wide inflation, while 22 percent of the increase was due to inflation specific to the medical care sector alone. Demographic changes—the growth and aging of the population—put increased demands on the system, particularly in terms of Medicare, retiree health benefits, and long-term care for the elderly, and was responsible for almost 10 percent of the increase (Levit, Lazenby, Cowan, and Letsch 1991).

The remaining share of the increase was due to factors such as increased intensity and utilization of medical services, including advances in medical technology. Such developments are double-edged swords; many high-tech medical procedures are cost-prohibitive and may or may not improve the quality of life of a patient. As one medical technologist points out: "Technologically, we can do more than society is capable of paying for" (Hamilton, Smith, and Garland 1989). Moreover, the particular means of payment of U.S. health care bills—a system of third-party-payers predominates—insulates the consumers of health care (patients) from the price of medical care, providing little incentive to be cost-conscious. Unlike in other industrialized countries, this consumer insulation is not balanced by measures to limit the services provided or the fees charged by health care providers.

Moreover, the cost involved in the administration of the multipayer U.S. health care system is significant. Diverse marketing, billing, and claims procedures of numerous third-party payers result in administrative costs that are estimated to represent almost one-quarter of total U.S. health care spending. These high administrative costs set the United States apart from other nations whose health systems provide universal coverage and a comprehensive package of benefits. Under these systems, coverage is universal, benefits are uniform, and provider fees are set according to a uniform schedule of rates. Consequently, it is unnecessary to spend large amounts of time and money to market different plans; to determine which individuals and what services are covered by insurance; and to determine the costs of each medical service.

Such health-related epidemics as the increased use of illegal drugs and the rise in AIDS pose a clear and present danger to our health care system. The drug epidemic takes its toll on future generations—babies are born without prenatal care and addicted to drugs—as well as on the present generation, both through addiction and injuries sustained in drug-related crimes.

The dramatic increase in the number of individuals who are HIV positive is clearly one of the biggest health challenges this and other nations face. According to figures from the World Health Organization, there were 15.6 AIDS cases per 100,000 people in the United States in 1990. By contrast, the rate in Canada is 3.4, in Germany 2.1, and in Japan, 0.2. The success of the drug AZT in delaying the symptoms of, and death related to, the AIDS virus has important implications for the U.S. health care system. This one drug has the potential to increase health care costs by billions of dollars, and thereby to provide further impetus to devise a nationwide strategy for health care reform (Hilts 1989).

While businesses are the primary health care payers for workers, the government pays for health care coverage for the elderly, poor, and disabled. As noted above, public programs contributed 42 percent of health care financing in 1990. Two of the largest government programs, Medicare and Medicaid, together represented 28 percent of total health expenditures, and the costs of these programs have been increasing even faster than the growth of overall health expenditures. Expenditures for Medicare increased at an average annual rate of 14.3 percent from 1970 to 1990, while Medicaid payments increased 21 percent in the one-year period from 1989 to 1990 (Jencks and Schieber 1991; Levit, Lazenby, Cowan, and Letsch 1991).

Implications for Corporate America

Policymakers and government officials are now joined in the quest for health care reform by captains of business and industry who are bedeviled by rising health care costs. Such costs have become the primary human resource and financial concern for businesses. According to the Employee Benefits Research Institute (EBRI), employer-financed health plans cover two-thirds of the U.S. population under age 65 (Snider 1992). Health costs per employee have tripled over the past ten years; average annual costs per worker exceeded $3,000 in 1991 (Wyatt Company 1992).

These spiraling costs have led companies to alter the structure of their benefits packages, ranging from increasing deductibles and co-payments to expanding use of managed care arrangements such as health maintenance organizations (HMOs) and preferred provider organizations (PPOs) (Wyatt Company 1990a). Indeed, the use of alternative delivery systems increased rapidly throughout the 1980s. Enrollment in HMOs, for example, grew from 9.1 million in 1980 to 35.1 million in 1991. Whereas 98 percent of full-time employees of medium and large private establishments were covered by fee-for-service medical plans in 1980, this number declined to 74 percent in 1989 (Snider 1992).

Such changes notwithstanding, surveys conducted by the National Association of Manufacturers (NAM) revealed that corporate management believed escalating health care costs were more of a threat to the health of corporate America than the budget deficit, while another NAM survey of more than 9,000 small companies indicated that escalating health care costs were perceived to be one of the greatest drags on their competitiveness (Jasinowski and Canner 1989, 1).

Such corporate concern is driven by fears that rising health care costs are seriously eroding the ability of American companies to compete in an international arena filled with lower-priced goods from countries with nationalized health care systems. The ability of corporate America to hold down health care costs is seen as vital to the survival of American businesses in the global marketplace. The frustration of the business community over what has come to be called the "health tax" was captured in a statement made by the chairperson of the National Association of Manufacturers to the *New York Times:* "Running those costs through business is one of the dumbest things we can do if we want to be internationally competitive" (Freudenheim 1989b).

This sentiment echoes throughout American business circles. In March 1989, Robert Mercer, chairperson of Goodyear Tire and Rubber Company, told the Conference Board's employee benefits conference that his company's $200.7 million annual health care bill increased the price of each Goodyear tire by $3.40 (Conference Board 1989). Chrysler's former chairperson Lee Iacocca, a vocal critic of rising U.S. health costs, decries the fact that Chrysler spends more than twice the amount spent by auto manufacturers in France and Germany and three times that spent by Japanese car manufacturers on health care. Iacocca expressed his frustration to the *New York Times:*

> American industry cannot compete effectively with the rest of the
> world unless something is done about the great imbalance between
> health-care costs in the U.S. and national health care systems in
> virtually every other country (Freudenheim 1989a).

Iacocca's remarks point to a major factor that sets the United States apart from other nations. The burden of health care costs in other nations is spread across the entire population, and no one industry or sector is overburdened. In the United States, on the other hand, industries with older work forces, such as steel and autos, do pay significantly higher health care costs. Indeed, in industries such as automobile manufacturing, health benefits costs are the largest nonwage factor in production costs. General Motors saw its annual health expenditures pass the $3 billion mark in 1988 (Freudenheim 1989a).

Many executives believe the rapid growth in health benefits costs is taking a toll on the bottom line: corporate profits. Indeed,

Table 2-1   Expeditures for Health Services and Supplies As a Percent of Business Expense or Profit: United States (in percent)

Year	Total compensation[b]	Labor compensation		Corporate profits[a]	
		Wages and salaries[b]	Fringe benefits[b]	Before tax	After tax
1965	2.0	2.2	22.4	8.4	14.0
1970	3.1	3.5	29.2	19.8	36.1
1975	3.9	4.5	28.5	21.3	34.3
1980	4.9	5.8	31.7	27.3	42.6
1985	6.1	7.2	38.9	51.3	89.9
1990	7.1	8.5	45.5	61.1[c]	107.9[c]

Source: Levit, Katherine R., and Cathy A. Cowan. "Business, Households, and Governments: Health Care Costs, 1990." *Health Care Financing Review* 13, 2: (83-93). HCFA Pub. no. 03326. Office of Research and Demonstrations, Health Care Financing Administration. Washington, D.C.: U.S. Government Printing Office, February 1991.

[a] Based on July 1990 data from the U.S. Department of Commerce national income and product accounts; a similar concept of "profits" of sole proprietorships and partnerships is not available.
[b] For employees in private industry.
[c] Estimated.

businesses' share of health care costs has risen dramatically over the past twenty-five years. Whereas private business spent $6.5 billion on health care in 1965, this amount soared to $186.2 billion in 1990. Health care spending by business equaled 14 percent of corporate after-tax profits in 1965; businesses spent more on health care than they earned in after-tax profits in 1990 (see Table 2-1) (Levit and Cowan 1991).

In that case, health care cost increases may be taking their toll on the corporate bottom line, but the process through which this occurs is very complex. In a product market with limited price competition, an employer may, at least in the short term, pass health care costs on to consumers through higher product prices. In that case health care costs may not affect corporate profits over the short term. It would not be as easy to pass along health care costs to consumers in a market with significant price competition, however, unless the employer's competitors also faced the same health care cost burdens. If some employers are affected by rapid health care cost increases and others are not, price competition will prevent those with higher health care costs from raising their prices. Short-term profits would indeed be driven down for those employers. This is particularly true for domestic producers who compete directly with foreign producers whose health care costs may not be as high.

Health care costs are part of an employer's overall labor cost, and employers can adjust other elements of the employee compensation package to transfer health care cost increases back to employees. Indeed, some of the slow growth of real cash wages over the last fifteen to twenty years may be directly attributable to the rapid increase in the noncash components of compensation, especially health care benefits. Total compensation may have grown over the period, but the rapid increase in health care benefits may have suppressed the growth in the cash element of compensation. For example, according to data on various elements of the National Income and Product Accounts published by the Bureau of Economic Analysis at the U.S. Department of Commerce, private employers contributed an amount equal to 2.2 percent of wages and salaries to finance their health benefits programs in 1965; by 1970, their contributions for health benefits had increased to 3.5 percent of wages and salaries; by 1990 it was 8.5 percent (see Table 2-1). Health benefit compensation increased fourfold relative to cash pay among private sector employers over the twenty-five-year period.

Over the same period, an analysis of other components of compensation, such as retirement benefits, reveals an entirely different trend. Employer contributions to pension and profit-sharing plans were 2.1 percent of salary in 1960, and 2.0 percent in 1990. While employer contributions to health benefits plans have increased rapidly, employer contributions to retirement plans have remained virtually flat (Wyatt Company 1991; Levit and Cowan 1990).

Shifting increases in health care costs to other elements of the wage bill may help businesses sustain their profit level for the short term, but it may have longer-term indirect effects on business operations that could in turn have an adverse impact on corporate profits. For example, when compensation is shifted from cash to health benefits, workers have less disposable income to spend in other sectors of the economy. If workers reduce their consumption of goods and services, it will ultimately make these sectors less profitable. If they reduce investments in their children's education or other productivity-enhancing expenditures, it will affect business productivity levels in the long run and further exacerbate the cycle of declining pay levels that threatens overall corporate profitability.

Cost-Shifting

U.S. employers pay directly for health care costs for their own employees, and they also indirectly subsidize the costs of providing health care for the uninsured. While there are hospitals that refuse to treat the uninsured, many hospitals provide treatment to those without insurance. The losses to these hospitals can be substantial; the American Hospital Association estimates that in 1989 approximately $9 billion in hospital charges were never paid (Kosterlitz 1992). Such costs are then passed on to those paying for insurance through increased premiums.

There has been a marked change in the source of cost shifting from uncompensated care associated with individuals to uncompensated care associated with the Medicare and Medicaid programs. Businesses believe that they bear the burden of costs that are shifted from public plans to private plans in the form of higher premiums. A study prepared by the Prospective Payment Assessment Commission (appointed by Congress to monitor Medicare's Prospective Payment System) revealed that uncompensated care is on the rise and that private payers do bear a disproportionate share of the burden. On average, private payers shoulder 128 percent of costs, while Medicare pays 91 percent, and Medicaid 74 percent (Chaconas 1992; Dobson and Clarke 1992; Wyatt Company 1992).

One analyst has coined the phrase "disjointed incrementalism" to describe the current situation. The term *incremental* refers to the piecemeal approach to health care reform; the term *disjointed* describes the way in which problems are not solved, but are pushed around as health care costs are transferred from one set of payers to the next (Kinzer 1990, 467). But the piecemeal approach to reform is not relieving any of the pressures on the system, and the cost-shifting arrangements are unraveling. In the words of James Morone, professor of political economy at Brown University, "the elaborate American system of health insurance cross-subsidies—the very concept of pooled risk—is eroding under the pressures of competition among payers" (Morone 1990, 140).

Corporate Response

The alarm of some corporate leaders over rising health care costs has spurred them to defy tradition and advocate a broader role for the federal government in the provision of health care. The call for government-financed health care amounts to nothing less than breaking a health care "taboo." Goodyear's Mercer, for example, explained to the *New York Times* that "I never thought I would be in favor of a Government health policy, but there are things that Government must do" (Freudenheim 1989b).

Growing numbers of industry executives are coming out in support of some form of national health insurance. A January 1989 Fortune 500/CNN Moneyline Poll of more than 200 CEOs of Fortune 500 and Service 500 companies revealed that 20 percent of respondents said their interest in some type of universal national health insurance had increased (Farnham 1989), while results of a survey of the views of executives on national health insurance conducted by *Business & Health* showed that 30 percent of those surveyed were in favor of national health insurance and 30 percent believed a system of national health insurance would be set up within five years (*Business & Health* 1990, 36). There is no consensus among business leaders, however; a 1990 survey of 2,000 executives revealed that 64 percent were opposed to a tax-financed universal health care system (Wyatt Company 1990).

Corporate support for an expanded role for government in the health care sector is a recognition of the failure on the part of business—through the use of such methods as requiring second opinions for surgery and participation in managed care arrangements such as HMOs and PPOs—to keep a lid on employee health care costs. Merrill C. Horine, a human resources director at Hershey Foods, explains that employee health costs continue to increase despite all Hershey's efforts at cost containment: "We've done all the things you're supposed to do ... changed our funding system, increased major medical deductibles ... shifted to a flexible benefits plan. Most of the things we've tried haven't worked, or not for a long period of time" (Kosterlitz 1989b, 2203). Because health care cost inflation is a systemic problem, it overcomes any one-time reductions in employer health costs.

Some companies, in an effort to identify strategies to control health care costs, are refusing to cover certain medical procedures. Employers, as the primary health care bill payers, are thus placed in the unenviable position of determining which expenses should be covered by corporate health care plans. The ultimate result is that corporate benefits managers are taking on a policymaking role in terms of limiting coverage of health costs. Hewlett-Packard, for example, decided it would no longer reimburse employee costs for heart, heart-lung, or liver transplants; Honeywell Corporation's policy on organ transplants limits reimbursement to cases in which the operation is critical to the survival of the patient. These decisions indicate that "allocation and rationing policy is being set increasingly by providers who are responsive to the interests of the organizations they represent" (Blank 1988, 93-95). It is clear that such decisions are being shaped by corporations that may want to preserve coverage for their employees' typical medical problems, but are desperate to control ever-increasing expenditures for unusual or high-tech health care interventions.

Large companies such as Gillette, Goodyear, and Nestlé have decided that the best way to keep health care costs under control is to hire their own physicians and run their own medical facilities. Other companies have developed additional strategies, including contracting with doctors and hospitals for discounted fees; running "wellness centers"; contracting with pharmacies and paying for drugs wholesale; and administering their own claims (Kramon 1990). Such cases, however, seem to be more the exception than the rule. There is a feeling shared by many executives that the problem of health care costs is a monster too large to battle on a company-by-company basis; such perceptions fuel the calls for reform of U.S. health care on a systemwide, nationwide basis (Kosterlitz 1989b).

Small Businesses

Small companies play an important role in the U.S. economy; in fact, this sector has been the most successful in creating new jobs. But small companies have been hit hardest by exploding health care costs. These companies pay higher health premium costs than larger companies, because the principle of spreading risk embodied in community rating has been abandoned in favor of experience rating—the practice of basing premiums on the claims history of an individual company. Small companies do not have large work forces so neither risks nor costs (such as administration and marketing) can be spread as widely as with a large company (Levit and Cowan 1991; O'Keefe 1992).

Many small companies are simply unable to bear the costs of these increased premiums for their workers. Less than one-third of workers in companies with fewer than ten workers were covered by employer-sponsored health plans in 1991 (Foley 1993). Small companies that cut health benefits for their employees contribute to the growing pool of the uninsured and increase the strain on larger companies that may end up covering those dropped through coverage for dependents.

Retiree Health Benefits

Employer concern over health care costs is not limited to current employees; the growing number of retirees and their attendant health care costs represent a significant burden on corporate finances. And the demographic pressures are mounting. Consider that twenty years ago the average Fortune 500 company had twelve active employees for every retiree. The current ratio is now three to one (Taylor and Newton 1991). Health care utilization rates are highest for the elderly. The elderly accounted for one-third of all health care expenditures in 1988, even though they represented only 12 percent of the population (Davis, J. 1991).

Retiree health care expenditures will become ever more critical in light of changes issued by the Financial Accounting Standards Board

(FASB) requiring many companies to list all future retiree health costs as liabilities on their balance sheets. The new rules take effect in 1993 and will have a profound impact on the corporate bottom line.

Pollster Louis Harris notes that the FASB requirements may be contributing to the increasing interest on the part of U.S. CEOs in some form of federal health insurance:

> These businessmen, almost all of whom are conservatives, and most Republicans, are not idealogues, to say the least. Instead, they are hard-headed capitalists who know a bottom line when they see one. And the bottom line for them is being twisted and placed in jeopardy by what is known as the "horror term," as one put it, of "unfunded liability" (Harris 1989, 10-11).

Given the magnitude of retiree health liability, many employers are redesigning their health benefit plans for retirees. Many companies are considering strategies including introducing a significant cost-sharing element for retirees; setting a cap on employer contributions to future health costs; linking employer contributions to employees' length of service; and requiring active workers to contribute to future health care benefits (Davis 1991). Other companies no longer include retiree health care as part of their benefits package, offering instead employee stock and savings plans. As more and more companies adopt this approach, one can expect pressure on government programs such as Medicare to increase (Freudenheim 1989d).

Organized Labor Enters the Fray

Organized labor entered the debate over health care as unions in industries such as steel, autos, and telecommunications joined with management in the call for health care reform. It is understandable why organized labor is increasingly concerned about health care costs. While wages have remained relatively stable, the cost of benefits has been increasing steadily. According to a report prepared by the Congressional Budget Office, workers are bearing the brunt of escalating health care costs through lower wages and reduced health care benefits (CBO 1992).

Involvement by organized labor cuts across industry lines. The United Steel Workers and Bethlehem Steel Corporation agreed to "develop and support an appropriate national health policy which will assure essential care to all citizens, control health care costs and equitably distribute those costs" among all economic sectors (Freudenheim 1989d). Both Chrysler and Ford have held discussions with the United Automobile Workers regarding a national health policy. Ford, seeing its health care costs reach the $1 billion mark in

1988, called for "public-private sector cooperation," while the new contract between the Communications Workers of America and AT&T contained a promise to "mutually work to achieve prompt and lasting national solutions to the health care crisis" (Bacon 1989).

Such cooperative statements notwithstanding, the health care issue has become a lightning rod for conflict, touching off numerous instances of labor unrest. Contract negotiations broke down in August 1989 between telephone workers and three of the seven U.S. regional telephone companies over health care benefits, specifically the transfer of some costs of medical premiums to employees. These cost-shifting attempts by companies subsequently sparked employee strikes nation-wide. According to one study, the issue of health benefits was the critical issue in 78 percent of all major strikes involving 1,000 or more workers in 1989, up from 18 percent in 1986 (Service Employees International Union 1990).

AT&T successfully averted a strike in May 1989 by dropping its initial demands for increased cost-sharing on the part of its workers and establishing instead a preferred provider network. The president of the Communications Workers union told the *Wall Street Journal* that the union's victory over AT&T was particularly significant because they "didn't want to send a signal that workers' health-care benefits could be reduced" (Karr and Carnevale 1989).

The battle over the preservation of health care benefits represents a watershed in labor-management negotiations. Companies once viewed health care benefits as a reasonably priced alternative to salary increases, but this is no longer the case as medical costs continue to escalate. Thus a dramatic reversal: workers have exhibited a willingness to accept smaller wage increases to maintain health benefits because, over the long-term, health benefits are worth more than salary increases given the higher rate of medical cost inflation. The fact that health benefits are tax-exempt has further stimulated workers' willingness to make the shift from cash compensation to health benefits.

Such trends will undoubtedly continue. A 1989 survey conducted by the Health Poll revealed that 34 percent of the respondents representing labor felt that health care benefits issues would be the paramount challenge to the business community in the 1990s, while only 20 percent said that wage increases would be most important (Ham 1989).

Limited Convergence

The 1980s witnessed dramatic changes within the U.S. health care sector, not least of which was the proliferation of measures aimed at controlling costs by increasing competition among health care providers such as HMOs and PPOs. In actuality, these structural changes represent forms of increasing regulation over health care providers in the predominately private sector-based U.S. system. Some analysts point to similarities between the way in which HMOs negotiate fees with health care providers and control benefits, and the ways in which Canadian provinces administer their health care plans (Woolsey 1990).

Increasing regulation is evident in other areas, particularly within the Medicare system. The establishment of the Prospective Payment System in 1983 changed the way Medicare reimburses hospitals for their services. Patients are assigned to 1 of 470 diagnosis-related groups (DRGs) that carries a set fee. Even though the emphasis during the 1980s was on the promotion of free-market competition within the health care sector, DRGs—what one analyst termed a "venture in national price fixing" (Kinzer 1988, 113)—actually represent just the opposite. DRGs provide an example of convergence toward systems of other countries, or at least an adaptation of certain features of other systems, for as one analyst notes, "these are regulatory mechanisms, imposed by payers, independent of user choice, and are thus closer to Canadian modes of control" (Evans 1987, 168).

Congress recently passed legislation that would provide a second regulatory pillar under the Medicare program. A new physician reimbursement system will now set doctors' fees according to factors such as skill level, training, time, and so on. (Fees will be phased in from 1992 to 1996.) This relative value scale will be buttressed by annual expenditure targets designed to prevent doctors from increasing the volume of their services (and thereby their overall fee level). Under this system, doctors yield a great deal of their power to set fees, again reminiscent of the Canadian and European health care reimbursement systems. Such fee schedules could signal movement away from open-ended financing of health care in the United States. Whether this practice will eventually spread to the private sector is still unclear. What is important, however, is that these changes can be seen as an indication of a reemergence of regulation in the health care sector (Iglehart 1990; Kinzer 1988; Morone 1990).

Increasing regulation—the decline of deregulation—combined with initiatives on the state level to set up universal health insurance plans can be seen as indications that the U.S. health care system is converging toward the systems of Canada and Western European nations. Such convergence will be limited, however, by the political and cultural forces that have shaped health care in the United States. The chances of the United States adopting cost-control measures such as a fixed budget for overall health expenditures as in the United Kingdom, or expenditure caps as in Canada, for example, are quite slim because this "would imply the acceptance of a philosophy of limits—an enormously difficult concept to sell in light of our material abundance, our fascination with technology and our resistance to the imposition of constraints" (Levey and Hill 1989, 1752).

New Directions for U.S. Health Care?

By now there should be no doubt that the U.S. health care system, with its crazy quilt of multiple payers and providers, is in serious need of reform. As Gail Wilensky, former director of the Health Care Financing Administration, noted, "the terms people use range from 'unacceptable' to 'intolerable.' You just don't find anybody left saying the system works fine" (Specter 1990). What is lacking is a consensus on a comprehensive national policy around which a nationwide health care reform program could be fashioned. Such a program would need to address the key problems of spiraling health care expenditures and declining access—the "paradox of excess and deprivation" (Enthoven and Kronick 1989, 29)—that seem to set the United States apart from other industrialized nations.

A wide array of alternatives for reform of the U.S. health care sector has emerged, from the highly charged health care debate—ranging from calls for some form of national health insurance—to the introduction of tax credits for the purchase of insurance. Central to this debate is the question of who is responsible for paying health care bills. What is the appropriate role of individuals, employers, and the government in financing health care? It is not only policymakers, health experts, and the two primary payers in the U.S. health care economy—the federal government and employers—who seek answers to these questions, but the individuals who are being asked to shoulder an increasing burden of health care costs.

A survey conducted by Robert Blendon, chairperson of health policy and management at Harvard University's School of Public Health, in conjunction with Louis Harris and Associates, found that 90 percent of Americans surveyed felt the U.S. health care system required fundamental change or a complete rebuilding (Blendon, Leitman, Morrison, and Donelan 1990). While polls indicate that Americans want "more health care," they reveal an unwillingness on the part of Americans to pay higher taxes to finance broadening of health care services—what some analysts have termed the "foolish inconsistencies" of Americans' views of health care (Gabel, Cohen, and Fink 1989).

Until the 1992 campaign season, health care had not been a major issue in elections despite seemingly widespread concern over rising costs, declining access, and an overall sense of crisis in the U.S. system. The fact that health care issues were relegated to the second tier in campaigns could be partly explained by the perception that health care was not a national problem (Blumenthal and Berenson 1989), and declining access and deteriorating quality of health care could be dismissed as problems faced only by isolated areas (Kosterlitz 1989c).

Presidents consequently took office without a mandate to change the health care system. In the absence of presidential focus on health reform, Congress addressed reform incrementally. Such a piecemeal approach to health care reform can be counterproductive, however. As health policy analyst Stuart Altman noted: "We make health policy in bits and pieces so the total picture is never seen. It may be that the collective set of decisions takes us in the wrong direction" (Blumenthal and Berenson 1989, 912).

It appeared that the two core ingredients of "ferment and leadership"—that is, a sufficient level of discontent and a key individual (or individuals) to set the course for health care reform—were missing. This in essence guaranteed the continuation of a "long tradition of equivocation on national health policy in the U.S." (Levey and Hill 1989, 1751). Adding to the inaction was the fact that health care reform efforts within Congress were dealt a lethal blow by the 1989 repeal of the Medicare Catastrophic Coverage Act only a year after it was passed by Congress. The bruising battle left congressional members licking their wounds and none-too-anxious to reenter the arena of health care reform.

All this began to change, however, with Democrat Harris Wofford's victory over former attorney general Richard Thornburgh in the 1991 Pennsylvania Senate race. Wofford tapped into voter anxiety over health care and made support for national health insurance the centerpiece of his successful come-from-behind campaign. The response from voters to Wofford's call for national health insurance affirmed the importance of health care as an election issue, second only to the economy (Smith, Altman, Leitman, Moloney, and Taylor 1992).

It would appear that the "present arrangement of unregulated multiple payers and insurers bargaining in the marketplace with an increasingly numerous and competitive army of fee-for-service and prospectively paid providers" will continue until public dissatisfaction reaches critical mass, consensus builds around a comprehensive health care reform program, and policymakers find the political willpower to push reforms through legislative channels (Relman 1989c, 590). The continuing dilemma of accelerating health care costs and increasing numbers of uninsured, however, ensures a prominent place for health care reform on the U.S. public policy agenda. The precise steps the United States will take toward resolving that dilemma, and how long the country will remain paralyzed by inaction, is still unclear.

What is certain is that as long as there are marked differences between the U.S. health care system and those of other industrialized nations—particularly in terms of expenditure levels and access to health care—the United States will continue to look at how other nations are addressing their health care challenges. No one nation has received as much attention as Canada, whose health care system is discussed in Chapter 3.

Canada's National Health Insurance System: U.S. Nemesis or Model for Reform?

Introduction

The previous chapter highlighted some factors fueling the widespread dissatisfaction with, and mounting concern over, the U.S. health care system and examined how these concerns have focused the attention of U.S. health care planners and policymakers on systems in other nations. The remaining chapters analyze the complex health care systems of five other industrialized nations and examine the ways in which they provide care for the majority of their populations while dedicating far less financial resources than the United States.

This journey through the "international health care landscape" (Evans 1988a) begins in familiar territory and moves on to the less familiar. The Canadian health care system is most often suggested as a potential model for reform for the U.S. system and will consequently serve as the point of departure for this cross-national analysis. This chapter will examine the origins of the Canadian system and the ways in which Canadian health care is organized, delivered, and financed. The discussion in this chapter will also focus on the reasons the system is praised by some, while others caution against adopting a similar system in the United States.

The Canadian system currently enjoys a place at the center of the U.S. health policy reform debate. Such attention pleases the Canadians to no end. As one Canada observer points out: "All of a sudden, a nation that has played permanent understudy to its self-absorbed neighbor to the south is in the limelight" (Kosterlitz 1989a, 1792). Almost as often as the Canadian system is cited as the model for restructuring the U.S. system, it is criticized as a totally inappropriate guide.

It is not surprising that the Canadian system is the most popular target for comparison; the United States and Canada share similar cultures, economies, geographic characteristics, and, for the most part, languages and political systems. Twenty years ago, the U.S. and Canadian health care systems were similar. However, Canada has since taken the path of universal insurance; the provincial governments are the sole providers of publicly insured health care services. The United States, in contrast, has remained on the privately based insurance track with multiple health care payers. That the two systems were once similar makes the comparison even more appropriate. Their experience "is the closest we are ever likely to come to a 'quasi-controlled experiment,' conducted in real time with real bullets" (Evans 1990, 110).

But does Canada's universal health insurance system represent a viable model after which the United States can pattern its own version of national health insurance? Furthermore, if the Canadian system does represent a viable alternative, would it be politically feasible to implement a Canadian-style health care system in the United States?

As discussed in Chapter 2, awareness of the fundamental problems of escalating health care costs and declining access has reached unprecedented levels as policymakers, academics, labor leaders, and corporate leaders all call for reform of the U.S. health care system. Perhaps more important from a public policy perspective, public opinion is in favor of change. One poll measuring the attitudes of American, British, and Canadian citizens about their health care systems revealed that a large majority of U.S. respondents felt the U.S. system was in need of fundamental reform. It is interesting to note that 61 percent said they would prefer a Canadian-type health care system (Blendon 1989a).

These results clearly reveal dramatic public concern about the state of health care in the United States. Blendon further noted that this was the first time Americans had exhibited a preference for a foreign system over their own—a significant change in public opinion. However, critics contend that the American preference for the Canadian system results from an inaccurate representation of the Canadian system. In the survey just cited, for example, the Canadian system was described as one in which "the government pays most of the cost of health care for everyone out of taxes, and the government sets all fees charged by doctors and hospitals." Critics assert that neither the fact that Canadians pay much higher taxes to support this system nor the potential rationing involved in such a system was clearly defined (Ham 1989).

Despite these claims, many Americans find the Canadian system intriguing. It may be the case that advocates of the Canadian system are more convinced of the weaknesses of the U.S. system than of the strengths of the Canadian system. It may also be a realization that other systems could provide valuable information for the United States. As an official of the National Association of Manufacturers noted, "the Canadian system may not be ideal, but it is food for thought" (Swoboda and Crenshaw 1989). It is unlikely that the United States would adopt—in the short term—a Canadian-type health care system, as we shall explore later in this chapter. Canada's accomplishments should not be ignored, however. Indeed, the mere existence of the Canadian system pushes the United States to focus on the weaknesses in its own health care system (Iglehart 1989).

The United States Looks Northward

American interest in the Canadian health care system seems to be cyclical. The United States set its sights on the Canadian system in the 1970s, when such public figures as Sen. Edward Kennedy (D-Mass.) and Joseph Califano, secretary of Health, Education, and Welfare in the Carter Administration, argued that the Canadian experience could provide beneficial lessons for the United States (Iglehart 1986a). American interest in national health insurance was usurped in the 1980s, however, by a commitment to the "magic of the marketplace." Such emphasis on competition was the hallmark of the Reagan presidency. The introduction of competition into the health care sector, or, "U.S. medicine's *perestroika*," in the words of one health policy expert, was promoted as the best way to solve the problem of escalating medical costs (Ellwood 1989). Given this environment, "the Canadian experience was of little relevance," notes Robert Evans, one of Canada's leading health economists (Evans, Lomas, Barer, Labelle, et al. 1989, 571). But the pendulum swung back as the 1980s came to a close. Health care costs continued to rise, access problems continued to increase, and the United States once again focused its attention on the health care system of its northern neighbors.

This period of renewed interest in the Canadian health care system has been marked by the participation not only of academics, but of government health policy professionals as well. William L. Roper, President Bush's former deputy assistant for domestic policy and former director of the Centers for Disease Control, remarked that "at the most basic political level, Canada's achievement says to the United States: 'our neighbors to the north have accomplished several important health policy goals. Why can't we?' " Roper went on to add a caveat that he

opposes Canada's approach to health care for the United States because
it goes against the American belief in limited government, but he did
stress the importance of Canada in intensifying the debate over the
future of U.S. health policy (Iglehart 1989, 1768).

The popularity of the Canadian system is based on the combination
of the system, its universal access, and lower overall health care costs
than the United States. Canada provides universal coverage for its
entire population of 26 million while containing health care expenditures at a level below 10 percent of Gross Domestic Product (GDP).
The United States, on the other hand, spends more than 12 percent of
GDP on health care. Despite these higher expenditures, between 35 and
40 million Americans lack health insurance.

Furthermore, the health of Canadians compares favorably with that
of Americans. Standard health care measures indicate that the Canadian health care system is effectively providing quality health care to its
citizens. For example, the average life expectancy at birth in Canada is
73 years for men and 79.8 years for women, compared with U.S. rates
of 71.3 years for men and 78.3 years for women. Moreover, the infant
mortality rate in Canada is 25 percent lower than in the United States
(OECD 1990). It is important to remember, however, that health status
is influenced by myriad nonmedical factors, including lifestyle, environment, and biological factors. Consequently, there are significant limitations on the use of these statistics as a measure of the performance of a
particular health care system.

Shades of Canada

Statistics on health status, particularly those on overall health care
costs, have renewed the interest of U.S. policymakers in the Canadian
health care system. A steady stream of U.S. lawmakers visit Canadian
health ministers, and Canadian health experts testify on a regular basis
at congressional hearings on U.S. health care reform. The reflection of
Canada's system can be seen in several U.S. legislative proposals and
recommendations. For example, the program designed by the Physician
Payment Review Commission to reform physician payment practices
under the Medicare system (discussed in Chapter 2) is similar to the
binding fee schedules for physicians in Canada.

Interest in the Canadian system is evident in proposed legislation in
several states to enact universal health insurance programs that bear
distinct similarities to the Canadian system. For example, the state of
Washington's legislature voted on a proposal to enact changes in the
state health care system based on the health insurance plan of the
Canadian province of British Columbia. Aaron Katz, co-author of a

comparative study of the health care systems of Washington state and British Columbia (B.C.), characterizes the relationship between the two regions as very close: "We probably have more in common with B.C. than with New York" (Priest 1990).

The bill considered by the state legislature—the Washington Health Access and Cost Containment Act—aimed to control costs while expanding access to health care. This is a particular need in Washington state, where 17 percent of the state's population is uninsured despite escalating health expenditures. As expected, the bill stirred up a large controversy, with opposition forces marshaled by the American Medical Association. The bill was passed by the state House but not the Senate. Even though the bill did not pass, Katz said it was important because it "catalyzed the debate." "It has gotten the interest groups here talking in ways they haven't before" (Kosterlitz 1990, 712).

Legislative proposals based on single-payer, universal health care systems similar to the Canadian system were also introduced (but not passed) in Ohio, Michigan, Wisconsin, Idaho, and Illinois. Of the more than eighty pieces of legislation to reform the health care system introduced in Congress in 1992, many envision a Canadian-style system wherein health care would be financed by tax revenues and physician and hospital fees would be set by a government agency.

U.S. Corporate Interest in the Canadian System

American corporations, one of the major purchasers of health care, are drawn to the Canadian system because of its ability to provide universal coverage at costs much lower than currently available in the United States. As noted earlier, many believe that these costs have a significant impact on a company's ability to compete. For example, Ford Motor Company's employee health care costs are significantly higher per car manufactured in the United States than per car produced by Ford's Canadian operations. Jack Shelton, Ford's manager of employee insurance, has argued that "the Canadian system has a lot to offer. For Ford, our costs are much lower in Canada than in the United States even though the benefits are similar." Shelton added that although he did not believe we should adopt the Canadian system wholesale, it was one of several options that deserves U.S. attention (Doherty 1989, 32).

Support for national health insurance in the United States has been strong among certain lobbying groups, but American industry has been unwilling to consider the Canadian system as a model for reform of the U.S. system. The U.S. business community has traditionally viewed the key role played by provincial governments in Canada's tax-financed system with distrust. These same critics have also viewed Canada's system as a close cousin to Britain's nationalized health service—a system not many in the United States would consider emulating. But in the late 1980s, some corporations, feeling powerless in the face of ever-increasing health care costs, began to think what was before unthinkable: national health insurance might be the only way out of the health care cost morass (Kaletsky 1989).

This change in position on the part of some U.S. corporate leaders may actually represent a logical progression rather than a revolutionary step. Henry Aaron, health policy analyst at the Brookings Institution, interprets the shift in the following terms: "One way of looking at it is that, confronted with practical problems, people tend to get pragmatic in a hurry. Even the largest companies have found they have no leverage over an industry that controls more than 10 percent of the Gross National Product" (MacKenzie 1989).

Opposition Remains Strong

As the level of interest in the Canadian system on the part of U.S. policymakers, business leaders, and the American public increases, certain groups in the United States are working to take some of the gleam off the positive image that the Canadian health care system enjoys. It is not surprising, given the vested interests at stake, that the more vocal critics of the Canadian system are members of the medical and insurance professions and trade associations. The American Medical Association (AMA), for example, has characterized the Canadian health care system as "socialized medicine managed by an ever-enlarging and more expensive bureaucracy, financed by ever-increasing taxation and featuring rationing, shortages, health care waiting lists and an absence of private-sector alternatives" (Freudenheim 1989b). The AMA launched a nationwide promotional campaign in 1989, funded by contributions from its members, to "alert Congress and the voters to the dangers of a Canadian-type health care system" (Iglehart 1989, 1772).

For its part, the Health Insurance Association of America (HIAA), a trade group representing the majority of U.S. insurers, recently published a study of the Canadian health care system. The study argued that Canada's health care cost-control record was not as successful as portrayed (Neuschler 1990). Carl Schramm, then-president of the HIAA, warned association members of the dangers posed by increasing U.S. interest in the Canadian system: "We cannot be mistaken about the implications of all this: a move in the United States to a Canadian approach to health care financing is antithetical to our interests" (MacKenzie 1990).

Other critics include the Heritage Foundation, which has stated that the Canadian system provides clear evidence that any health care system managed by the government can only have one outcome: "diminished and rationed health care resources" (Freudenheim 1989b). Moreover, although many corporations have paid lip service to support of a national health insurance system similar to Canada's, very few have gone beyond talk. As one analyst explains, "as defenders of the market, they will surely hesitate a long time before advocating that we eliminate the role of private health insurance companies" in health care financing (Ginzberg 1990, 1465).

Overview of Canadian Health Care

What is this system that has inspired U.S. legislation while engendering the interest and respect of some health experts, policymakers, and business leaders, and the disdain of others? There are many similarities between the U.S. and Canadian health care systems, but there are key differences, also, ranging from the underpinning philosophy of the system to the way in which health care costs are reimbursed. Such differences raise important implications for the way in which health care is managed and delivered in the two countries.

Most health care systems contain elements of the public and private sector, but Canada, to a greater extent, straddles the line between public and private. The Canadian health care system consists of twelve separate provincial and territorial plans financed almost exclusively through public revenues in the form of personal, sales, and corporate taxes. Doctors run private independent practices and are paid fees for their services. The majority of hospitals are operated by private, voluntary, nonprofit organizations. There is a high level of regulation within the Canadian health care system. Physicians' charges are fixed according to a negotiated fee schedule, and hospitals must operate within the parameters of an overall "global" budget. Given this mixture, Canada can be placed in the center of the market minimized/maximized continuum, because even though hospitals are private, nonprofit institutions, and physicians practice on a private fee-for-service basis, the government is the primary payer of health care services (Anderson 1989).

While Canada's health care system is a blend of public finance and private practice, the role of the private sector in Canadian health care has been limited intentionally. Whether controls on the involvement of the private sector are relaxed will determine whether the Canadian system will converge toward a more privately based health care system similar to that of the United States.

Canadian National Health Insurance:
A Long Time Coming

The roots of Canada's most popular social program can be traced to the British North American Act of 1867, which laid out the parameters of responsibility for Canada's health care system. All aspects of the hospital sector—from construction and maintenance of facilities to all medical care provided within hospitals—were to fall within the purview of provincial governments. The federal government was to be responsible for such groups as native Indians, Eskimos, and military personnel, as well as for food and drug legislation (Evans 1975).

The concept of a publicly financed health insurance program in Canada was first introduced in 1919, but it took the combined hardships of the Great Depression and World War II to bring national health insurance to the top of the legislative agenda. In the mid-1940s, public support for universal health care was strong. A 1944 Gallup Poll revealed that 80 percent of the Canadian population was in favor of federally supported health insurance plans for each province. More important, as Malcolm Taylor, a preeminent historian on Canadian health care, points out, the public was willing to shoulder the cost of a national health plan (Taylor 1986). The concept also had the support of the Canadian Medical Association (CMA), although the medical profession demanded representation on all public health insurance commissions and final say over compensation methods (Stevenson, Williams, and Vayda 1988).

Drawing on such broad-based public support, the federal government, as an enticement to encourage each of the provinces to set up provincial health insurance plans, offered to contribute funds to help defray some of the cost of health services. In return for these federal funds, the provinces had to turn over all personal and corporate income taxes to the federal government. This requirement proved to be too bitter a pill for the provinces to swallow, and the federal proposals were abandoned in 1945 (Taylor 1986).

Blue Cross, Blue Shield, and commercial insurance plans filled the void left by the unsuccessful attempt to set up a nationwide system of provincial health insurance plans. The development of these insurance plans eroded the initial base of support for a comprehensive national health insurance system, as medical, hospital, and insurance groups developed their own power bases. The CMA, meanwhile, shifted its position from support of public insurance to opposition; the collapse of federal proposals allowed the medical profession to create their own physician-controlled health insurance plans. These plans took hold in all the provinces (Stevenson, Williams, and Vayda 1988). At the same time, however, federal-provincial relations—which had been strained by conflict over the initial proposals—gradually began to relax, and a consensus in support of national health insurance reemerged among provincial leaders (Taylor 1986).

Hospital Insurance

The initial federal proposals were brought back to life when the province of Saskatchewan introduced a hospital insurance program in 1947. British Columbia followed suit in 1949, as did Alberta in 1950. When Newfoundland became part of Canada in 1949, approximately half its population was already covered by government hospital insurance. Thus, even though attempts to create a national health insurance program had failed five years earlier, four Canadian provinces had functioning public hospital insurance plans by 1950.

The "demonstration effect" of these provincial programs should not be underestimated (Tuohy 1986). In 1957, the federal government passed the Hospital Insurance and Diagnostic Services Act, which served as the basis for a universal system of hospital insurance. Each province would receive federal grants that were to cover approximately half of the program's total cost. It is important to note that this was not a smooth, quick process; it took at least a decade for the federal and provincial governments to settle all the financial and administrative details (Anderson 1989).

While the plans were being formalized on the provincial level, concern arose that Canada might allow plans to develop in the provinces without federal oversight to ensure equity and regulate a standard level of benefits (Anderson 1989, 63). The granting of federal funds was made contingent upon four conditions. First, each provincial plan had to be *comprehensive,* providing all medically necessary services with no benefits limitations. Second, plans had to be *publicly financed and administered by an agency accountable to the provincial government.* Third, plan benefits had to be *universal*—available to all— and provided on *uniform terms and conditions.* Fourth, the interprovincial *portability* of plan benefits had to be assured so that Canadian citizens traveling outside their province of residence would still be covered.

As long as these four conditions were met, the federal government would allocate funds to contribute to the costs of the provincial hospital plans. This method of cost sharing ensured a nationwide standard of health care. Citizens of such poorer provinces as Newfoundland would have access to the same standard of health care as those in such wealthier provinces as Ontario. Even though the provinces had to cede a certain amount of autonomy to the federal government in terms of control over the provincial plans, the cost-sharing offer was too good to refuse. By 1961, all ten provinces had hospital insurance plans that fulfilled the four criteria (Taylor 1986).

The establishment of hospital insurance plans did not mean that the government took over the hospitals. Canadian hospitals remained voluntary, not-for-profit organizations under the direction of a board of trustees. What changed was the system of reimbursement: provincial governments became the sole payers of hospital services (Barer 1988).

Medical Care Insurance

The success of the hospital program generated public support for an expansion to include medical care provided in areas other than hospitals (in other words, physicians' services). A Royal Commission appointed by the federal government in the early 1960s recommended the creation of a program to provide a wide range of medical benefits, partially supported by federal subsidies and administered by the provinces.

The medical care insurance program was not universally welcomed. In fact, it met large-scale opposition from the medical profession, the private insurance industry, and even several provincial governments. In order to win over the physicians, the federal government had to make certain assurances to the medical profession that their professional freedom would not be jeopardized by government intervention in the health care sector (Rachlis and Kushner 1989). But professional autonomy was not all the doctors were concerned about; there were more than ten private insurance plans controlled by physicians that covered four million people, and "business was booming" (Regush 1987, 28). The government assured the doctors (and tempered their opposition somewhat in the process) that the fee-for-service payment system and the system of fee schedules that existed in the physician-controlled insurance plans would be preserved.

The federal government pushed its program through despite the opposition of physicians and insurance groups, and the Medical Care Act went into effect in 1968. The same four conditions applying to the hospital plans governed disbursement of federal funds for physicians' services. Physician opposition declined as it became apparent that the new system was a boon to the income of physicians; the doctors were less likely to complain in the face of "windfall professional income gains" as a result of payment basically being guaranteed by the new provincial plans (Stevenson, Williams, and Vayda 1988, 69).

Medicare Is Born

All ten provinces had full physician and hospital coverage by 1971, and the Yukon and Northwest territories followed a year later. Canada finally had a national health insurance program—known as Medicare—in place more than fifty years after the idea was first conceived. Almost all hospital and physician services are covered under the plans, and all legal residents receive health care that is free at the point of service (although not "free" in the financial sense; residents pay taxes that fund health care services) (Lomas, Fooks, Rice, and Labelle 1989, 82). The removal of financial barriers to care was a crucial principle guiding the Canadian health care system's formation. Another key feature of the system is the freedom it allows both patients and physicians: Patients are free to choose their own physicians and hospitals, and physicians are free to choose where they want to practice.

The Canadian system of universal, comprehensive health care is rooted in the deeply held conviction that health care is a right, not a privilege. This conviction is illustrated by this statement by the Royal Commission: "What we seek is a method that will provide everyone in Canada with comprehensive coverage regardless of age, state of health, or ability to pay, upon uniform terms and conditions" (Brown, K. 1989, 213).

Preventing a two-tier system of health care comprised of those who could pay and those who could not was a high priority. The federal government determined that the best way to avoid such a two-tier system was to take the dramatic step of outlawing private insurance coverage for any services covered under the provincial plans. Provincial universal hospital and medical plans thus took the place of all the various forms of insurance—private, not-for-profit, and public—that had existed up to that point. The provincial governments became the single purchasers of publicly insured hospital and medical care services (Taylor 1986).

The shift in financing from private to public channels brought about by the advent of the Canadian provincial health insurance plans is traced in Table 3-1. By the mid-1970s, approximately 95 percent of all costs of hospital and medical care services were paid through the provincial health plans. The shift in financing is particularly striking in the medical care sector. In 1960, only 14 percent of all medical care expenditures were covered by public funds; fifteen years later this figure had increased to 95 percent (Evans 1984).

The federal government, as discussed previously, was not granted constitutional authority to set up and manage a national health system. As a consequence, the health system that exists in Canada is actually a

Table 3-1   Health Insurance Coverage, Canada 1950-1981

	1950	1955	1960	1965	1970	1975	1978	1981
Percent of spending in public sector								
All health	n.a.	n.a.	43	51	70	77	76	74
Hospitals	n.a.	n.a.	72	89	94	95	93	91
Medical care	n.a.	n.a.	14	18	77	95	96	96
Percent of population with medical care insurance								
Private comprehensive	14	27	36	45	1	0	0	0
Private limited	5	10	14	16	0	0	0	0
Public	n.a.	n.a.	8	12	96	100	100	100
Percent of hospital expenses paid by third parties	71	86	98	100	100	100	100	100
Percent of population with some medical coverage	20	38	50	62	95	100	100	100

Source: Evans, Robert G. *Strained Mercy: The Economics of Canadian Health Care*, p. 29. Toronto: Butterworths, 1984. Reprinted with permission.

federal-provincial system that is essentially a patchwork of separate provincial and territorial plans (Evans 1988a). The provinces are free to determine how their health care plans will be organized and their health care dollars spent. This is a crucial point, for, as Evans notes, "the division of powers between the federal government in Ottawa and the 10 provincial governments is Canada's longest and most carefully defended border" (Evans 1975, 129). At the same time, the federal government imposes certain regulations that tie the plans together.

Political and Cultural Underpinnings of Canadian Health Care

Social institutions such as health care systems are not created in a vacuum; they are reflections of societal values and expectations. Appreciation of the political and cultural environment in which the Canadian health care system evolved is essential to an understanding of the system itself, and how resources are allocated and costs controlled. Canada's universal, publicly administered, tax-financed system stands in contrast to the U.S. system, which although it is not a true free market, does rely to a large degree on market forces to determine prices (except under Medicare and Medicaid) and is based on a limited role for government in the health care sector. Every Canadian citizen is eligible for coverage under the provincial health insurance plans. Canada has thus successfully avoided the casualties of the U.S. system—the large number of U.S. citizens who face financial barriers to health care. This difference highlights what one observer calls the "remarkable egalitarian quality about Canadian health care that reflects a society that attaches a higher value to social equity than does the United States" (Iglehart 1986b, 781).

The Canadian and American political cultures share similar features: both are multiparty systems based on democratic ideals. Both are also federal systems with state (province) and local level government participation in public policy matters (Tuohy 1986). Despite these similarities, distinct features of each political culture have had a significant impact on the creation of each nation's social programs, particularly their health care systems.

One important feature—as noted by political theorist Louis Hartz— is that societies such as the United States, English Canada, French Canada, and Australia are "fragments," or offshoots, of European countries that developed independently in non-European lands. Despite shared British origins, the U.S. and English Canadian societies and their institutions evolved differently. Most notably, the American war of independence buried all vestiges of "tory" origins in the United States, while the "loyalists" in Canada kept their "tory touch" (Tuohy 1986, 396).

Yet in Canada, this "tory" strain did not predominate. Instead, a rather strange mixture evolved, one containing remnants of the British tory conservatives combined with socialism. A socialist party was able to establish itself in Canada because its ideas did not differ significantly from the prevailing beliefs in society. Socialism in Canada, in the words of political theorist Gad Horowitz, "is British, non-Marxist and worldly," in contrast to the U.S. view of socialism as "German, Marxist, and other-worldly" (Tuohy 1986, 396).

One Canadian journalist described Canada's distinctive political culture, known as collectivism, as a combination of "capitalism with social responsibility—a kind of liberal conservatism or vice versa" (Brown, B. 1989, 28). According to one analyst, Canada's collectivist culture "encourages a collaboration between the leadership of corporate groups and the state in the pursuit of redistributive policies" (Tuohy 1986, 396). The implications of this particular type of political culture are significant for the development of social programs:

> The coexistence of these elements has produced distinctive hybrids: "tory touched" liberals less distrustful of concentrated

power than their U.S. counterparts; "red tories" supportive of
redistributive policies implemented through public and private
hierarchies; and democratic socialists willing to pursue collectivist
goals through the institutions of the state (Tuohy 1986, 398).

The existence of this collectivist culture is central to the evolution
of a health care system in Canada far different from its American
counterpart. Canada's parliamentary system is a product of this
political culture and thus focuses on consensus building. One
analyst suggested that a present day illustration of Canadian
efforts at compromise and consensus building is found in the oxy-
moronic name of the ruling party—the Progressive Conservatives
(Linton 1990b).

Such consensus building is not a feature of the U.S. system, whose
diffuse bicameral political structure makes conflict the rule rather than
the exception. Indeed, U.S. governmental institutions were created to
check and balance power, in part, through the use of vetos; the
Canadian system does not contain such mechanisms (Tuohy 1986).
Other differences have important implications for the formulation of
policy. In Canada, for example,

> The majority party (or a coalition of minority parties) governs
> until the electorate votes it out of office. Private interests
> tend to have less influence in a parliamentary system, because
> governments generally try to fashion policy that appeals to a
> national majority. Thus, Canadian policy is designed with
> greater unanimity of purpose at the national and provincial levels
> and there are fewer checks and balances than in the U.S.
> (Iglehart 1989, 1770).

The inherent distrust of government on the part of many Americans
precludes such an arrangement in the United States. Brown University professor James Morone argues that this aversion to government
leads Americans to search for "mechanistic, self-enforcing, automatic
solutions" as a way of avoiding government intervention. The U.S.
reliance on market forces in the health care sector can be clearly
understood in this context (Morone 1990, 133). Canadians, in contrast, have shown a greater willingness than Americans to grant
government the key powers to finance and regulate health care
programs (Lomas, Fooks, Rice, Labelle 1989). Canada places a strong
emphasis on using the government as a vehicle to attain goals
consistent with the collective good. As Evans notes, "In Canada . . .
the natural focus for collective activity has always been government.
As residents of a small country . . . Canadians have instinctively

turned to the state as the instrument of collective purposes. A multiplicity of competing organizations is a luxury we cannot afford" (Evans 1988a, 169).

Such a distinction can be seen in the contrasting objectives spelled out in the constitutions of the United States and Canada. Life, liberty, and the pursuit of happiness are the stated goals in the United States; peace, order, and good government are the stated goals in Canada (Linton 1990b). The concept of the government as the promoter and guardian of the collective good may seem strange to many Americans. This was the case for Vickery Stoughton, an American who manages Toronto General Hospital:

> The thing that struck me was that there's a social conscience in this country that says *"we value the collective good over the individual"* [emphasis added]. Canadians trust government and it's part of the social fabric of this country. That kind of societal attitude must have made it easier to introduce a universal health care system and it has become the most popular social program in this country, bar none (Kosterlitz 1989b, 1874).

The emphasis of the collective good over the individual shapes Canadian health care policy, particularly the Canadian approach to the distribution of scarce health care resources. Resources are allocated on the basis of need, not on the patient's financial standing, as " 'equality before the health care system' has been established as a . . . principle similar to 'equality before the law' " (Evans 1988a, 165). With this distinction and others in mind, let us now take a closer look at the Canadian system, how it operates, and how it differs from its American counterpart.

Health Care Delivery in Canada

Since health care in Canada is financed through tax revenues, and provincial governments play a key role as the primary bill payers within the system, Canada's system is often equated with "socialized medicine," similar to the system provided by Britain's state-owned National Health Service. In fact, health care in Canada is provided through a private delivery system: Patients have free choice of physician, physicians are in private practice and are paid fees for the services they provide. This combination of public financing and private delivery can be described as socialized insurance. In Canada, public control is exerted by the provincial governments, but health care services are delivered privately. Some key characteristics of the Canadian provincial health insurance plans are discussed briefly below.

Coverage under the Plans

Canadian provincial health insurance plans cover a broad range of services. All legal residents are covered regardless of income level and health status. Coverage is portable and not linked to employment. Health coverage, therefore, does not limit job mobility—a growing concern in the United States. All medically necessary physicians' services provided in hospitals, clinics, and doctors' offices are covered, as are all in-patient hospital services, all necessary drugs (if supplied in the hospital), supplies, and tests. A wide range of outpatient services are also covered; psychiatrists' services and mental hospitals are also covered under the plans (Iglehart 1990). Depending on the province, the public plan may cover services such as podiatry, physical therapy, chiropractic treatments, prescription drugs for the elderly, and dental care for children.

Long-term care services are provided under the plans as a result of the Extended Health Care Services Program passed in 1977. Such services include health care, personal care, and social services provided in nursing homes or in the community. The individual's inability to function without the services is the criterion used to determine eligibility for nursing homes; the individual's income does not affect his or her eligibility status, and therefore the elderly do not have to exhaust their savings, as in the United States (Kane and Kane 1985).

Hospitals

The hospital insurance plans in six provinces are organized under a provincial department. In the remaining four provinces, the hospital plans are run by special committees that report to the ministry of health. The vast majority of Canada's 1,243 hospitals are public community or university hospitals, owned by voluntary corporations, religious organizations, or local governments. They are funded primarily by the provincial health plans and are operated by independent boards on a nonprofit basis (Hastings and Vayda 1986; Iglehart 1990a).

Certain hospitals in the United States, particularly in the inner cities, have become de facto hospitals for the poor, but no such separation exists in Canada. Indeed, it is almost impossible to determine a patient's economic status since the only question asked on admission is whether the patient has private insurance coverage to cover the cost of a private hospital room (Iglehart 1986b, 781).

Physicians' Services

The majority of doctors in Canada are in private practice, generally solo practice, and are paid on a fee-for-service basis. The price for each service performed is set according to a fee schedule. This schedule is determined through negotiations between the provincial governments and the medical associations. Doctors do not bill patients directly, but are paid by the provincial health plans. Physicians practicing in the public system are not allowed to accept private payments from patients. Doctors cannot be both in the system and out of it. As Evans has said, "The Canadian physician who chooses to go private must go all the way" (1988a, 166). Very few physicians have opted out of the provincial plans.

Alternative Health Care Delivery Mechanisms

In the United States such alternative forms of health care delivery as Health Maintenance Organizations (HMOs) are being used with greater frequency by employers as a cost-control strategy (Wyatt Company 1990b). In contrast, Health Service Organizations (HSOs— modeled after U.S. HMOs) in Canada have yet to move from the periphery of the health care sector, and are viewed by many as experimental in nature. Canadian interest in the U.S. experience with HMOs can be expected to increase as Canada examines new strategies of controlling health care costs. For example, Toronto General Hospital opened its first HSO in 1990.

Such new arrangements are not welcomed by all; many Canadian doctors warn against "blind acceptance of evidence from the U.S." (Linton 1989, 20). Physicians are particularly opposed to the con- straints on the freedom of providers imposed by HMOs. As one former director of the Ontario Medical Association put it, "The managed care component of American medicine is being held like a Damocles' sword over the heads of Canadian physicians, while our universal health insurance system is held like a Damocles' sword over you" (Iglehart 1990a, 563).

One Canadian health expert asserted that it is unlikely that Cana- dian-style HMOs would expand in the near future due to the structure of the Canadian health care system; Medicare serves as insulation against managed care because doctors in Canada provide fully insured services that are free at the point of service. Private prepayment agencies are limited by Medicare's first-dollar coverage. Moreover, the freedom of Canadian patients to choose their own doctors prevents HSOs from "locking in" patients as HMOs do in the United States.

These factors create what is essentially "an inhospitable environment" for alternative arrangements to fee-for-service (Naylor 1990).

Canadian Health Care Financing

As we have seen, Canada's universal health insurance system is financed primarily through tax revenues. Steady economic growth (and the tax revenues generated in the process) are consequently the lifeblood of the health care sector. The Canadian provinces are very powerful. Provincial governments have extensive taxing powers and regulate health programs as they wish. The provinces earmark amounts ranging from 19.5 percent (Newfoundland) to 32.2 percent (Ontario) of their entire budgets to administer and operate their health plans (Rachlis and Kushner 1989).

Although Canadian health care is essentially free at the point of service (patients never see a bill), it is by no means *free* to the individual. Individual income taxes are 15 to 20 percent higher in Canada than the United States. In addition, sales taxes are higher, which in turn causes products to be more expensive in Canada than in the United States. Sales taxes vary in Canada; the province of Alberta, for example, does not charge any sales tax, while sales taxes in Ontario are 8 percent and in Newfoundland are 10 percent (Claiborne 1990).

Residents of British Columbia and Alberta pay monthly income-based premiums on health care. Many employers pay these premiums for their employees. The province of Ontario did away with its monthly individual premiums in 1990, replacing them with an employer-paid payroll tax of 1.9 percent.

Financing Changes: 1977 and 1984

The way in which health care in Canada is financed was markedly altered by two pieces of federal legislation. First, the enactment of the Federal-Provincial Fiscal Arrangements and Established Programs Financing Act (EPF) in 1977 effectively instituted a cap on the federal contribution to provincial health plans. Second, the passage of the Canada Health Act in 1984 ushered in one of the more controversial periods in the history of Canadian health care by pitting the medical profession against the public.

The EPF. By the mid-1970s, the Canadian federal government had become concerned about rising health care expenditures. Although the federal government matched all provincial expenditures, it had no control over total expenditures. For their part, the provinces were not overly concerned with holding down costs because they were spending "50-cent dollars"; they knew whatever amount they spent would be matched by federal funds (Taylor, M. 1986).

The federal government rectified this situation by retreating from its open-ended commitment to fund provincial health plans, enacting the EPF in 1977. This law set out a new method of cost-sharing in which the government traded its prior arrangement of matching provincial health costs on a 50-50 basis for a system of per capita health care payments in the form of block grants. In return, a certain amount of personal and corporate income tax revenue was to be shifted to the provinces. This new financing scheme tied increases in federal financial support for provincial health plans to economic growth measured by increases in GNP. The provinces would therefore be bound to cover a larger share of the health care costs when these costs increased faster than the nation's overall economic growth (Iglehart 1986b). In this way, the federal government could use the cap on federal funds to foster cost control at the provincial level.

Thus the EPF effectively shifted the responsibility for cost control to the provinces. The federal government would maintain a measure of control over the system, however, as disbursement of the block grants was linked to compliance with national standards. Federal funds were contingent on fulfilling the four criteria (comprehensiveness, public administration, universality, and portability) outlined earlier.

The EPF was a watershed in the development of the Canadian health care system for two reasons. First, it "represented the most massive transfer in history of revenues (and therefore of the substance of power) from the federal to the provincial governments" (Taylor, M. 1986, 25). Second, it completely changed the ratio of federal-provincial funds for health care. From 1977 on, the annual rate of health cost increases would have to stay in line with GNP increases. The difference would be borne by the provinces if health care expenditures outpaced GNP growth.

The ultimate result of the EPF legislation has been a significant increase in the provincial share of health care costs, as those costs have increased faster than the Canadian economy in eight of the past thirteen years. In 1979 to 1980, the federal government covered 44.6 percent of total health care expenditures. Current figures put the federal share at 36.7 percent, while future predictions indicate the share will slip even further (Iglehart 1990a, 564).

The Canada Health Act of 1984. The second major piece of legislation with important financial implications for Canadian health care was the Canada Health Act of 1984. The Act was partly a consequence of a series of wage and price controls implemented by the federal government during an inflationary period in the mid-1970s. When the government relaxed these controls, physicians used the vehicle of balance billing—that is, charging more than the fee schedule would allow—to make up for the previous period of austerity. This practice was seen to be in direct conflict with the philosophical core of Canadian health care: equal access for all. A commission created by the federal government to study this issue found that balance billing (or extra billing, as it is sometimes called) was indeed compromising access to care for those unable to pay the extra fees (Taylor, M. 1986).

According to health economist Morris Barer, then-prime minister Pierre Elliott Trudeau, with his reelection hanging in the balance, seized upon the issue as a political life raft and proposed the Canada Health Act (Barer 1988; Iglehart 1986b). The act made extra billing by physicians illegal. The medical profession opposed the act on the grounds that extra billing was a safety valve offering protection from the powerful provincial governments that set physicians' fees. Provincial governments opposed the bill on the grounds that it infringed on their constitutional rights (Iglehart 1986b). Whereas the EPF transferred power to the provinces, the Canada Health Act was considered an "unwarranted and powerful federal intrusion into a field of provincial jurisdiction" by the provincial government and the medical associations (Taylor, M. 1986, 25).

The Canada Health Act enjoyed tremendous public support, and no government official with any survival instinct would vote against it. So the bill breezed through Parliament unopposed, despite strong opposition from the medical profession and provincial governments. The act imposed a strict penalty on those provinces that permitted extra billing: federal grants would be reduced in direct proportion to the extra billing charges. In other words, for every dollar charged directly to a patient, the province would lose one dollar in federal funds.

The reaction to the passage of the Canada Health Act was particularly heated in Ontario, where the Ontario Medical Association challenged the legality of the bill and called a strike to put pressure on the provincial government to repeal it. The strike, the longest in Canadian history, was called off after twenty-five days. The conflict over extra billing "drew sharp lines of battle between the majority of the physicians in the country and the majority of the population. The population won" (Evans 1988a, 168). All ten provinces had passed legislation by 1987 to ban extra billing. However, the deep rifts that developed over the extra billing issue continue to this day.

Financing Benefits Not Covered by the Provincial Plans:
The Role of the Employer

Unlike their U.S. counterparts, Canadian employers rarely, if ever, are faced with employee strikes over the issue of health benefits. As Perrin Beatty, Canada's minister of national health and welfare, stated during an October 1989 presentation to the Families U.S.A. Foundation in Washington, D.C.:

> Businesses like our system, not just because it is cheaper, but also because the burden of paying for it is spread more fairly. In Canada, health care is paid for by taxes—personal taxes, corporate taxes, sales taxes, payroll taxes and other taxes. All Canadians share in the burden according to their ability to pay, and all Canadians benefit (Health and Welfare Canada 1989).

Canadian employers do subsidize the health insurance of their employees through contributions to Workmen's Compensation boards in the majority of the provinces, and many employers pay employee health insurance premiums in the provinces that levy such charges.

As noted earlier, the final seal on the establishment of universal health insurance in Canada was the enactment of a federal law prohibiting private health insurance companies from covering any medical services that fall within the scope of the provincial health plans. Supplementary health insurance plans are available, however, to cover medical costs for services not covered by the plans. These services include dental care, vision care, prescription drugs, and semi-private and private hospital rooms. Approximately 80 percent of the population has such supplemental coverage (U.S. Congress 1989). The majority of such coverage is financed by employers and provided through Blue Cross or a range of commercial health insurance plans.

According to a 1990 survey of more than 750 Canadian companies, 99 percent of employers provide their employees with a supplemental health benefit plan, and 94 percent provide dental benefits. The survey found that 70 percent of employers require no employee contribution toward their supplemental health plan (Wyatt Company 1990a).

The biggest item covered by supplemental health plans by far is prescription drugs. The survey revealed that 60 percent of supplemental health plans reimburse 100 percent of prescription drug expenses (Wyatt Company 1990a). These costs absorb almost three-quarters of all employer-financed supplemental benefits (Doherty 1989). Prescription drug costs are soaring; between 1983 and 1988, the average prescription cost increased by 10.6 percent per year. Employers are consequently searching for ways to cut down on these costs. Cost-control efforts include increasing deductibles and co-payments, using generic drug plans that cover only the least expensive drug available, or forming preferred provider arrangements to obtain discounts on drugs (Harrietha 1989).

The era of tightening fiscal restraint in Canada increases the likelihood that shifting costs from the public to the private sector will become more common. Measures such as the taxation of dental and prescription drug benefits and the introduction of user fees are being considered. In anticipation of their share of employee health care costs increasing, Canadian employers are currently examining such U.S. cost-control measures as managed care and flexible benefits programs (Doherty 1989).

Health Care Cost-Control, Canadian-Style

In 1970, Canadian and American health expenditures were on par with one another at 7.1 and 7.4 percent of GDP, respectively. Within the following ten years, however, U.S. expenditures shot up to 9.2 percent of GDP while Canadian expenditures remained steady at 7.4 percent of GDP. Canada kept its health expenditures below 9 percent of GDP throughout the 1980s while U.S. health costs soared beyond 11 percent of GDP (see Figure 3-1).

The broad divergence in U.S. and Canadian health care expenditure trends during the period 1971 to 1981 is due almost entirely to differences in expenditures for hospitals and physicians. Although hospital and physician services are the largest single outlay in provincial budgets, health economist Evans notes that during the ten-year period:

> U.S. expenditures on hospitals, as a share of the GNP, rose very rapidly, from 2.86 percent to 4.02 percent; while the Canadian share was actually falling from its initially higher level of 3.33 percent to 3.16 percent. For physicians' services the fall was even more pronounced, from 1.32 percent to 1.10 percent, while the U.S. share was rising from 1.48 percent to 1.87 percent (Evans 1986b, 29).

The differences can be explained by the particular methods of reimbursement that form the centerpiece of the Canadian system. Unlike the U.S. multiple-payer system, the Canadian provincial governments are the only payers for publicly insured services. One economist draws an analogy between Canadian cost-control processes and a U.S. HMO: "In a sense, our provincial plans are super HMOs, each with a

Figure 3-1   Total Health Expenditures As a Percentage of Gross Domestic Product, Canada and the United States, 1970-1990

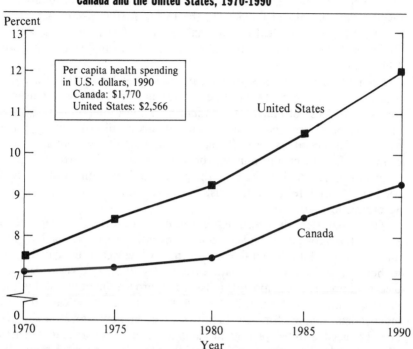

Source: Schieber, George, Jean-Pierre Poullier, and Leslie M. Greenwald. "U.S. Health Expenditure Performance: An International Comparison and Data Update." *Health Care Financing Review* 13, 4: (1-15). HCFA Pub. no. 03331. Office of Research and Demonstrations. Health Care Financing Administration. Washington, D.C.: U.S. Government Printing Office, September 1992.

geographical monopoly, negotiating with a fractious group of providers, and under political rather than market constraints to keep costs down" (Evans 1986a, 34). Provincial governments use their monopsony (sole purchaser) power to control expenditures, drawing on two major weapons from their cost-control arsenals: global budgets for hospitals and tight control over physicians' fees.

Global Hospital Budgets

Controls on hospital budgets are important because hospital expenditures absorb the largest share of provincial health care budgets. Hospital operating expenses are kept separate from funds for capital expenditures. Annual global (total) hospital budgets for operating expenses are negotiated between the provincial governments and each individual hospital. In Ontario, for example, hospitals are given an annual global budget (in the form of a lump-sum payment) by the Ministry of Health that "serves as a fiscal envelope within which each hospital must function for the following year" (Naylor 1991, 111).

Each hospital then has to allocate resources for all the different hospital services from its one budget. Annual budgets are not usage-sensitive. It does not matter if a patient comes in for a coronary bypass operation or to seek care for a sprained ankle: all costs are applied against the hospital's overall budget. A hospital will budget, for example, for a certain number of elective coronary artery bypass surgical procedures. If more than the predetermined number of patients need the procedure, a waiting list is created and patients are ranked according to need.

The separation of operating expenses from capital expenditures enables the provinces to exert control over increasing capacity, and ultimately over total hospital expenditures. All new capital expenditures to build new facilities, renovate existing facilities, or procure major pieces of medical equipment must be approved in advance by the provincial ministry of health. Although hospitals can raise capital from independent sources for new facilities or equipment, government approval is needed to use provincial plans to cover the operating expenses of the new facility or procedure. In other words, a hospital might be able to raise enough money to purchase a magnetic resonance imager (MRI), but the hospital would need the provincial ministry's permission for funds necessary to operate the machine.

Most major advanced technologies are concentrated in hospitals. For example, all computerized tomography (CT) scanners are in hospitals (a rule enforced by law in Ontario). This concentration of high technology services in hospitals, and the control over hospital budgets by provincial governments, slows the diffusion of technology. For example, the city of Toronto has only one radiation therapy treatment center while the city of Boston, Massachusetts, a city of similar population, has thirteen machines used to administer radiation therapy (Iglehart 1986b). The United States has eight times as many MRI units per million people than does Canada (Rublee 1989). This concentration of medical technology thus forces physicians to prioritize treatment on the basis of need.

The highly centralized hospital budgeting process in Canada contrasts sharply with the decentralized hospital budgeting process in the United States. The absence of limits on procurement of expensive, highly advanced equipment and procedures in the United States also stands in sharp contrast to Canada, where technology control is an integral component of cost control.

Physicians' Fee Schedules

The second cost-control mechanism, the process of negotiating physicians' fee schedules, has also contributed to Canada's success in controlling health care costs. Doctors in Canada are paid directly from the provincial budgets on a fee-for-service basis. Their incomes are based on a fee schedule that establishes a price for each medical service. The total percentage increase in the fee base is hammered out during negotiations between the provincial ministries of health and the provincial medical associations. The provincial medical association then determines how the increase will be divided among the different medical specialties and services.

The negotiating process has evolved over time. The transition from physician-controlled plans to the establishment of provincial insurance plans with the government as major paymaster markedly altered the structure of fee negotiations and caused a shift in the balance of power between the health care providers (physicians) and payers (provincial governments). Barer sheds light on this important transition:

> Whereas previously the physician-controlled insurance programs had essentially administered an orderly escalation of fees and incomes, under the new regime provincial governments had to bear the political costs of raising the necessary funds. Fee schedules were subsequently negotiated, not promulgated, and the negotiations became serious (1988, 12).

Even in the early years of national health insurance, provincial governments tended to accept the medical associations' fee schedules and agreed to pay physicians 85 to 100 percent of the amounts set out in those schedules. Physicians agreed to less than full reimbursement because they would no longer have to be concerned with bad debts—patients not paying their bills—as the government would be the sole payer. As the system matured, however, formal negotiations replaced the province's nearly automatic acceptance of the medical associations' fee schedules (Lomas, Fooks, Rice, and Labelle 1989).

The negotiations—once described as "large-scale political theater with all the rhetorical threats and flourishes that political clashes require"—are designed to determine the total percentage increase for physicians' services (Evans, Lomas, Barer, Labelle, et al. 1989, 576).

Tuohy argues that the fee schedule negotiations are beneficial for both the government and the medical profession because they:

> galvanize the entrepreneurial majority of the profession into a display of defiance; they symbolize to the public at large that professional power is being held in check by a government concerned about costs; and they offer a catharsis for the mutual suspicions of physicians, bureaucrats and politicians, without fundamentally challenging existing power relationships or familiar ground rules (1986, 412).

Recent negotiations reveal the strong bargaining position of the provincial governments. Doctors contend that fee negotiations occur only in theory; in practice provincial governments impose their will on physicians because "in the end the provincial government can determine what fees it will pay on a 'take it or leave it' basis" (Barer 1988, 15). This is precisely what happened in Ontario during the 1989 fee schedule negotiations. The medical associations and the provincial government reached a stalemate in the negotiations. The government unilaterally imposed a 1.75 percent increase in the fee schedule, rejecting the physicians' demand for a higher increase (Linton 1990a). Such exercises of absolute control over fee schedules have resulted in a significant amount of physician disaffection in Canada.

The process of physician fee negotiation is inherently contentious because it "requires the direct confrontation of interests with substantial build up of stress" (Evans 1990, 101), but it has played a key role in Canada's ability to control health care costs. And despite the fee controls, doctors are the highest paid professionals in Canada. Average incomes of physicians have consistently surpassed those of lawyers, dentists, and accountants for the past fifteen years (Iglehart 1990a, 567).

Taking Aim at Physicians

Negotiations over physician fees is not the only way Canada exerts its cost-control muscle. Controls are also applied to physician service utilization and physician supply.

Controlling Utilization. The Canada Health Act effectively banned billing beyond the amount indicated on the physician fee schedule, leaving physicians only one option for augmenting their incomes above those levels: that is, to provide more services. Indeed, an unanticipated byproduct of the ban on extra billing has been actual increases in utilization levels. One study revealed that in Ontario the volume of physicians' services increased 2.5 percent each year from 1986 to 1988; the previous rate of increase had been 1.2 percent. Such increased utilization levels, combined with sluggish economic growth, have prompted five of the ten provinces to implement mechanisms to discourage increasing utilization by linking such increases to fee schedules (Lomas, Fooks, Rice, and Labelle 1989).

Two different approaches are used to limit utilization increases. The first method, the *threshold approach,* has been adopted by British Columbia, Manitoba, Saskatchewan, and Ontario. The approach entails setting a level of utilization that is usually based on the previous year's level with some adjustment for such factors as population increase, increased number of physicians, new technology, and so forth. If physicians exceed the predetermined level, the provinces have several ways of recouping some of their expenditures:

- the next year's fee increase is scaled back, as is done in Ontario and Manitoba; or
- physicians are paid lower fees for a specific period of time, as in British Columbia; or
- physicians' fees are lowered to offset an expected increase in utilization for the year, as in Saskatchewan (Lomas, Fooks, Rice, and Labelle 1989, 86).

Quebec is the only province to use the second method, the *capping approach.* Quebec sets quarterly billing caps for General Practitioners (GPs) and income targets for specialists. The billing caps for GPs work in the following manner: doctors can bill up to a certain amount each quarter. Once the limit has been reached, their fees are reduced by 75 percent until the next quarter begins. The capping approach makes some physicians view Quebec as the "medical equivalent of purgatory" (Kosterlitz 1989b, 1795). In many cases, doctors approaching their limit will go on vacation for two weeks every three months and let another doctor use their office, in return for a healthy share of that doctor's billings (Brown, B. 1989).

This approach seems Draconian by U.S. standards. Indeed it is important to note that Quebec's approach is also unique within Canada. Quebec's particular culture and French-speaking populace create the unique conditions for such a strategy. Language barriers prevent medical professionals from looking for jobs outside Quebec, thus enabling the government to exert much stronger control on physician payment than would be possible elsewhere (Lomas, Fooks, Rice, and Labelle 1989).

Canadian expenditures for physician services are significantly lower than those of the United States, even though there are more physicians per capita in Canada than the United States. One might assume that Canada controls its expenditures by providing fewer physician services. However, a recent study revealed the opposite to be true. The study concluded that Canada provides more services than the United States at a lower overall cost because the United States uses more resources to provide a given service than does Canada. These resources drive up the cost of providing physician services and include such factors as billing and other administrative overhead costs, a higher level of amenities in U.S. doctor offices (such as higher quality offices with more expensive furnishings and decor), and the existence of more procedure-oriented specialists in the United States (Fuchs and Hahn 1990).

Moreover, U.S. physician incomes are one-third higher than physicians in Canada. In 1987, for example, the average income of a physician in Canada was $82,740; the average income for a physician in the United States was $132,300 (Iglehart 1990a). Part of the income difference can be traced to higher overhead costs for U.S. physicians and larger outlays for malpractice premiums, which average nine times higher in the United States than in Canada.

Malpractice suits are considerably less common in Canada than in the United States. This can be explained in part by a cultural difference: Canadian society is less litigious than American society. It can also be explained by several legal and institutional factors. In Canada, the losing party pays the costs of litigation; there are limited awards for pain and suffering; and juries are not used as frequently as in the United States. Moreover, attorneys do not usually take cases on contingency (Coyte, Dewees, Trebilock 1991).

Physician Supply.   Canadian provincial governments flex their considerable fiscal muscles as the single buyer of publicly insured health care services to keep not only the *prices* of physicians' services (fees) under control, but the *volume* of services provided as well. But such measures are not sufficient for controlling costs unless they are accompanied by efforts to limit physician supply. The number of physicians in Canada has increased more than 40 percent over the past dozen years, while the population has increased by only 13 percent (Rachlis and Kushner 1989). It is not possible to control physicians' costs if physician supply continues to increase (unless physicians accept lower incomes).

The number of foreign doctors allowed to immigrate to Canada is limited by law. In addition, provincial governments use their control over the purse strings for medical schools to wield significant influence over the number of physicians that will be trained and will ultimately enter the health sector in Canada. For instance, the province of Manitoba cut its first-year medical school enrollment in health-related courses by 10 percent in the early 1980s, while Ontario elected to reduce the number of specific post-graduate training positions.

The provincial governments also use their control over funding of medical education programs to control the type of medical positions—primary care physicians versus specialists. The province of Ontario, for example, has a formal policy that the ratio of general practitioners to specialists should be 55 to 45. As a whole, Canada has more general practitioners or primary care physicians than the United States (Whitcomb and Desgroseilliers 1992). This difference in physician specialty mix has important implications for the control of health care costs.

Other efforts have focused on the geographic distribution of physicians. The provincial government of Quebec, in an effort to discourage physicians from practicing in the capital city, warns medical students that they will receive only 70 percent of the established fees if they choose to practice in Montreal (Kosterlitz 1989a, 1795).

The province of British Columbia used controls over billing numbers to discourage physicians from practicing in heavily serviced areas. Although doctors could practice without a billing number, they could not be reimbursed from the provincial plans without one. This policy did serve as a strong disincentive, but was later ruled unconstitutional by the courts (Barber 1989).

As the previous discussion reveals, Canada has relied on an integrated approach to control health care costs that attacks expenditures on several fronts: physicians' fees, service utilization, and physician supply. This integrated approach enabled Canada to keep its health care expenditures below 9 percent of GNP throughout the 1980s. But the HIAA, in their analysis of the Canadian system, argued that Canada's cost-control record is not as strong as is portrayed, particularly in terms of health expenditures per capita. From 1960 to 1987, health care costs per capita increased faster in Canada than in the United States (Schieber and Poullier 1989). The HIAA concluded that Canada has been able to contain its health expenditures as a percentage of GNP despite increases in per capita spending because Canada's economy grew at a much faster rate than the U.S. economy during that period (Neuschler 1990).

Some health care analysts contend that it is inappropriate to use real per capita health care costs as a measure for international comparison. Increases in GNP per capita will raise wages in the health care sector that will result in higher health care costs per capita. Because per capita health care costs are influenced by changes in the economy as a whole, they are not a valid measure of comparison. The analysts argue that health care costs as a percentage of GNP are a more appropriate measure for international comparison, and it is by that measure that Canada has fared better than the United States (Barer, Welch and Antioch 1991).

Administrative Costs

One of the biggest differences in health care spending levels between the United States and Canada—and among the most controversial—is in the area of administrative costs. Real per capita expenditures for health insurance administration in the United States have grown at an average rate of 6.2 percent since 1971, while such costs in Canada have remained almost constant (U.S. GAO 1991). U.S. administrative costs amounted to $95 per person, or 0.66 percent of GNP in 1985; Canada's administrative costs, in contrast, were $15 per person, or 0.11 percent of GNP (See Figure 3-2).

The large cost differential can be traced directly to the way the two systems are organized and financed. Canada's single-payer, universal coverage system allows administrative cost savings because it precludes many of the processes that drive those costs in the United States. In the United States, more than one thousand insurance companies offer an extensive range of policies, each with a different set of benefits. The costs of marketing policies and processing claims is significant, not to mention the funds devoted to claims reserves, taxes, and profits. In contrast, in Canada everyone is covered, and for the same benefits, so resources do not have to be devoted to establishing insurance eligibility or risk status (Evans et al. 1989).

Moreover, the payment system in Canada is streamlined and the patient is not involved (except for services not covered under the plans). Each individual receives a health card similar to a credit card that is used each time the individual receives health care services. The health care providers use the individual's number to complete a computerized bill that is sent directly to the provincial ministry for payment. This automated claim card processing results in large administrative cost savings.

One study by two Harvard physicians estimates that in 1987 U.S. administrative costs totaled between 19.3 and 24.1 percent of total health care expenditures. The corresponding costs for Canada were between 8.4 and 11.1 percent of total health care expenditures. Based on their calculations, the authors contend that if U.S. administrative costs were similar to those of Canada, savings of more than $70 billion could have been realized in 1987 (Woolhandler and Himmelstein 1991).

Figure 3-2 **Costs of Insurance and Administration As a Percentage of Gross National Product, Canada and the United States, 1960-1985**

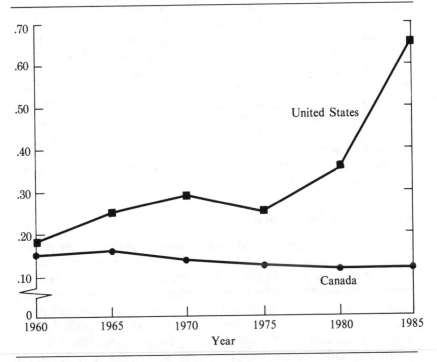

Source: Costs of Insurance and Administration as a Share of GNP, Canada and the U.S., 1960-1987, from "Tension Compression and Shear: Directions, Stresses and Outcomes of Health Care Cost Control" by Robert G. Evans published in the *Journal of Health Politics, Policy, and Law* 15:1. ©1990 Duke University Press. Reprinted with permission of the publisher.

Trouble in Paradise

With the dawn of a new decade, shrinking resources are forcing Canada to look to more stringent methods of cost control in their health care system. The provinces are being put in a fiscal vice by a particularly dangerous combination of a slowdown in the economy, a burgeoning federal budget deficit, and cuts in federal transfer payments. Health care expenditures are the largest single expenditure category in provincial budgets and therefore are large and highly visible targets for cost containment.

One of the strongest pressures to hold down costs in Canada's $52 billion per year health care industry comes from the growing federal budget deficit. This deficit has serious implications for the Canadian health care sector. The federal government once covered half of all provincial health care expenditures, but now covers only slightly more than one-third of all provincial health care costs. As a result, the provinces must devote growing shares of their budgets to health care. The province of Ontario, for example, dedicated 27 percent of its budget to health care in 1978; this share has risen to 33 percent.

The pressures of reduced federal funding, aging medical facilities, increasing physician supply, to name just a few, are intensifying. These problems are the consequence of an inherent conflict in a system that promises universal access, comprehensive coverage, professional freedom for physicians, patient choice of provider, and control over health care costs (Iglehart 1990a). These problems manifest themselves in different ways, but perhaps the most obvious is in how limited health care resources are allocated.

Allocating Health Care Resources

Canada's system of universal comprehensive health insurance was created during a period of economic prosperity; rationing of care was rarely, if ever, an issue in the 1970s. Yet, as escalating costs begin to erode government's ability to be all things to all people, resource allocation issues have been pushed to the forefront of health care policy and planning decisions, as competing demands for limited funds necessitate implicit and explicit rationing of health care. This is true for most industrialized countries. The mechanisms chosen to ration health care differ from country to country. Many nations have developed unequal systems of health care provision, wherein one's access to care is based on one's ability to pay. Some countries limit the number of beds per population, while others limit the amount of medical technology per region.

A key distinction between the American and Canadian systems is in the willingness in Canada to use explicit rationing to address the problem of finite resources for health care. One observer of the two systems notes that "Americans shrink from the notion that care must be rationed; Canadians don't. It's not a question of whether either country must ration, they say, but rather how it is done" (Kosterlitz 1989a, 1793). A member of the AMA House of Delegates concurred: "We do ration health care in this country by [tying it to individual] financial resources. We're the only Western nation in the world that hasn't solved the problem of universal access. It's a me-oriented society" (Kosterlitz 1989b, 1873).

Canada has relied on such explicit forms of rationing as limiting the distribution of medical technology—the number of CT scanners and dialysis machines, for example. According to the former president of the Ontario Medical Association, "rationing is inevitable" in today's economy (Linton 1989, 20). Many believe that explicit rationing policies in Canada have given way to implicit rationing. Hospital budget restrictions, for example, have led to "blind rationing," such as the totally "random reduction in the number of hospital beds in Ontario" (Linton 1989, 20). Indeed, the *Toronto Star* reported in June 1989 that more than 2,000 hospital beds had been "closed" in Toronto since the autumn of 1988. As a result, one in six beds in Toronto hospitals was empty. Approximately one-half the total number of closed beds were to be reopened in the following year, but the other half were to remain closed indefinitely due to personnel shortages and inadequate funding (Toughill 1989).

Certain Canadian cost-control methods serve as de facto rationing mechanisms. Setting global budgets for hospitals keeps expenditures down, but also limits the number of available services in the process. Many provincial governments have adopted a policy of refusing to cover hospital budget deficits. Hospitals are then forced to close off wards and limit the number of operations performed. Canada's determination to preserve rather than sacrifice the feature of universality of access to health care has led to the establishment of specific limits on the levels of care that can feasibly be provided. Canada consequently uses methods of allocating scarce resources to health care according to need. Such a system seems logical, for "under circumstances of universal coverage, queuing is the most likely substitute for differential insurance status as a rationing mechanism" (Vladek 1986, 444).

Dr. Morton Lowe, coordinator of health sciences at the University of British Columbia, compared the U.S. marketplace rationing approach to the Canadian queue-based approach: "You have to wait your turn for a hip transplant even if there are three poorer people in front of you. In the U.S. if you're rich you get it fast, and if you're poor you don't get it at all. That's how they ration" (Brown, B. 1989, 30). Canada's system of queue-based rationing of limited health services relies on physicians to act as "triage agents," classifying patients according to need (Naylor 1991). According to U.S. Sen. David F. Durenberger (R-Minn.), Canadians "really believe in equity and equal access and are willing to go without some things that we take for granted. . . . Rather than pay the price in dollars, they pay the price in waiting time" (Freudenheim 1989b).

Investment in Technology. As discussed earlier, a prominent cost-control feature of the Canadian system is highly regulated budgets for hospitals, which limit the procurement of expensive, high-technology

Figure 3-3   Comparative Availability of Medical Technologies: Canada, Germany, and the United States

Units per million persons

Legend:
- Magnetic resonance imaging (MRI)
- Radiation therapy
- Organ transplantation
- Open-heart surgery

United States (1987)   Germany (1987)   Canada (1989)

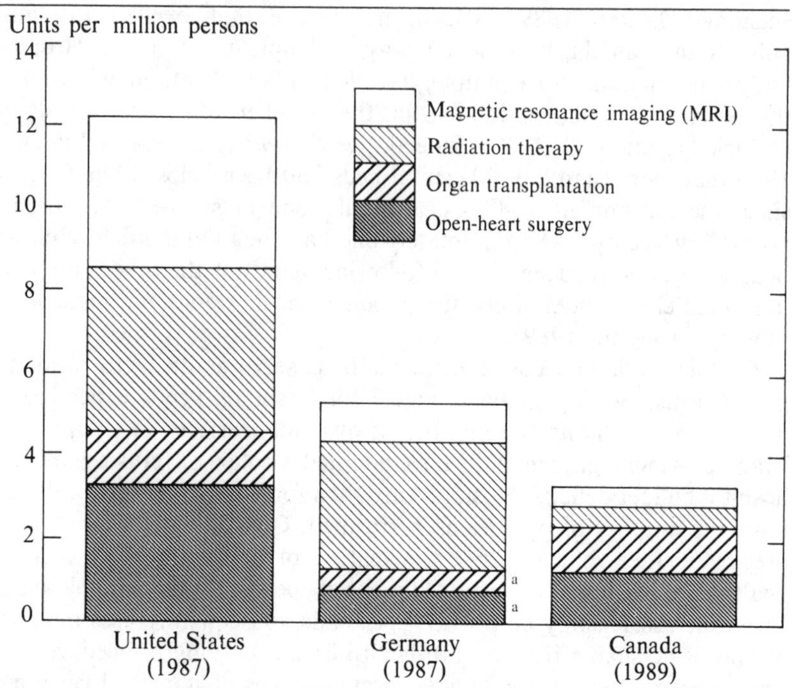

Source: Rublee, Dale. "Medical Technology in Canada, Germany and the United States." *Health Affairs* 8, no. 3. Reprinted by permission from *Health Affairs,* Fall 1989: p. 100.

a 1988.

medical equipment and other investments in technology. Provinces attempt to distribute high-tech equipment to areas in which they are most needed, and the most highly advanced equipment tends to be concentrated in teaching hospitals (Iglehart 1989).

A study of the availability of medical technology in Canada, West Germany, and the United States found that Canada has taken the biggest steps toward controlling the introduction of major technologies (see Figure 3-3). The researcher who conducted the study was careful to point out the difficulty in interpreting the study's findings, however, particularly when comparing the United States and Canada. It is unclear, for example, whether there is overprovision of technology in the United States, or underprovision in Canada. Moreover, such differences may indeed be more a reflection of cultural preferences than anything else. The researcher concluded that "the differences in levels of major technology, in themselves, indicate little about the overall effectiveness, achievements, and weaknesses of the health care systems of any of the three systems studied" (Rublee 1989, 181).

An expected result of limits on technology is long delays for particular procedures. An article in the popular *Macleans* magazine described long waiting periods for coronary surgery; an estimated one thousand people were facing waiting periods of up to a year for coronary bypass operations at three Toronto hospitals in 1989 (Barber 1989). In Toronto, three-and-a-half million people share two magnetic resonance imagers. In Montreal there are twenty-one computerized tomography scanners to service a population of more than two million. In one Canadian province there is only one CT scanner for one-half million people. A patient can only have a CT scan on referral by a specialist, at which point the waiting time begins, often lasting more than two months. Even such routine procedures as pap smears and mammograms can now involve waiting as long as several months. These waiting times, according to the *Macleans* article, are "only one highly visible symptom of an underlying crisis that is undermining Canada's health care system" (Barber 1989).

During a June 1989 conference on health care in Canada, Les Foster, an official of British Columbia's Ministry of Health, justified such investment policies on the basis of significant "cost savings to be realized through the judicious use of technology." He explained that new technology must be introduced "in a controlled manner so we can secure the benefits and the savings." He added that "It will appear at times that we are limiting access to the latest procedures, devices, drugs, etc. And, indeed we will be" (Foster 1989, 38).

Although there are often accounts in the press indicating that Canadians are forced to come to the United States for specific treatments, two separate surveys of American hospital administrators conducted by the Pepper Commission and the American Medical Association concluded that "border-jumping" is not a pervasive phenomenon. Canadian patients represented less than one percent of total admissions in each of the nine border hospitals surveyed (U.S. GAO 1991).

Many Canadians argue that the system is dangerously "underfunded"—a term rarely, if ever, applied to the U.S. health care system. Looking at health care expenditures of other industrialized countries indicates that Canada spends more than Germany, Japan, and the Netherlands. The United States is the only country that spends more than Canada.

Arnold Relman, former editor of the *New England Journal of Medicine,* notes that complaints about underfunding are difficult to gauge because it is hard to know whether complaints reflect serious weaknesses of the system or a natural response by providers to what they perceive as unfair cost controls (1989c). One serious defect, pointed out by Rachlis and Kushner in their critical analysis of the Canadian health care system, *Second Opinion: What's Wrong with Canada's Health Care System and How to Fix It,* is that the most cost-effective health care settings are not used:

> [W]hen you read in the news that hospitals are "dangerously underfunded," does anyone mention that 20-50 percent of all patients in acute care hospitals don't belong there? Many are elderly or disabled. Often what they need isn't medical care at all, but personal care—regular assistance with bathing or housekeeping chores. Yet they languish in the most cost-intensive setting we provide, because appropriate alternatives—nursing homes, home care services and the like—are unavailable (1989, 3).

Indeed this use of hospital beds by long-term care patients—known as "bed-blockers"—often prevents physicians from treating other patients.

The debate over funding levels will certainly rage on, but clearly more information is needed. As Relman correctly points out, "until we invest much more in the assessment of technology and the measurement of quality of care, we will be at a loss to evaluate the medical effectiveness of any health care system, regardless of how it is organized and financed" (1989c, 590).

The Future of Canadian Health Care

Pressures on the Canadian system are increasing. As two decades of experience with national health insurance take their toll, new stress points appear. Renewed concern over how long the precarious balance can be maintained will lead Canada to take a closer look at the funding basis of its health care system (Iglehart 1990a).

While cost-control methods such as global budgets and negotiated fee schedules have worked with a reasonable degree of success for some years, this is due in part to "some slack in the system that allowed it to tolerate restraint without much damage." But many fear that there is no longer any slack in the system, and the cost-control methods employed in the Canadian system are too rigid (Linton 1990a, 198).

Such pressures put the doctors in the middle, as governments squeeze health care budgets while patients continue to demand more services. A significant amount of doctor disaffection has been a dangerous byproduct of this situation, particularly because of physician strikes or the threat of strikes in several provinces, as "the absence of any alternative system of care and the adversarial stance of provincial governments leave doctors with a feeling of impotence and impair the profession's ability to contribute to the development of the system" (Linton 1990a, 191).

User Charges

Concern over the increasing demands on the Canadian health care system has rekindled debate over the introduction of user fees as a method of reducing unnecessary medical visits. One deterrent may be to include the cost of minor medical services as part of an individual's taxable income (Barber 1989).

The issue of user charges is the source of great controversy, and is the stuff of which political campaigns are made. One candidate running for office in Ontario, for example, called for user fees as a necessary cost-control tool, justifying their use as a control mechanism: "There are no checks on cost, there are no controls on usage, (and) there are no controls on those billing the system." In response, the candidate's opponent charged that "anybody who has taken a look at the history of the implementation of a user fee ... will tell you that it discriminates against the poor" (Ferguson, D. 1990).

The inherent paradox in the debate over financing health care is that the provinces have to sacrifice investment in other areas (education, environment, infrastructure) to maintain the level of resources (tax dollars) dedicated to health care. But if private funding were introduced, the egalitarian principles on which the Canadian health care system was constructed could be sacrificed in the process (Iglehart 1990a).

It is important to note that provinces can impose user charges, but the Canada Health Act of 1984 ruled that federal monies will be reduced in direct proportion to the charges levied against patients. No province has yet taken the step of introducing user charges, but the debate continues in many of the provinces.

Private Sector Involvement

The debate over user fees is part of a much broader issue: the role of the private sector in Canadian health care. Indeed, the key features that set Canadian health care apart from health care systems in most other industrialized nations is the outlawing of private health insurance and a strong resistance to developing private-sector alternatives (Iglehart 1990a). But this may change. Noting the large federal deficit, the former president of the Canadian Medical Association remarked: "In a country that now spends 35 cents out of every [tax] dollar servicing its debt, we have to ask ourselves whether we can maintain our high standards of health care without any involvement from the private sector" (Iglehart 1990a, 564).

Outside the realm of health insurance, however, the private sector has been involved in several areas within the Canadian health care sector. First, it provides services under contract, such as the construction of hospitals and the operation of pharmacies and ambulance services. Second, the private sector has been involved in nursing home care in Canada. In Ontario, for example, 90 percent of nursing home care beds are privately owned. Third, private corporations (such as Extendicare) administer particular departments of hospitals, or entire hospitals. The government of Ontario, for example, has a contract with a subsidiary of American Medical International (AMI) to manage a public hospital there. These companies are directly accountable to the public hospital boards.

Support for increased private sector participation in health care is growing. A former minister of health for Ontario advanced the concept of a partnership of public and private sector mechanisms in the provision of health care in Canada during a June 1989 health care conference. The former minister argued that while "private management is no panacea," it is not "a capitalist plot to destroy Medicare" either (Timbrell 1989, 68).

A certain amount of concern accompanies the extension of the private sector's reach into other areas of the Canadian health care system. This is particularly the case as private clinics have become more pervasive. The Gimbel Clinic in Calgary, Alberta, for example, performs 5 percent of all eye surgery in Canada. Rather than waiting for care, an individual can go to the clinic and pay out-of-pocket for the cost of the operation (Brown 1989).

Some see the irony in Canadian support for increased private sector involvement in health care. An editorial in the Canadian newspaper, the *Financial Post,* for example, pointed out that "crisis-mongering in Canada leads to suggestions of privatization along U.S. lines at the very time Americans are looking to Canada for models of how to restrain a system that really is out of control" (1989).

System Maintains Popular Support

Despite the problems and weaknesses in the system and the uneasy truce that exists between the various conflicting forces in Canadian health care outlined above, Canadians are satisfied with their system of health care and take a deep sense of pride in it. Indeed, one thing Canadians probably fear most is the loss of their universal comprehensive coverage. A former minister of health remarked that the best way to stir the normally complacent Canadians into "ballot-box revolt" would be to do something to threaten the health care system (Timbrell 1989). For example, many Canadians feared their health care system would be jeopardized by the passage of the U.S.-Canada Free Trade agreement. Canadians opposed the Agreement until fears that their health care system would have to be scrapped—due to American insistence that Canadian companies had an unfair advantage—were proven unjustified (Manga 1988).

One Montreal doctor provides what seems to be an accurate description of the present and future state of Canadian health care: "We're close to being excellent, but we're also dangerously close to the abyss—and I'm not at all sure which direction we're going in" (Barber 1989). An overhaul of the system does not seem likely in the near future, and certainly not in the direction of a U.S. system of health care. Indeed, many Canadians view the U.S. system as a "horrible example of how *not* to provide and pay for health care" (Evans 1986a, 25). The Blendon poll revealed that while 61 percent of Americans polled would prefer a Canadian-type system, only 3 percent of Canadians surveyed would prefer an American-style health care system. Compared to 89 percent of Americans polled who said that the U.S. system requires fundamental change, only 43 percent of Canadians believed their system needed broad-based reform (Blendon 1989a).

A 1987 Canada-wide survey found that 77 percent of those polled believed the quality of health care was good or excellent; another survey conducted in Ontario that year revealed that 91 percent of respondents were satisfied with the system (Barkin 1988). Authors of a study of health care in Ontario and Quebec prepared for the American Association of Retired Persons found almost universal satisfaction among the individuals interviewed for the study. The authors admitted that they "tried to find severe criticism of the system, but heard none in any quarter (including organized medicine)" (Leader, Guildroy, Kennan, Lehrmann, and Skinner 1988, 24).

A poll conducted by Louis Harris and Associates, in conjunction with the Harvard School of Public Health and the Institute for the Future, revealed that of ten nations surveyed, the citizens of Canada were the most satisfied with their health care system. A majority of the respondents reported that only minor changes were needed to make the system work better (Blendon, Leitman, Morrison, and Donelan 1990).

Lessons from Canada

Canada's two decades of experience with national health insurance provides valuable lessons for the United States. The Canadian experience appears to indicate that health care costs can be controlled while still maintaining universal access to health care. The existence of a single purchaser of health care services—the provincial governments—is key to Canada's successful record on cost control, as health care providers have nowhere else to turn for payment (Lomas, Fooks, Rice, and Labelle 1989). The provincial government as the single paymaster, "acts as a consumers' cooperative [that] equalizes the bargaining power, compared with the situation in which individuals confront professionals directly" (Evans 1987, 169). Global budgets for hospitals and negotiated fee schedules for physicians are essential elements of Canada's cost-control arsenal, as are limits of the diffusion of technology and streamlined administrative processes.

Cost constraints in the Canadian health care system are applied to the system as a whole, through the provincial budgeting process. In the United States, on the other hand, such constraints are directed to the level of the individual patient; ability to pay determines access to health services (U.S. GAO 1991).

A salient feature of the Canadian system is the government's central role in determining how much money will be spent on health care. This can be a "bruising political process" as health policy debates and conflicts over cost control are very visible and politicians are held accountable for their decisions. Provincial governments cannot shirk their considerable responsibility for financial decisions regarding health care and are forced into the combative arena of cost control (Evans 1990, 119). Such lessons from Canada are the antithesis of U.S. health care policy experience, which has reflected American preference for "hidden, implicit policies" over "explicit, programmatic decisions" (Morone 1990, 141).

Convergence

The U.S. General Accounting Office (GAO) prepared a comprehensive analysis of the Canadian health care system and concluded that adoption of a Canadian-style system would generate enough savings to cover the cost of expanding access to the uninsured. But the GAO recommended that the United States keep some form of a cost-sharing requirement (except for low-income persons) to offset the costs of implementing such a broad-based reform program. In addition, the

GAO concluded that the United States would want to implement more flexible cost-control mechanisms than Canada's global hospital budgets, for example, so that queues would not be required (U.S. GAO 1991).

There are developments and trends common to the U.S. and Canadian systems. As one analyst notes, "In Canada, conflict and accommodation will occur over private encroachments on an essentially publicly funded system; in the United States, the issue will be the extent of public intervention in the private sector" health care system (Tuohy 1986, 425). There may be some common middle ground where the two systems will meet.

Perhaps the clearest sign of convergence among the Canadian and U.S. health care systems is a shared approach to cost control by containing physicians' incomes. Recent U.S. legislation regarding physician reimbursement methods under Medicare is indicative of this trend (Iglehart 1989). Further signs of convergence may be seen in the actions on the state level in the United States to establish universal health insurance; if the United States chooses to pursue such a decentralized strategy, the Canadian system would certainly deserve close inspection. If the United States decides to adopt a more centralized system, however, the health care systems in place in Europe may be more appropriate models for the United States to follow (Marmor 1982).

Limits to Convergence

Americans continue to view the Canadian system with interest despite the cultural and political differences of the two nations. Several of the factors that would hinder adoption of a Canadian-type system include the following:

- *Size and composition of the U.S. population:* Canada's population is one-tenth the size of the United States, and the U.S. population is much more heterogenous. (Canada does not have as large an underclass as the United States);
- *Organizational nightmare:* a federal health insurance program would be much more difficult in a country with fifty states than a country with only ten provinces; and
- *Pervasive mistrust of government:* Americans fear placing health care in the hands of government bureaucrats.

It should be noted that a very significant obstacle is ideology. Many Americans liken national health insurance to socialism, a perception that is advanced by such organizations as the American Medical Association. As one analyst points out:

[T]he policy positions and political activities of organized medicine, particularly the AMA, have used the language of free enterprise and freedom of choice and alliances with business interests, to make the case opposing state intervention in the health care arena (Tuohy 1986, 419).

The large U.S. health care economy, which in and of itself is larger than the entire Canadian economy, has many vested interests determined to preserve the status quo. Such economic interests include hospitals, which are among the largest employers in most U.S. cities; doctors, who would not be willing to give up as much financial freedom (or clinical freedom to have access to necessary technology) as their Canadian counterparts; and the multi-billion-dollar insurance industry. These interests would not support a system such as Canada's wherein the "government pays the piper and calls the tune" (Kosterlitz 1989b, 1873). Indeed, government-funded health insurance is denounced by critics as offering "all the compassion of the IRS, the efficiency of the Post Office, at Pentagon prices" (Stout 1992).

Former representative Willis D. Gradison, Jr., (R-Ohio), of the House Ways and Means Subcommittee on Health, noted: "To make their system work, the Canadians had to outlaw private [health] insurance. We're not going to do that in this country . . . it's not even on the table" (Kosterlitz 1989b, 1873). Indeed, usurping the powerful U.S. private insurance industry would be quite a coup: The industry's assets amount to almost $2 trillion (Welles and Farrell 1989). An August 1989 *Business Week* cover story argued, however, that "some insurance markets face possible government takeover. The auto and health markets have become so dysfunctional, with millions of people unable to get affordable coverage, that the market may be increasingly assumed by state and federal insurance mechanisms" (Welles and Farrell 1989). As large employers such as Chrysler Corporation and American Airlines come out in support of a national health program, the "socialization" of insurance in the United States may not be as far-fetched as it initially seemed.

These developments notwithstanding, broad-based support for a Canadian-type system in the United States faces two major obstacles: (1) the issue of access to services, and (2) the cost of setting up such a system in the United States. Americans would not accept the sacrifices involved in Canada's built-in cost-control mechanisms. Such arrangements as waiting lists for nonemergency surgery are seen as Draconian measures by many Americans. A report prepared for the Heritage Foundation by the Fraser Institute, a Canadian think tank, warns that adoption of a Canadian-type system would have deleterious effects on the quality of health care in the United States. The report states that although average Canadians are satisfied with their system of health care, "average Canadians do not require significant medical services. For those who do, the Canadian system increasingly means waiting lists, chronic shortages of new technology, and the rationing of many procedures" (Walker 1989, 14).

If health care rationing is inevitable, as many experts contend, Canada may just be one step ahead of the United States in this regard. Canada, according to U.S. Rep. Pete Stark (D-Calif.) "has clearly made some trade-offs on resource use that the United States, sooner or later, simply must address" (Iglehart 1989, 1769). The state of Oregon has already made a move in this direction: In an effort to expand Medicaid coverage, Oregon has prioritized health services and created a list of specific services that will be covered, and those that will not be covered under the Medicaid program. The Oregon plan was rejected by the federal government, but did represent an explicit approach to rationing that may be considered in the future.

The second major obstacle centers on the dilemma of how to broaden a social program as massive as health care during a period of fiscal austerity and revenue-driven legislation. Henry Aaron, a health policy analyst at Brookings Institution, reminds us that, "as long as the deficit is the major issue, we aren't going to see any programs that add to new federal spending" (MacKenzie 1989). Rep. Dan Rostenkowski (D-Ill.), chair of the House Ways and Means Committee, explains how the budget deficit limits the government's ability to maneuver:

> Every program—health, drugs, education, aid to Eastern European countries—is compared to and competes with the deficit. . . .
> [The deficit] has reduced our ability and flexibility to address social problems and it has dramatically complicated the process of enacting major health and other social legislation (Iglehart 1990a, 44).

One study estimated that the establishment in the United States of a national health insurance system similar to Canada's would require $339 billion in new taxes (Robbins 1990). The HIAA estimates that if a Canadian-style health care system were to be implemented in the United States and financed through the federal government, a 46 percent increase in income taxes would be required. If the states were to be the sole financing agent of the system, a 71 percent increase in state tax revenues would be required (Neuschler 1990).

While Canadians have accepted higher taxes as a means of financing health care, in 1988 Americans elected George Bush who ran on a platform whose centerpiece was "Read my lips: no new taxes." Given the negative reaction to Bush's about-face on his anti-tax stand, there is little indication that Americans would be willing to pay higher taxes to fund universal health insurance. Public opinion polls continue to reflect conflicting views over the role of the federal government in U.S. health care, as well as who should pay for health care (Blendon and Donelan 1990). A 1990 Gallup poll for Blue Cross/Blue Shield, for example, revealed that while 86 percent of respondents supported a role for the federal government in health care, a significant majority mistrusted government management and believed that government-run programs are inefficient and wasteful (Taylor and Reinhardt 1991).

The repeal of the Medicare Catastrophic Coverage Act of 1988 underscores the fierce opposition by the elderly to paying more for health care, and dulled congressional enthusiasm for health care reform. Sen. Dave Durenberger (R-Minn.) commented that "the impact of the campaign against the Medicare Catastrophic Bill has scared a lot of us into feeling that we can't do what we should do." Durenberger added that "nobody seems to want to give up anything for the greater good" (Tolchin 1989). This is not only true for the elderly; one survey revealed that less than 20 percent of Americans would be willing to pay an extra $25 per year so that the uninsured could receive health insurance coverage (Reinhardt 1989b).

Princeton University professor Uwe Reinhardt couches the dilemma over who should pay for a society's health care in terms of whether health care is treated as a private consumption good (economic product) or a community service collectively financed (social good). In Canada, it is clearly the latter. Canada has chosen egalitarian access to health care over economic freedom; economic freedom is eclipsed by global budgets and fee negotiations. But the burden of being ill is spread over the entire population, because the health care system relies on a broad funding base (income and sales taxes) (Evans 1988a). Indeed, one of the major differences between the Canadian and the U.S. systems is that:

> the government of Canada believes that a civilized and wealthy nation, such as Canada, should not make the sick-bed a financial burden of health care. Everyone benefits from the security and peace of mind that comes with having prepaid insurance. The misfortune of illness, which at some time touches all of us, is burden enough. The cost of care should be borne by society as a whole (Reinhardt 1989b, 135).

The United States has chosen the route of economic freedom via the market, but egalitarian access is the tradeoff, as health care is rationed by price mechanisms. It appears likely that the United States will maintain its reliance on the free market for health care, as evidenced by President Bill Clinton's interest in "managed competition" as a preferred method of reforming the U.S. health care system. At the heart of the managed competition approach are managed care networks formed by employers and individuals. These networks would use their purchasing clout to force doctors and hospitals to compete for their business on the basis of price and quality.

The sacrifices involved in restructuring the health care system along Canadian lines—setting limits on which services are covered, and increases in taxes to name just two—make the adoption of a Canadian-type health care system in the United States unlikely in the near future. But Dr. Arnold Relman contends that "by the end of the century, I'd be willing to bet that's where we'll come out" (Tolchin 1989).

The Canadian system will undoubtedly remain a subject of analysis for U.S. health care experts and policymakers, and the popular press will continue to report on the Canadian system. Academics and private foundations will also keep their eyes focused on the Canadian system. Stanford University's Victor Fuchs, for example, is analyzing health care spending levels in the United States and Canada to determine what impact, if any, differences in spending have in terms of mortality and morbidity rates, and quality of life in the two countries. Moreover, the Robert Wood Johnson Foundation, Pew Charitable Trust, and the Commonwealth Fund continue to finance studies and projects comparing the two systems (Iglehart 1989).

Health care reform is a dynamic, ongoing process occurring in most industrialized countries. The Canadian unwillingness to allow private sector alternatives stands in contrast to the situation in the United States and, as further chapters will show, contrasts with the experience of the United Kingdom. In the United Kingdom, "conflict and accommodation" are occurring as health care reform measures are being implemented that could dramatically alter the British National Health Service. Before turning our sights on the United Kingdom, however, we will first examine the health care systems of Germany, the Netherlands, and Japan.

CHAPTER 4

German Health Care: Does Bismarck's Grand Design Hold Lessons for the United States?

Introduction

The Canadian system has monopolized the attention of U.S. health experts, policymakers, medical professionals, and business leaders for many years. But American interest in adopting the Canadian system has been tempered by the inevitable sacrifices that adopting such a plan would entail. Questions have consequently been raised about the appropriateness of the Canadian health care system as a model for U.S. health care reform.

Although interest in the Canadian system is by no means evaporating, there are signs that Canada may have to move over and share the spotlight with another country: Germany. Analysts are focusing on the German health care system, which embodies an employer-mandate approach, as another potential model to guide U.S. health reform efforts. One indication of Germany's imminent ascendancy into the center of the U.S. health care reform debate is that the Physician Payment Review Commission—created by Congress to examine physician reimbursement methods under Medicare—dispatched a fact-finding team to Germany in the summer of 1990 to study the German system, and a congressional delegation followed in the summer of 1991.

At first glance, the United States and Germany would seem to have less in common than the United States and Canada, which share cultural, geographic, and linguistic characteristics. On closer inspection, however, quite a few parallels exist between the United States and Germany. First, Germany, like the United States, has a federal system of government whose constitution prescribes responsibilities for local, state, and federal government. Second, both the U.S. and German health care systems are a mix of public-private financing and federal-state responsibility, and employers are directly involved in financing both systems (Altenstetter 1987; Reinhardt 1981; Schulenburg 1983). Third, German national health insurance, like U.S. Medicare and Medicaid programs, was designed to address the needs of a specific population group and has expanded its coverage over the years (Stone 1977). Finally, the organization of health care delivery systems in Germany is similar to that of the United States.

The German health care system, like the Canadian system, is offered as working proof that universal health insurance coverage can be provided without invoking the specter of socialized medicine (Henke 1990a). Unlike the British National Health Service, the German health care system is neither government-owned nor government-run. Instead of public ownership or public provision of health care services, there is public regulation and oversight of the system (Lockhart 1981). Indeed, the German system represents a compromise that might be acceptable in the United States as government interference in the German health care system is kept to a minimum. In Germany, the government does set the overall framework and establishes the rules, but it is the health care providers and the sickness (insurance) funds that are at the center of the system—the government remains on the sidelines (Glaser 1978).

The German health care system has multiple payers and providers, and features a key role for employers, therefore resembling more closely the U.S. system than does the Canadian system. Health care in Germany is provided through private hospitals and physicians, but tight control is exerted over physicians' fees, hospital budgets, and capital investment.

While German and U.S. total health care expenditures as a percentage of gross domestic product (GDP) were relatively equal in the mid-1970s, Germany implemented certain cost-control policies that have effectively reined in health care expenditures (see Figure 4-1). Germany is one of a few nations whose health-to-GDP ratio has actually declined over the past decade. German health expenditures represented 8.4 percent of GDP in 1980, and 8.1 percent in 1990, reflecting a national health care cost-containment policy that links growth in health care expenditures to increases in wages and salaries (Schieber, Poullier, and Greenwald 1992). Such experience merits close examination by the United States. And because the German system has a role for insurers and multiple payers, restructuring the

Figure 4-1   Total Health Expenditures As a Percentage of Gross Domestic Product, Germany and the United States, 1970-1990

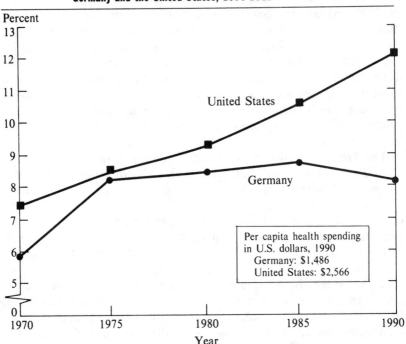

Per capita health spending in U.S. dollars, 1990
Germany: $1,486
United States: $2,566

Source: Schieber, George, Jean-Pierre Poullier, and Leslie M. Greenwald. "U.S. Health Expenditure Performance: An International Comparison and Data Update." *Health Care Financing Review* 13, 4:(1-15). HCFA Pub. no. 03331. Office of Research and Demonstrations. Health Care Financing Administration. Washington, D.C.: U.S. Government Printing Office, September 1992.

U.S. system along German lines would not be as disruptive as the systemwide overhaul necessary for adoption of a Canadian single-payer system.

The organization and financing of the German system and the achievement of comprehensive, near-universal coverage (less than 1 percent of the population is uninsured, and the wealthy are the ones who choose not to have insurance) at a lower overall cost than in the United States, are clearly issues relevant to the ongoing American health care reform debate (Hurst 1991). Moreover, commonly accepted measures of health status indicate that the quality of health care provided in Germany is quite high; infant mortality and life expectancy rates compare favorably with those of the United States.

The First 100 Years

The German system provides a study in continuity. As the system enters the 1990s, one can only marvel at its resilience over a century that included two world wars. Germany pioneered national health insurance: Chancellor Otto von Bismarck made history in 1883 by implementing a system of health care for workers under certain incomes. The statutory health care scheme was the first pillar of the broad-based German social security system, which, like the U.S. social security system, is financed through contributions from employers and employees (Stone 1979). Unlike Canada, where universal health care is financed primarily through general taxation, employment-based, income-related contributions provide the bulk of health care financing in Germany.

Bismarck's system has certainly withstood the test of time, but structural reform continues to be proposed, debated, and implemented to preserve and strengthen the system and to adapt it to changing demographic needs and economic requirements. The reunification of Germany represents an unprecedented challenge, as the century-old system expands to provide coverage to the erstwhile residents of East Germany. Unified Germany is now the undisputed economic powerhouse of Europe, accounting for more than one-quarter of the Gross Domestic Product (GDP) of the twelve-nation European Community.

The former East German nation, formally dissolved on October 3, 1990, had a centralized, publicly owned and operated health care system. Most of the population was covered through the Free German Trade Union Federation, the primary organization for social insurance, and health care was lumped together with social security and funded through payroll and general tax revenues. Physicians were salaried state employees and hospitals were owned by the state (Hurst 1991; Swabey 1990; Stone 1991).

That system will gradually be restructured along West German lines. This merging of the very different social systems of the former "rich and poor cousins"—most of the more than 16 million residents of the former East Germany are poor in comparison to their West German neighbors—is putting significant economic strain on the health care system (Marsh 1990b). For example, unemployment rates in the states of the former East Germany are more than double those in the western states. And although income levels are gradually increasing in the east, they are still only half of those in the west. How Germany manages its costly unification will define the future shape of its health care system.

ℐ of Health Care in Germany

ℐhe German state combines a freemarket economy with extensive social welfare programs (Kirkman-Liff 1990). Germany stands out among the OECD countries as one of the highest spenders on social security programs, according to the broad definition of social security used by the International Labor Organization.[1] German expenditures for social security, plus health care, are equal to almost a third of Germany's Gross National Product (GNP)—approximately one-and-a-half-times the amount dedicated by the United States to such social programs (Simanis 1990).

The decentralized public/private German system is situated toward the middle of the market-minimized/market-maximized continuum. The public and private sectors are linked and consensus provides the glue that holds the system together (Anderson 1989). Physicians are in private practice and hospitals are mainly independent, nonprofit institutions. The role of the government is limited to three major areas: (1) delineating broad legal parameters within which the system operates; (2) acting as the final arbiter in deadlocked negotiations; and (3) financing capital expenditures for the hospital sector (Reinhardt 1981b).

German health insurance is characterized by its collectivization— most of the insured are mandated by federal law to become members of a "sickness fund," which is a nonprofit insurance organization. These organizations represent the patients in their dealings with health care providers (Stone 1979). The sickness funds collect premiums in the form of employee and employer-paid payroll taxes and pay the providers from these revenues. The German system is known as an "all-payer system," because all sickness funds in the same area pay providers the same fee for the same service.

A network of approximately 1,150 sickness funds provides coverage to approximately 90 percent of the population, according to the German Federal Department of Labor (Spencer and Associates 1989-1992). These funds, which have been likened to Blue Cross/Blue Shield groups in the United States (Kirkman-Liff 1990), are decentralized and governed by independent administrative boards. The funds are distinguished by their almost complete autonomy from both the federal (*Bund*) and the state (*Land*) governments. This mixture of federal mandate and decentralized administration exists throughout Europe (Henke 1990a).

---

[1] The definition of social security includes payments for retirees, survivors, and those who are disabled, as well as health care programs, unemployment insurance, and family allowances.

The importance of collectivization is evident in the legal requirement that all physicians and dentists practicing under the sickness fund system join an organization of sickness fund physicians. These sickness fund physician associations are different from professional trade associations such as the American Medical Association because they are organized on a regional basis and given the legal authority to control the process of physician payment, as well as to monitor the services provided by physicians (Schneider 1991).

The sickness funds are also organized on a regional basis. Regional associations of sickness funds negotiate with regional organizations of sickness fund physicians to set payment rates for ambulatory medical services. In the hospital sector, the negotiation structure is different as sickness funds negotiate with each hospital separately. The key roles played by these two groups—the physicians' organizations and the associations of sickness funds—distinguish the German health care system from the health care systems of other nations (Hurst 1991; Schneider 1991).

The rest of this chapter takes a closer look at how the German health insurance system was developed and how it has evolved and expanded, in terms of membership and benefits provided, over its more than one-hundred-year history. The first section examines the ideological and political underpinnings of the system that continue to shape German national health insurance, and further sections discuss health care financing and cost control in Germany.

Present at the Creation: Tracing the Roots of National Health Insurance

Social solidarity and the concept of a strong state were the guiding forces in the newly founded German Reich of the late nineteenth century (Blanpain, Delesie, and Nys 1978). Otto von Bismarck, as chancellor of the imperial government—formed in 1871 through an alliance between the *Junker* (landed aristocracy) class and the Prussian military—devised the health insurance plan as a manifestation of his government's concern for the health of its citizens (Glaser 1983). At the same time, the government was responding to new needs for social programs generated by the interrelated forces of "industrialization, population growth, urbanization, increasing wage dependence and the geographical concentration and political awareness of new industrial workers" (Zollner 1982, 5-9).

The importance of a strong state was firmly anchored in German history. As noted social historian Ralf Dahrendorf points out, one of the peculiar features of German industrialization was a strong involvement on the part of the state in all aspects of the industrialization process—particularly in the area of workers' welfare (Dahrendorf 1976). That Bismarck would champion the first system of social insurance in Europe was quite consistent with his approach to government and industrialization and his view of the relationship between the state and society. As historian Theodore Hamerow explains, Bismarck "believed that government had a right to regulate the interaction of classes and interests for the advancement of the general welfare. He was never a doctrinaire supporter of individualism, whether in politics or economics." For Bismarck, "the preservation of the established order took precedence over the immunities and liberties of the citizen" (Hamerow 1973, 233).

Bismarck's response to the challenge of encouraging industrial development while at the same time preserving the political status quo was to bring about "reform from above"; in other words, the state, rather than the workers, would be the engine of change (Stone 1980, 21). This strategy relied on the provision of social benefits by the state as a means of ensuring workers' loyalty. Bismarck acted in his own political self-interest by introducing "social rights to avoid granting wider political rights" (Starr 1982, 239). Bismarck used an expanded welfare system to check the power of a growing socialist movement. Through this method he sought to establish what has been termed a "welfare monarchy" (Starr 1982, 239).

This strategy differed considerably from what occurred in England during the industrial revolution. Dahrendorf compares the British with the German experience:

> In contrast to the applied Social Darwinism of publicly tolerated misery of industrial workers, their wives and children in England, which Marx took as the emotional point of departure in his demand for state action, public agencies in Germany consistently felt responsible for the welfare of their workers. There was poverty, illness and misery in industrializing Germany as elsewhere; but the official attitude to the social question strikingly documents the preindustrial combination of a severe and paternal authority (1976, 37).

Thus, industrialization in Germany was distinguished from industrialization in other European nations by the role of the state, which was dedicated to preserving and protecting the status quo while simultaneously supporting economic progress (Stone 1980).

While Bismarck's advocacy of national health insurance in Germany stemmed from his belief in a strong yet benevolent state, it had overt political underpinnings. By offering health insurance to factory workers in the newly industrializing Germany, Bismarck hoped to make them loyal followers of the state and to preempt the growth of a nascent socialist party in Germany (Light 1985; Stone 1979). In the late 1800s, Germany was characterized by harsh economic conditions as noted earlier. These conditions fueled "a mass following for a labor movement which promised to build a new order of society founded on equality and justice" (Hamerow 1973, 235). Bismarck believed that the only way to extinguish this movement was to fight fire with fire: prove to the working class that the state would protect them so they would not be compelled to form trade unions or join the ranks of the Social Democratic Party. Eventually Bismarck used social legislation as a "tool of social and political control" (Blanpain, Delesie, and Nys 1978, 24).

1883 Sickness Insurance Act

Business and labor groups fought against Bismarck's transparent attempt to consolidate his power. During the legislative debates following the introduction of proposals for health insurance in 1881, those groups strove to limit the reach of the federal government and to maintain "Germany's long tradition of autonomous groups" (Glaser 1983, 355). State legislators opposed federal attempts to take over responsibility for social programs, which they wanted to remain at the state level. Moreover, the existing mutual aid societies argued that they alone had the exclusive right to head the new insurance program (Light 1985).

These mutual aid societies were created by guild—and later union—members prior to the establishment of national health insurance. The societies, run by employers, employees, or both, collected dues from their members and in return provided access to medical services. Thus, health care programs were run by societies on a local basis, funded by members' contributions. The concept of premiums was therefore not an alien one; workers were already paying premiums to these societies, and in some cases employers contributed some amount toward the total. The mutual aid societies facilitated the implementation of national health insurance, a new program built on an existing foundation (Light 1985).

The 1883 Sickness Insurance Act was the first of three pillars of social security legislation in Germany. It was followed by accident insurance legislation in 1884 and old-age and disability insurance in 1889. The 1883 legislation required that all workers earning a certain income or below be insured by a sickness fund or mutual aid society. The law also mandated employer-employee contributions (premiums) and stipulated a minimum level of benefits. The 1883 legislation ensured that all members of a sickness fund would receive physicians' services, medication, eyeglasses, and hospital treatment without charge at the point of service. Sickness funds were also required to provide income-replacement benefits, which were more important than medical benefits to workers at that time (Blanpain, Delesie, and Nys 1978).

Passage of the 1883 legislation was a success for Bismarck on two counts. First, social benefits for workers would be derived directly from an employment relationship, rather than from the state. The mode of financing health care through employer-employee contributions, rather than through general tax revenues was, and remains, a linchpin of the German health insurance system. Second, using the sickness funds as employer-employee organizations "undermined any future effort of trade unions to capture social protection as an exclusive function of labor organizations" (Stone 1980, 23). Bismarck's ability to draw health programs already in existence under the banner of the state was an effective response to the growing strength of the socialists (Lockhart 1981).

Bismarck's social insurance system was based on the concept that a nation is responsible for the provision of social systems such as health care for its citizens. This "principle of social solidarity" also ensured that the costs of health care would be spread across the population. Hence the reliance on income-based premiums for health care financing (Iglehart 1991a; Wysong and Abel 1990).

German Corporatism

The final shape of the national health insurance program reflected both the social-solidarity/state-as-agent-of-social-welfare approach and earlier mutual-aid society arrangements. Although Bismarck did push through his version of national health insurance, he failed in his effort to secure a key role for the state governments in the administration of the program. That role fell to the sickness funds, which were similar to the mutual aid societies (Light 1985).

The "sickness funds compromise" was the embodiment of a particularly German organizational arrangement known as corporatism. German corporatism is characterized by a "quasi-public form of representative government over a specific program area" (Light 1985, 619) and stems from the belief that occupational groups are the best equipped to articulate political interests.

There are two main features of German corporatism in the health care context. First, mandatory organizations whose membership is based on occupational status serve as intermediaries between the government and individuals. Second, these organizations are granted the legal authority to regulate "work-related aspects of their members' behavior and to administer government programs related to their members" (Stone 1980, 20). The compulsory organizations in this context are the sickness funds to which employees earning below a certain income must belong and the associations of sickness-fund physicians, of which any physician wishing to be paid under the sickness-fund system must be a member. The role of the state in this arrangement is to act as a referee with power to set the rules. The state can change the rules of the game through legislation if it feels that the system is off track (Light 1985).

The sickness funds were given legal responsibility over the financial and organizational aspects of health care services for their members. The funds were consequently responsible for staffing and operating medical facilities (Glaser 1978). The governing boards of the early sickness funds included representatives of employers and employees. Representation on the boards was in proportion to the share of premiums paid, and the unions volunteered to pay two-thirds of the premiums. The "resulting union control of the majority of seats would have a profound impact in the years to come" (Light 1985, 618), as the boards have always been responsible for determining such important factors as the size of premiums to be charged (Glaser 1983).

Premiums are income based and, unlike insurance premiums in the United States, risk factors are not a consideration in premium calculations. The German health insurance system thus had a redistributive bent right from the start, as workers received similar (but not identical) benefits even though they did not necessarily contribute the same amounts (Glaser 1983). Through its income-based financing, the system enacts significant financial transfers between income groups, individuals with families and individuals without, healthy and sick alike (Wysong and Abel 1990).

System Expands

The 1883 law initially required manual laborers to join, but membership in the national health insurance system increased gradually over the years. Ten percent of the population was covered two years after the program's introduction. In 1911, the National Health Insurance Act increased the legal income limit for workers to be insured under the statutory program, and 23 percent of the population was insured by 1914. The number of insured has grown steadily since that time, to a current coverage rate of approximately 90 percent of the population (Henke 1990a; Schneider 1991; Spencer and Associates 1989-1992).

German national health insurance was implemented in the absence of opposition from doctors' groups (Anderson 1989). It was not surprising that physicians did not play a role in the initial formulation of national health insurance in Germany since "they were not [then] recognized under law as a profession and did not have the extensive legal privileges of a profession" (Light 1985, 620). But as membership in the statutory system increased, private physicians came increasingly to believe their livelihood was being jeopardized by the stronger position of the sickness funds. Workers were attracted to clinics run by sickness funds because they were conveniently located and kept after-work hours. Moreover, the sickness funds applied capitation (per person rates) or fee schedules to physician rates, which helped to contain costs (Light 1985; Zollner 1982).

The relatively weak position of physicians changed dramatically over the history of German national health insurance, as the doctors ultimately usurped the sickness funds to become the most powerful professional group in the health care sector (Light 1985). This trend started in 1900 with the founding of the Hartmann Bund, a physicians' organization dedicated to protesting the growing control of the sickness funds over the practice of medicine (Stone 1977). Indeed, as membership in the statutory health insurance program expanded after 1911, the number of funds decreased (see Table 4-1). Physicians were thus confronted with larger organizations comprising larger patient constituencies (Stone 1980).

Thirty years after the formation of the Hartmann Bund, the Emergency Regulation of 1931 created associations of sickness fund physicians to represent those physicians participating in the national health insurance scheme. As will be discussed in more detail in following sections, these physicians' associations were given the legal authority to negotiate fee schedules with the sickness funds as well as to conduct monitoring of physicians' practice. This granting of authority laid the groundwork for the evolution of physicians' organizations into very powerful political entities (Stone 1977).

Cornerstone of German Health Insurance: The Sickness Funds

The cornerstone of the German system is a network of approximately 1,150 sickness funds. Membership in the sickness funds is mandatory for all residents earning less than the government-established income ceiling (approximately $41,000 in the western states, and $30,000 in the states of the former East Germany in 1993). And, as in the U.S. Social

Table 4-1   Coverage under German Statutory Health System, 1885-1986

Year	Number of insured in millions[a]	Percent of population insured[b]	Number of insurance funds
1885	4.7	10.0	18,942
1911	10.0	21.5	22,000
1914	16.0	23.0	13,500
1932	18.7	30.0	6,600
1951	20.0	48.1	1,992
1960	27.1	85.0	2,028
1970	30.6	88.0	1,827
1976	33.5	90.0	1,425
1982	35.8	89.8	1,286
1986	36.5	90.2	1,184

Source: Reprinted with permission from *Advances in Health Economics and Health Services Research,* Supplement 1 (1990), p. 146. "The Federal Republic of Germany." Jean Jacques Rosa, Klaus-Dirk Henke.

[a] Without family dependents   [b] With family dependents

Security program, only earned income up to this ceiling is taxable for health insurance. As the tax rate and the ceiling on taxable wages are fixed, an employee who earns $3,000 per month with four dependents will pay the same amount as one without any dependents earning the same salary (Stone 1980).

The mandatory coverage group ranges from self-employed farmers, artists, and students, to the unemployed, disabled, and retirees, and includes all family members. The membership of the sickness funds is currently 85 percent mandatorily insured, 15 percent voluntarily insured. Individuals who earn more than the income ceiling have the option of purchasing private insurance coverage, but most choose sickness fund coverage because the contribution rates are lower than private insurance (Hurst 1991).

Covered Benefits

The German health insurance program is among the most comprehensive in the world. Government regulations establish a basic benefits package that all funds must offer. Medical, dental, in-patient hospital care, and prescription drugs are covered. Patients do not pay deductibles, and there are minimal co-payments for certain services. Additional benefits are provided to cover care of the sick at home, and even rehabilitative treatment at health spas. Generous maternity benefits provide an interesting contrast with the current U.S. debate over family leave legislation. Maternity allowance (full pay) in Germany is paid during the period six weeks before birth through eight weeks after birth. The sickness fund pays a small portion of the allowance and the employer pays the rest.

Another measure of the breadth of German national health insurance is in the area of income replacement. If an insured person is unable to work due to an illness, employers are obligated to pay the employee's full salary for the first six weeks. After this period, the insured person can collect 80 percent of covered earnings from the sickness fund—up to a maximum of seventy-eight weeks in any three-year period (Stone 1979). According to one analyst, benefits such as these indicate that German national health insurance over the past century "has been fundamentally transformed into an all-inclusive health protection and income maintenance program for which the term 'insurance' may be a misnomer" (Altenstetter 1987, 507).

Fund Organization and Financing

The sickness funds fall under two general categories: state insurance (RVO) funds, and so-called substitute funds, whose predecessors were the early mutual aid societies discussed earlier (Schneider 1991). Initially, sickness funds were organized around one's occupation. For example, there were funds for miners, seamen, factory workers, and so forth. However, currently the majority of the insured belong to local funds, whose members are located in a specific geographic area (Stone 1980). Approximately one-quarter of all sickness funds are local funds that provide benefits for 44 percent of all individuals for whom membership in a fund is mandatory. Although more than 60 percent of the funds are industrial funds (factory funds), these funds cover only slightly more than one-tenth of those insured under the sickness fund system (see Table 4-2). A separate fund exists for civil servants (Henke 1990a; Wysong and Abel 1990).

Individuals who earn more than the income ceiling set by the government for mandatory coverage can choose to join a substitute fund, which generally offers better benefits and tends to have lower contribution rates. As shown in Table 4-2, more than one-third of the covered population belongs to a substitute fund. Although there is limited competition between the funds in terms of supplemental benefits and contribution rates, selection by insurers according to the risk of the individual is forbidden by the government (Wysong and Abel 1990).

Table 4-2 German Sickness Fund Membership, 1986

Fund	Membership (in millions)	Membership (as percent of covered population)
Local (community)	44.0	16.1
Substitute	33.9	12.4
Factory	11.6	4.2
Craft	4.4	1.9
Miners'	2.2	1.0
Farmers'	2.1	0.8
Seamen's	0.1	0.1

Source: Wysong, Jere, and Thomas Abel. "Universal Health Insurance and High-risk Groups in West Germany: Implications for U.S. Policy." *Milbank Quarterly* 68, 4 (1990): 534. Reprinted with permission of the Milbank Memorial Fund.

Each sickness fund is supervised by a board of employee-employer representatives. While these private nonprofit sickness funds are subject to federal guidelines, they are solely responsible for their own financial health (Reinhardt 1981b). The funds calculate the amount of revenues they will need to keep themselves solvent and set the employee-employer contribution rate accordingly (Iglehart 1991a).

In the early days of the sickness funds, the ratio of contributions was two-thirds employee, one-third employer. In 1951, contributions were set at an equal level. An employee's contribution is not determined by risk status nor family status, since premiums are a set portion of income and cover all dependents, but rather by an individual's ability to pay (Reinhardt 1981b). The employer-employee contribution varies across funds and ranges from 8 percent to 16 percent of an employee's gross income (see Table 4-3). The average contribution rate in 1992 was 12.5 percent. As will be discussed in more detail in following sections, the sickness funds transfer the employer-employee contributions to the regional physicians' associations, which then pay the doctors.

Coverage for Retirees, the Unemployed, and Citizens of Former East Germany

Retirees receive benefits through their sickness funds. A certain percentage of a retired person's pension is transferred to the sickness fund. This percentage equals the average employee payroll contribution. However, these retiree contributions cover only approximately 40 percent of the health care costs of the elderly. Sickness funds subsidize the rest through payroll taxes paid by employed sickness-fund members. Retiree health care costs in Germany are thus spread among the

Table 4-3   Payroll Tax Rates of German Sickness Funds, 1988

| | Employer-employee contribution as percentage of gross income | |
Type of fund	Range	Average
Local (community)	10.8 to 16.0	13.5
Substitute	10.9 to 12.8	12.7
Craft	9.8 to 15.6	12.8
Factory	7.5 to 15.5	11.4

Source: Wysong, Jere, and Thomas Abel. "Universal Health Insurance and High-risk Groups in West Germany: Implications for U.S. Policy." *Milbank Quarterly* 68, 4 (1990): 553. Reprinted with permission of the Milbank Memorial Fund.

government, retirees, the employed, and the sickness funds (Iglehart 1991a; Reinhardt 1990a; Wysong and Abel 1990).

The unemployed and their dependents are protected by a federal law that requires sickness funds to provide the same benefits to the unemployed as to the employed. The covered unemployed numbered 7.4 percent of the work force in June 1990 (prior to reunification). The Federal Labor Administration pays the premiums for the majority (two-thirds) of the unemployed, while the remainder of the unemployed are covered through local social welfare agencies (Iglehart 1991a). Although German health insurance is employment-based, loss of one's job does not necessarily entail loss of health insurance coverage—a significant problem in the United States.

As part of the agreement to restructure the former East German health system along West German lines, a network of local sickness funds was created in 1991. Because of their low income levels, the vast majority of the population of former East Germany will have to join a sickness fund. More than 14 million former East Germans are now covered by the sickness fund system, but statistics from the German Federal Department of Labor indicate that only slightly more than one-half million people are voluntarily insured by the sickness funds (Spencer and Associates 1989-1992).

The average contribution rate for the sickness funds was set at the average rate prevailing in West Germany. Physicians' fees and hospital charges were to be set at a level of slightly less than half that in West Germany, however, to reflect the gap in the standard of living between the east and west. These levels will gradually be increased as the gap in the standard of living closes (Schneider 1991).

Company-Sponsored Sickness Funds

There has been a steady increase over the years in the number of health insurance plans sponsored by private companies. Approximately seven hundred employer-sponsored funds presently cover about 12 percent of all individuals insured by sickness funds. Similar to self-insured plans in the United States, such company-sponsored plans tend to be offered by larger employers and have a distinct cost advantage over the statutory sickness funds. Costs (both for employers and employees) tend to be lower because company-sponsored funds generally provide coverage for workers who are in lower-risk groups. For example, the average contribution to company-sponsored funds in 1989 was 11.4 percent of taxable salary while the average contribution rate for the statutory funds was 12.8 percent. Premium rates for company-sponsored funds range from a low of 8.5 percent to a high of 16.0 percent (Spencer and Associates 1989-1992).

The German government has grown increasingly apprehensive about the number of company-sponsored plans, arguing that by attracting the good-risk individuals, these funds increase the costs of the statutory sickness funds. Indeed, one could argue that the availability of lower costs for only certain employers and employees belies the underlying principle of equality in German social policy. The German government is looking into ways of correcting the discrepancy between the contribution rates for company-sponsored funds and other sickness funds, with the possibility of a major reorganization of sickness funds (Spencer and Associates 1989-1992).

Private Insurance

Germany has not outlawed private insurance for benefits covered under the national health insurance program, as we saw in the Canadian system. Any individual earning more than approximately $3,400 per month (for those in the western states) can purchase insurance from about forty-five private insurers. This alternative coverage represents to many the "escape valve for the affluent" that is absent in the Canadian system (U.S. GAO 1991). Those who purchase private insurance as their sole coverage tend to be single people with high incomes (Schneider 1991).

Private insurance provided coverage for slightly more than 11 million people, according to a microcensus conducted by the German Federal Statistical Office in April 1989. This number included 6.4 million individuals who were exclusively privately insured and 4.8 million who had private coverage to supplement sickness fund coverage.

If an employee opts to purchase private insurance rather than join a statutory sickness fund, the employer contribution to the private plan is the same as if the employee had joined a statutory sickness fund. Once an individual opts out of the statutory sickness fund system, however, that individual cannot rejoin the system (Reinhardt 1990b).

Private insurance premiums are calculated according to age in five-year cohorts. The premiums do not increase as the individual ages, so individuals pay more when they are younger, thus setting aside a reserve needed to cover higher costs as they age (Iglehart 1991a; Reinhardt 1990a). Private insurance premiums for married couples and families with children are higher than sickness fund premiums (Schneider 1991).

As noted earlier, almost 5 million Germans covered by sickness funds also purchase private insurance for supplementary coverage. Such supplemental coverage plans generally cover private or semi-private hospital rooms, a cash allowance for each day in the hospital, medical coverage during overseas travel, and coverage for dentures and eyeglasses.

Health Care Financing

Germany's comprehensive system of health care is financed by revenues from five major sources (Henke 1986, 341-342):

1. general taxes (local, state, and federal);
2. payroll taxes (shared equally between employer and employee);
3. private insurance premiums (in addition to, or in place of, payroll taxes);
4. direct payments (out-of-pocket expenditures, co-payments); and
5. financial charges imposed on public and private employers (to pay a sickness allowance for up to six weeks; after six weeks it is financed by the sickness funds, in other words, out of payroll taxes).

Employer/employee contributions represent 60 percent of health care expenditures, while federal, state, and local government tax revenues make up 21 percent and co-payments and out-of-pocket expenditures represent 11 percent. Private insurance represents approximately 7 percent of health care expenditures (Hurst 1991).

Co-payments were first introduced in 1970, when a small charge for prescription drugs and minimal co-payments for eyeglasses, dentures, and prostheses were instituted (Stone 1979). Additional co-payments have since been introduced. Patients now pay a small co-payment (approximately $6 per day) for the first two weeks in a hospital, a small co-payment for prescription drugs, and a per diem charge for in-patient rehabilitation treatment (Hurst 1991).

Hospital Financing

Three major pieces of legislation have reshaped hospital financing in Germany over the past two decades. The Hospital Financing Act of 1972 formally separated the responsibility for hospital operating expenses from capital investment funds. The latter were to be covered by federal and state budgets, while operating expenses were included in the hospital per diem rate paid by sickness funds for the treatment of their members (Godt 1987).

Hospital services in Germany are financed on a per diem basis, regardless of the type of care required or the length of hospital stay. Physicians belong to associations of sickness fund physicians through which they negotiate fees, but the three thousand German hospitals negotiate the per diem rate directly with the sickness funds.

In contrast to the United States, where hospitals charge patients separately for room, board, lab tests, physicians' fees, and so on, the daily charge in a German hospital is all-inclusive. Hospital-based physicians are employees of the hospital and are paid a salary that is set according to a physician's area of specialty and years of experience. The per diem, therefore, has to be sufficiently large to cover all operating costs of the hospital, including labor costs (salaries for hospital physicians and nurses). All health care payers (sickness funds) in the same region pay the same per diem rate, regardless of the patient's illness (Henke 1986; Iglehart 1991a; Schneider 1991; Stone 1980).

The federal government ceded its shared responsibility for the hospital sector to the states as a result of a second major piece of legislation: the Hospital Financing Reform Law of 1984. Under the 1984 law, state governments have the final say over the financing of all capital expenditures for medical facilities and equipment; this authority gives the states control over hospital capacity (Altenstetter 1987; Godt 1987; Jonsson 1990).

The third major piece of legislation affecting the hospital sector was the Federal Hospital Payment Regulation of 1986. This law instituted a prospective global hospital budgeting system for hospitals. Operating budgets are now calculated in advance based on expected rates of hospital occupancy for the following year. Each hospital negotiates its budget with the sickness funds. These negotiations determine the per diem rate paid by sickness funds to the hospital (Altenstetter 1987; Hurst 1991; Schneider 1991).

Thus the responsibility for policymaking in the hospital sector is divided. The states control capital budgets and must approve all requests for capital expenditures, but operating budgets are covered by the per diem rates negotiated between the hospitals and the sickness funds. This makes for an uneasy alliance since states may not be sensitive enough to the impact of their decisions regarding capital expenditures because they do not have to take responsibility for the latter. For example, while the states might purchase new equipment, they might not take into consideration the cost of operating the equipment that the hospitals will incur (Iglehart 1991b; Schneider 1991).

Physician Payment

In Germany, as in many other European countries, there is a distinct legal separation of the services of ambulatory (office-based) physicians and hospital physicians. A physician is generally allowed to provide either in-patient hospital care or office-based care only (Stone 1977). An office-based physician cannot treat his or her patient once that patient enters the hospital. In the same way, hospital physicians are not allowed to conduct such prehospital procedures as diagnostic workups, nor are they allowed to provide follow-up care (Stone 1980).

Each physician sends vouchers covering the type of service a patient received to the regional association of physicians for payment (see Figure 4-2). These regional associations serve not only to pay physicians, but also to monitor the volume of services performed by each physician. In this way, the associations play a critical cost-containment role as will be discussed further in following sections (Schneider 1991).

Physicians must accept payment from the sickness funds as payment in full. Again, as Germany has an all-payer system, all regional sickness funds pay the same fees for the same services to regional associations of sickness fund physicians. It should be noted, however, that private insurance pays physicians and hospitals at fee levels that are more than twice that of the sickness fund fee levels (Schneider 1991).

Evolution of Physician Payment Methods. Physician payment in Germany has evolved over the past several decades. The seeds of the current relationship between health care providers and payers were planted in 1931 and 1932, when, as noted earlier, physicians' associations were created to represent physicians in negotiations with sickness funds. Negotiations with individual physicians were no longer allowed and sickness funds were required to negotiate with physicians as a group (Kirkman-Liff 1990).

Figure 4-2 Flow of Funds and Sickness Vouchers in the German System

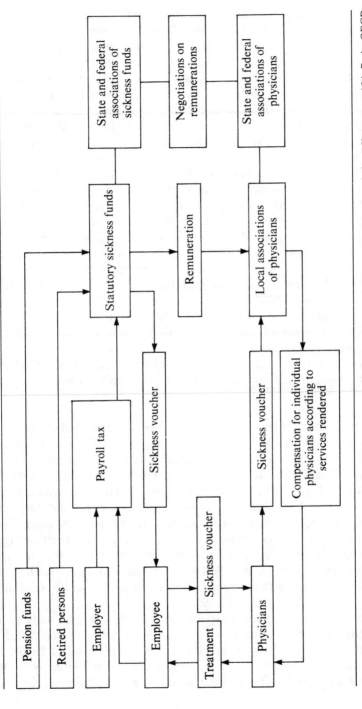

Source: Henke, Klaus-Dirk. "Federal Republic of Germany" in *Health Care Systems in Transition: The Search for Efficiency.* p. 104. Paris: OECD, 1990.

The 1931 and 1932 regulations also established a two-step physician reimbursement process. First, the sickness funds would make lump-sum capitation (per person) payments to the physicians' associations. The physicians' associations were then responsible for dividing this revenue pool and distributing individual payments to their physician members. These payments were generally made on a fee-for-service basis according to a fee schedule. The size of the pool and the specific fees for medical procedures were hammered out through collective bargaining between the physicians' associations and the sickness fund associations (Stone 1980).

Each physician's share of the total pool was determined by a relative value scale that applied a certain number of points to each medical service rendered. The total number of points accruing to each physician determined his or her share of the pool. The financial risk was thus spread among physicians because a sickness fund with a majority of low-income members would pay a lower capitation rate into the pool than a fund with mainly high-income earners. In this way, the funds with wealthy members subsidized the funds with poorer members (Kirkman-Liff 1990).

The sickness funds contributed to the pools on a capitation basis for the next two decades, during which time a system of fixed budgeting essentially governed physician payment methods. But a 1955 reform empowered sickness funds to select their preferred method of calculating the pool: fee-for-service, fee-per-visit, capitation, or any mix of these (Stone 1980).

From Capitation to Fee for Service. The first sickness fund changed to a fee-for-service method of calculating the pool in 1958. The physicians' associations then staged a campaign that pitted the statutory sickness funds (which were still using the capitation method) against the substitute funds, which had made the switch to a fee-for-service method. The physicians' associations argued that as the statutory funds were still using a capitation method, the care they provided was of lower quality than the other funds. The statutory funds were therefore faced with loss of membership if they did not change to a fee-for-service method (Stone 1980). By 1968 the physicians' associations had succeeded in changing the payment system to a fee-for-service reimbursement system (Kirkman-Liff 1990).

Payments were made each quarter by the sickness funds to the regional physicians' associations; these payments were calculated by examining the claims in the previous quarter (Kirkman-Liff 1990). The limit on total expenditures for physicians' services was effectively wiped out by the new fee-for-service method of pool calculation. This new method allowed physicians to increase their share of the pie without detracting from that of their colleagues (Stone 1980). Indeed, the change from capitation to fee-for-service was a real windfall for physicians and would sound the death knell for efforts to control physician reimbursement.

Health Care Cost Control

Health care expenditures increased significantly throughout the early 1970s. Between 1970 and 1975, for example, German health care expenditures increased at a rate of almost 20 percent a year (Henke 1990a). Faced with such rising expenditures, the federal government turned to regulatory measures. The efforts of the government made Germany "one of the first countries to impose budgetary discipline upon national health insurance" (Glaser 1978, 111). Physicians in Germany were as enamored of government intervention as their American counterparts—in other words, they were not happy about it—and opposed the government's efforts (Kirkman-Liff 1990). Nevertheless, several landmark health care cost-control measures were enacted.

Health Care Cost Containment Act of 1977

Germany took its cost-control mission seriously and formalized procedures—codified in the federal Health Care Cost Containment Act (HCCCA) of 1977—to rein in health care expenditures. This law was designed to reduce health care expenditure growth and create a framework for stabilizing the payroll tax rate for health insurance (Henke 1986). The law sought to introduce predetermined budgets for all health care expenditures (Reinhardt 1981a), and to that end created a national health conference (*Konzertierte Aktion*). The so-called Concerted Action is an advisory body made up of approximately seventy representatives of all the major shareholders in the health care system (see Figure 4-3).

The conference meets twice a year. Its mandate is to bring all the various groups together in an effort to work toward agreement on a uniform, nationwide, operational framework for the German health insurance system (Henke 1990a). All aspects of the system are discussed and negotiated, from overall expenditure levels to specific increases in physicians' fees. A key objective of the conference is the establishment of guidelines for the maximum annual increase in expenditures for physician and dental services

Figure 4-3   Health Care Negotiation Structure in West Germany, Late 1980s

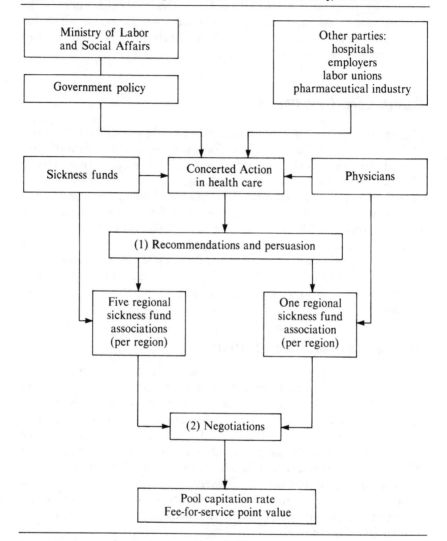

Source: Kirkman-Liff, Bradford. "Physician Payment Reform and Cost-Containment Strategies in West Germany." *Journal of Health Politics, Policy, and Law* 15: 1. Copyright 1990 Duke University Press. Reprinted with permission of the publisher.

and prescription drugs. The conference's guidelines are nonbinding, but do bear significant influence; if the groups are incapable of agreement, compulsory arbitration may be imposed (Kirkman-Liff 1990; Stone 1980).

A significant outcome of the 1977 legislation was a series of reforms that resulted in a new contract between the sickness funds and the physicians' associations. This contract established a target for physician expenditures. The target was calculated based on health costs for the previous year and could be adjusted to accommodate changes in demographics, new medical technology, and so forth. More importantly, the target was to reflect changes in wages and salaries of employees. This was the centerpiece of a new strategy known as income-related expenditure growth. Increases in expenditures would be tied to increases in the wage base of the sickness funds' members (Kirkman-Liff 1990; Schneider 1991).

In addition to establishing a target for physician expenditures, the 1977 law also formally established a national relative value scale (Godt 1987). Negotiations between the sickness funds and the physicians' associations were held on a national level to determine the point value assigned to over two thousand different medical treatments (Kirkman-Liff 1990). Whereas the relative value scale was negotiated between national associations of sickness funds and national associations of sickness fund physicians, the conversion factor used to arrive at a monetary equivalent for each point on the scale is set in annual negotiations between the regional associations of sickness funds and their physician counterparts. As a result, there is a series of regional fee schedules for physicians, but no single nationwide fee schedule (U.S. GAO 1991).

Conspicuously absent from the HCCCA were regulations affecting cost containment in the hospital sector. The hospital sector was able to elude the government's net as the states, which had primary responsibility for the hospital sector, wielded their veto power in the national parliament. It was not until 1982 that the hospital sector was formally included within the Concerted Action forum (Godt 1987).

The HCCCA was a watershed in the development of health care policymaking in Germany, for it was the first time in many decades that the federal government directly intervened in the health care sector (Henke 1986). Whereas other reform attempts had failed, such as those undertaken in the 1960s to introduce cost-sharing, the successful implementation of the 1977 legislation can be attributed to three major factors. First, the public was well aware of escalating health care expenditures. Second, these health care costs were widely perceived to be jeopardizing the financial standing of the social security system. Third, public opinion was enraged by the wide disparity in income levels between physicians and other workers (Godt 1987; Stone 1980). Indeed, physicians' incomes were almost five to six times the national average wage from 1970 to 1975. The federal government, with strong public support for reform, was able to "mobilize a coalition of labor and business leaders [the primary financiers of the health care insurance system], who were hostile to the doctors' positions" (Godt 1987, 475).

From Expenditure Target to Cap

A second major health care cost-control reform measure was enacted in 1986. While the expenditure target appeared to be a plausible approach in theory, in actuality, health care expenditures during the period that the target was in use (1978 to 1986) always surpassed the target figure. Targets were essentially nonbinding; when spending exceeded the target, future expenditures were not reduced accordingly. Tighter control over physician expenditures was needed, and it was decided that an expenditure cap would be a more effective method of cost control. Expenditure caps were given the teeth that expenditure targets lacked and set binding limits on annual expenditures for physician services. Increases in the expenditure cap were directly linked to increases in the average wage level of sickness funds' members (Kirkman-Liff 1990).

The expenditure cap was set every year through negotiations between the sickness funds and the physicians' associations. A certain amount of money was allocated for each person insured by the sickness fund system; a total budget amount was determined by this figure. The sickness funds would pay the physicians' association a lump-sum payment; the association would then pay the doctors on a fee-for-service basis. Under the expenditure cap, when the volume of services exceeded the limit set by the cap, the point value used to determine physicians' fees was reduced.

As Reinhardt notes, the system of downward adjustment of fees worked because all physicians were part of a "zero-sum-game" as they all drew from the same revenue pool. The physician associations consequently "police[d] their own members" (Reinhardt 1990b, 9). Expenditure caps addressed the weaknesses of the previous cost-control mechanisms since not only could the caps enforce spending limits, but they contained a built-in mechanism to prevent physicians from increasing the volume of services to increase their incomes.

Health Reform Law of 1988

A third cost-control regulatory effort came in the form of the Health Reform Law of 1988 (effective January 1, 1989). Driven by escalating employer-employee insurance contributions, this law was designed to enact a comprehensive overhaul of the German health insurance system. Employer-employee contributions reached a high of almost 13 percent of income in 1988 and 1989 (see Figure 4-4). There was heightened concern that increasing contribution rates were inflating labor costs (already among the highest in Europe), and would ultimately render German industry uncompetitive. Moreover, the federal government was concerned that the continued increases in spending on health care might reduce any gains derived from a gradual reduction in income taxes (Goebel 1989).

The reform law implemented a series of cost-control measures, including:

- co-payment for each of the first fourteen days in the hospital is to be increased from DM 5 to DM 10 as of January 1, 1991 (approximately $6 per day as of 1991);
- co-payments per prescription are now DM 3; fixed prices for certain medicines were set; incentives were established to encourage patients to use less expensive generic medicines;
- reimbursement of transport and travel costs was scaled back; travel costs are now only reimbursable in case of hospital emergency, or if costs exceed DM 20;
- new benefits for home care were to be phased in from 1989 to 1991 in an effort to discourage reliance on more expensive nursing home care;
- co-payments for dental care were increased; bonuses were awarded for preventive care;
- funeral (death) grants for newly insured were eliminated, such grants for those already insured were reduced; and
- lump-sum birth grants were eliminated (Goebel 1989; Will 1989).

These reforms were designed with the objective of shaving about 10 percent off the total German health care bill. The specific measures targeting the pharmaceutical industry, for example, are very important. Drug prices in Germany are twice as high as those in any other industrialized country. Pharmaceuticals account for more than 20 percent of total health care expenditures, compared with slightly more than 8 percent in the United States (Schieber, Poullier, and Greenwald 1991).

The price controls on pharmaceuticals have been largely successful. The Health Care Reform Act fixed the price of pharmaceuticals at the level of their generic equivalents and the sickness funds will not reimburse beyond that price. Fixed prices are approximately 30 percent below those of brand name products and a person must make up the difference if they wish to use a more expensive medicine. Faced with a loss of market share, many pharmaceutical companies have reduced their prices. Prices of drugs with fixed rates were reduced by more than

Figure 4-4   Contribution Rates for Sickness Funds, Germany, 1973-1992

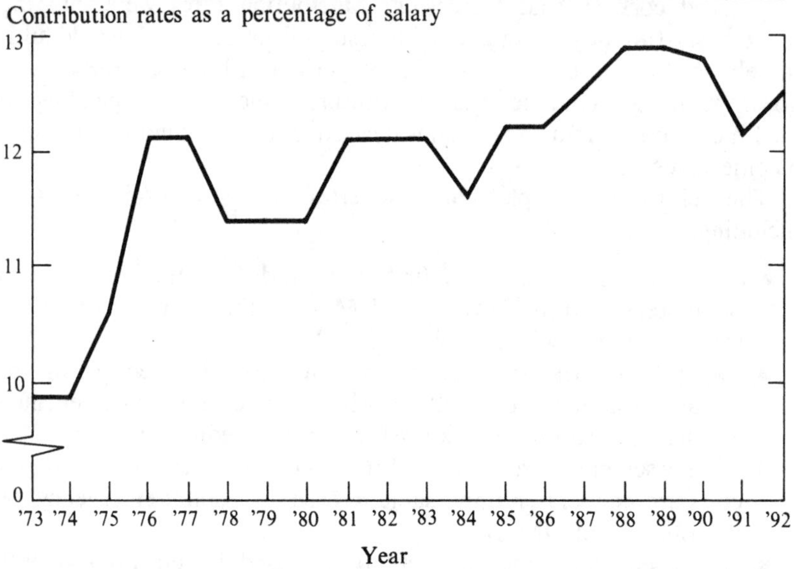

Contribution rates as a percentage of salary

Year

Source: Ministry of Labor and Social Affairs, 1990, and Charles D. Spencer & Associates, International Benefits Information Service, 1992.

20 percent in the first year of implementation of price controls (Schneider 1991).

One Hundred Years of Health Care Reform?

The government's health care cost-control efforts continue with the implementation of the Health Reform Law of 1993. As with previous cost-control measures, this new law does not restrict services covered by the comprehensive public plan. Rather, it calls for shared sacrifices on the part of patients and providers. For instance, the amounts patients pay out-of-pocket for prescription drugs will be increased. Previously, patients paid a flat co-payment of DM 3 per prescription. The new law scales the co-payment to the price of the drug, to a maximum of DM 7 (approximately $4.50) per prescription. Co-payments for the first fourteen days in the hospital are to be increased from DM 10 to DM 11 (Spencer and Associates 1989-1992).

The second cost-control weapon embodied in the controversial law is very unpopular with the medical profession. Physicians, dentists, and hospitals will face limitations on increases in their fees. Providers' fees will be tied to increases in workers' incomes and will essentially not be allowed to increase more than 4 percent per year (Fisher 1992). In addition, the law targets the supply of physicians. Germany has among the highest number of physicians per capita in the industrialized world—and the number continues to outpace population growth. This growth in physician supply can be attributed in part to the German system of education, which guarantees free education to all students who pass the required exams. But medical schools are now beginning to reduce their class sizes based on the claim that large classes are having a negative effect on the quality of teaching (Iglehart 1991b). The new law takes this one step further by setting limits on the number of physicians allowed to practice under the sickness fund system.

These reform measures are designed to stabilize the level of premiums that employers and employees pay for health care without restricting access to services. Given Germany's rapidly aging population and the rising cost of advanced medical technology, it is unclear whether future cost-control efforts will leave intact the comprehensive package of benefits covered under the public plan.

German System Faces Challenges

Although the German system sounds almost too good to be true—universal coverage, comprehensive benefits, effective cost-control mechanisms—it is not without its drawbacks. The problems faced by the German health care system will be compounded by the challenge of bringing the health care system of former East Germany into line with the system in the west. An estimated DM 20 billion of investment is needed, for example, to raise the standards of the hospital sector in the east to those in the west (Hurst 1991). There are also other weaknesses in the system that are the object of reform efforts, several of which are described in the following section.

Weaknesses of the System

There is significant variation among the contribution rates paid by members of the different sickness funds. Sickness fund contribution rates are set according to the costs of covering all members of a fund. Therefore, the varying composition of a sickness fund affects the contribution rates. Sickness funds not only cover individuals with different age and health risks, but different numbers of family dependents as well. Moreover, certain sickness funds cover mainly lower-income workers, while other funds cover higher-income workers. Those funds that cover primarily lower-income workers, or those whose membership comprises mainly higher-risk individuals or individuals with many dependents, must charge higher contribution rates in order to generate enough revenues to cover the health care costs of all of their members (Rublee 1992).

To date health care reform efforts have not narrowed the rate differential of contributions. In 1978, payroll tax rates ranged from 7 to 14 percent; in 1990, the range was 8 to 16 percent (Schneider 1991). The local sickness funds, which have the highest contribution rates, are pushing for legal reforms that would create financial transfers between the funds to help equalize the different risk levels (Reinhardt 1990b).

A second weakness is the division between ambulatory medical care on the one hand and in-patient hospital care on the other. One consequence of this division is a "lengthy referral chain" between ambulatory doctors and hospital-based physicians (Hurst 1991, 76). Among patients that need to be hospitalized there tends to be unnecessary duplication of tests and procedures that have already been conducted by the ambulatory physicians who have advanced medical equipment at their disposal (Hurst 1991, 76; Schneider 1991). The division between in-patient and out-patient physician services has resulted in battles fought over how health care resources should be allocated among the different health care delivery settings (Iglehart 1991b).

A third weakness is that the German system is financed on a pay-as-you-go basis. In other words, the current health care costs are financed by premiums for that year. Under this approach, financial reserves are not built up to pay for higher expenditures required for the aging population. As mentioned earlier, Germany has one of the largest elderly populations in the world, with more than 20 percent currently over age 65. This number is expected to rise to 27 percent by the year 2010. As the ratio of workers to retirees declines, many experts question whether this system of financing will be sustainable in the future (Rublee 1992).

Another issue related to the aging of the population is the need for long-term care services (such as those provided by nursing homes) that are currently not covered by the sickness fund plan. Legislation is currently under consideration to create a long-term care program that would pay a cash benefit up to a certain monthly limit for full-time nursing home care and a reduced amount for home care. Long-term care coverage would be mandatory for all those covered under the sickness fund system. The program would be financed by employer/employee contributions. The proposed legislation would eliminate employer-paid cash sickness benefits for the first day of illness. The cost savings from this change are expected to offset the employer cost of the proposed long-term care coverage. If approved, the law would take effect in 1996 (Hurst 1991; Spencer and Associates 1989-1992).

Finally, as in the United States, an absence of cost-consciousness by patients plagues the German health care system. Patients insured by the statutory health insurance fund are not given a bill for their medical treatment, so they are not aware of the actual cost of their care. Moreover, since co-payments are still quite minimal, "cost-consciousness of the patient is severely underdeveloped" (Henke 1986, 349). It has been suggested that Germany should consider changing its health insurance system to a cost-reimbursement system, in which the patient pays the medical bill first, then is reimbursed by the sickness fund. If indeed it were possible to implement such a radical change, it is believed that the introduction of co-insurance would then become a definite possibility (Henke 1990a). But any changes made to alter the insurance premium system from income-based to actuarial-based contributions would jeopardize the risk-sharing and free access to care that are the cornerstones of the German system (Altenstetter 1987; Schneider 1991).

German System Receives High Marks

Despite the problems and weaknesses outlined above, this imperfect system receives high marks when judged in the court of public opinion. A poll by Louis Harris and Associates in conjunction with the Harvard School of Public Health revealed that a little more than a third of German citizens polled believe fundamental changes are needed to make the system work better. Thus it seems that Germans are more satisfied with their health care system than Americans are with theirs; as much as 60 percent of Americans polled believe fundamental changes are needed to improve the U.S. health care system (Blendon, Leitman, Morrison, and Donelan 1990). Indeed, of the ten countries surveyed, Germans are among the most satisfied with their health care system (see Figure 4-5).

Lessons from Germany

This brief survey of the complex workings of the German national health insurance program yields several important lessons for the United States. On a general level, the German experience with universal, comprehensive health insurance should disabuse many Americans of the view that the presence of national health insurance

Figure 4-5   **The Public's View of Their Health Care System in Ten Nations, 1990 (in percent)**

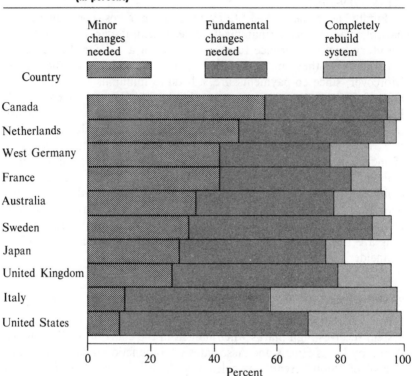

Source: Blendon, Robert, Robert Leitman, Ian Morrison, and Karen Donelan. "Satisfaction with Health Systems in Ten Nations." *Health Affairs* 9, no. 2. Reprinted by permission from *Health Affairs,* p. 188. Summer 1990.

necessarily means that government controls not only the practice of medicine, but limits choice for the patient as well (Glaser 1983). The German experience should also disabuse the misconception that health insurance systems that are mandated by the government must also be administered by the federal government (Henke 1990a).

The Role of Government

In Germany, the federal government sets the broad legal framework within which the health care system operates, and then steps back and gives the main health care actors (payers and providers) both the room to work out the operating details and the legal standing to negotiate fees. While the German health care system is neither government-owned nor run, government intervention in the health care sector is viewed as necessary to achieving universal access to health care (Henke 1990a). The German approach to health care policymaking and cost control—what one analyst terms "the third way" between a procompetition strategy and a governmental regulatory strategy (Henke 1986, 348)—grants "prime responsibility for managing the health care system to collective groups of actors involved . . . and under the watchful but aloof supervision of the state" (Godt 1987, 474).

Some of the German health care arrangements that are derived from this "third way" would seem to be attractive to U.S. reform efforts. For example, one analyst argues that the creation of the Concerted Action "reflected an approach to conflict management and problem solution [sic] in tune with American political preferences." In setting up the Concerted Action forum, the government gave primary health care policymaking and cost-control responsibility to an advisory body consisting of the major health care payers and providers (Altenstetter 1987, 506). The threat of stronger government intervention ensures that the system of consensus-building will continue to work (Abel-Smith 1985). The spectre of a nationalized health service with all physicians on salary haunts the health care system and acts as a counterweight to providers' desires for higher fees.

The experience of German health care also shows that the "increasing role of the state in health care . . . did not diminish the organizational strength of the medical profession" (Stone 1977, 38). This should be of interest to the American Medical Association, which vociferously opposes adoption of the Canadian health care model for fear of having to cede all professional autonomy to the government. In Germany, Bismarck's compulsory government health insurance predated any significant organization on the part of the medical profession. German medical organizations actually became powerful and capable of exerting influence only as the national health insurance program expanded. The German system gives physicians a formal role in health care policymaking. German physicians consequently enjoy a position of greater power and influence than they did prior to implementation of national health insurance (Iglehart 1991b; Stone 1977). Based on German experience, the implementation of a nationalized system of health insurance in the United States would not necessarily sound the death knell for the autonomy and influence of the U.S. medical profession.

Cost Control

The lessons from Canada are reinforced by this examination of the German experience; monopsony power enhances a nation's ability to control health care costs. In Canada this is achieved through a payment system in which the provincial governments act as central paymasters. In Germany, multiple payers are closely regulated, creating in effect a single payer (Evans 1990).

Reinhardt notes that Germany and Canada share a "skepticism of the market." The U.S. approach to health care cost control through free-market competition has not been adopted by these countries (Reinhardt 1981b, 161). Kirkman-Liff concurs, tracing the eschewal of market forces to the particular corporatist arrangements that exist in the German health care system, and noting that the physician payment methods developed in Germany reflect a strong reliance on "corporatist and bureaucratic rather than market mechanisms" to allocate resources (Kirkman-Liff 1990, 74).

The Canadian and German health insurance systems employ similar processes for controlling health care costs. The German system uses state regulation of hospital planning, coupled with negotiated per diem rates and physician fee controls. In this way, health care cost control is achieved by regulating the flow of revenue between payers and providers. This control is not exerted by the government, as in countries such as the United Kingdom, but by the sickness fund associations that use their "quasi-governmental powers" to negotiate fee schedules with the regional associations of physicians (Reinhardt 1990a, 107).

Indeed, a critical feature that distinguishes the German health insurance system from the U.S. health insurance system is that the primary participants in the health care sector—the payers and the providers—deal with each other "not as individual buyers/sellers in a market, but rather as members of large organizations that engage in collective bargaining" (Stone 1980, 75). This bifurcation of the insured and the providers into separate camps (whose membership is compulsory) is the linchpin of the system. The government's involvement is limited to having legally created the two groups that represent the patients and the providers. The legal status of the groups brings with it no small amount of power. Rather than being directly regulated by the government, these autonomous groups are guided by the principle of self-regulation in their dealings with one another (Hurst 1991; Stone 1980).

The German government's strategy to balance power within the health care sector is unique, for "instead of fragmenting the medical profession to keep it weak, the government deliberately consolidated organizations" (Stone 1980, 18). Thus, we return to the collectivization mentioned at the outset of this chapter. Unlike in the United States, neither patients nor physicians in Germany are "expected or allowed to represent their own interests individually in the health care system" (Stone 1980, 28). All battles are waged among the groups representing the physicians and those representing the insured.

The results of the German approach to health care financing and organization speak for themselves. Trend data from the period 1970 to 1990 reveal that the United States and Germany had similar health-to-GDP ratios in 1975 and how dramatically their expenditure paths have diverged since that time. German health care expenditures as a percentage of GDP declined at an annual rate of 0.4 percent from 1980 to 1990. The U.S. health-to-GDP ratio, in contrast, increased at an annual rate of 2.7 percent over that same period. In terms of per capita health expenditures over the period 1980 to 1990, Germany experienced a 5.7 percent annual growth rate, while U.S. per capita health expenditures grew 9.2 percent a year from 1980 to 1990 (Schieber, Poullier, and Greenwald 1992).

Convergence

The German health care system has already served as an important guide for certain U.S. health reform efforts. During discussions over the recent physician payment-reform measures under Medicare, for example, a cap was found to be a "more radical approach than a target." The Physician Payment Review Commission viewed an expenditure target "as substantially similar to Congress' current practice of determining fee updates through its budget reconciliation process." An expenditure cap, on the other hand, was rejected as an option because it represented a dramatic shift in Medicare policy (Iglehart 1989, 1717).

The establishment of an expenditure target for physician payment under Medicare is important because it signals a change in U.S. physician reform efforts. It "reflects a movement—by both government and physicians' associations—away from market principles as the favored method of allocating medical resources and toward government policy as the way to achieve equity among patients, payers and providers" (Iglehart 1990a, 1251). In this way, one can see signs of convergence of the U.S. system toward other systems.

The United States may want to look closely at the German system's approach to financing care for the elderly. The German arrangement enables a high-risk group such as the elderly to be covered by the same plans that cover other groups in the population. The cost of health care for the elderly is consequently spread across a broader spectrum of the population: the elderly themselves, the government, and the employed through sickness fund contributions. This cost-sharing approach, if adopted in the United States, could replace the Medicare program, and even the Medicaid program, or any other publicly funded program that covers a specific high-risk group. The current pressure to cut back on Medicare and Medicaid expenditures makes it even more important to look at alternative funding arrangements for such programs (Wysong and Abel 1990).

Uwe Reinhardt noted in his June 1990 report to the U.S. Bipartisan Commission on Comprehensive Health Care that "it is probable that the American health system will eventually stumble toward an arrangement that will resemble Germany's in important respects, with a tightly regulated, private health insurance industry taking the place of Germany's sickness funds" (Reinhardt 1990b, 4). One major obstacle to such change in the past, however, has been apparent lack of leadership on a national level. In the words of Bradford Kirkman-Liff, professor of health administration and policy at Arizona State University: "George Bush is no Otto von Bismarck" (Stevens 1992, 155). It remains to be seen how President Bill Clinton will fulfill his campaign promise to revamp the U.S. health care system.

In the event that Medicare payment reforms are extended to the rest of the health care system and fee schedules are adopted by private insurers, the United States may take the first step in Germany's direction. Moreover, as the battle lines are drawn and redrawn over U.S. health care reform alternatives, the strengths of the German system—such as comprehensive, universal coverage; the prominent role of employers; uniform fee schedules for physicians; strong cost-control mechanisms; and lack of direct governmental control—will continue to intrigue U.S. health policy planners and lawmakers.

C H A P T E R **5**

Health Care in the Netherlands: Should the U.S. Go Dutch?

Introduction

The health care system of the Netherlands features a combination of public and private financing and private delivery of care. The majority of the population is covered under the mandatory public insurance program, and approximately one-third of the population is privately insured. Health care is financed through employee-employer contributions to a network of independent nonprofit sickness funds and private insurance organizations. The Dutch system is actually a hybrid of German social insurance and American private insurance (Janssen and van der Made 1990), and thus joins Germany in the middle range of the health care continuum.

Public and private insurance plans provide coverage for the entire population of the Netherlands, yet overall health expenditures, both on a per capita basis and as a percentage of Gross Domestic Product (GDP), are lower than those of the United States. Indeed, Dutch per capita health care expenditures in 1990 were lower than those in the United States, Canada, and Germany. Throughout the 1980s, Dutch health care expenditures as a percentage of GDP have remained fairly stable, rising only from 8.0 percent of GDP in 1980 to 8.2 percent in 1990 (Schieber, Poullier, and Greenwald 1992). (See Figure 5-1.)

Despite this stability in health care expenditure levels, there has been increasing concern about the future burden of health care costs. In addition, concerns have been raised over certain inequities in the health care system. A health care reform program was initially drafted in 1987 to respond to these concerns, and has since been undergoing continued

Figure 5-1   Total Health Expenditures As a Percentage of Gross Domestic Product, the Netherlands and the United States, 1970-1990

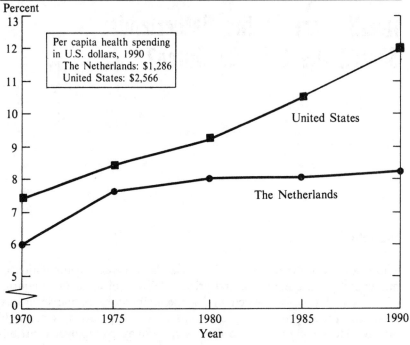

Source: Schieber, George, Jean-Pierre Poullier, and Leslie M. Greenwald. "U.S. Health Expenditure Performance: An International Comparison and Data Update." *Health Care Financing Review* 13, 4:(1-15). HCFA Pub. no. 03331. Office of Research and Demonstrations. Health Care Financing Administration. Washington, D.C.: U.S. Government Printing Office, September 1992.

refinements. Influenced in part by a concept developed by Stanford University professor Alain Enthoven, the reform program will introduce market-based changes to improve the health care system. The Dutch approach to regulated or managed competition in the health care sector will rely on price competition among providers and insurers to control costs and enhance efficiency.

The proposed reforms signal a change in course away from heavy government involvement in the health care sector toward an approach that is based on strengthening market forces and shifting responsibility of health care cost and quality control to providers and insurers. But the government will still play an important regulatory and oversight role. Whether the Dutch health care reform program accomplishes its goal of creating a health care system that provides unimpeded access to affordable health care for the entire population will be instructive for the United States.

Dutch Health Care Organization

Health insurance in the Netherlands, as in Germany, is an outgrowth of medieval guilds. Each guild set up a health organization for its members; the system that developed was consequently one of occupation-based health insurance. The guilds gave way to other groups such as small farmers and other workers who set up their own health insurance groups, followed by firms and nonprofit groups in the mid-1800s. By 1933, numerous health insurance groups provided voluntary coverage to 41 percent of the population (Abel-Smith 1988).

National health insurance in the Netherlands was introduced in 1941 under German occupation during World War II. At that time a network of 650 sickness funds provided coverage for one-half the population. The introduction of national health insurance in the occupied Netherlands was important to the Germans for two reasons. First, they could use the sickness funds as tools to achieve their political and propaganda goals; they aimed to build support for national socialism by instituting a popular social program such as health insurance. Second, they sought to create a level playing field between German and Dutch industry since Dutch employers would now have to contribute toward the costs of their employees' insurance, as did their German counterpart (Blanpain, Delesie, and Nys 1978, 132).

After the War, the Dutch retained the national health insurance set up by the Germans. The Dutch health care system is undergoing dramatic changes, but at the end of the 1980s, the system consisted of four separate programs (see the box on page 118). The public insurance program (ZFW) is compulsory for all residents earning below a specified salary level (approximately $32,000 in 1992). The ZFW is the insurance component of the Dutch social security program for employed persons and is financed through employer-employee contributions in the form of payroll taxes. Approximately 62 percent of the population is covered under the ZFW plan, which provides standard benefits such as coverage for hospital and physician services, as well as dental care up to age 18 (Ministry of Welfare, Health and Cultural Affairs 1988; 1989).

The Dutch health care system bears distinct similarities to the German system in that sickness funds form the heart of the system for the majority of the population. There are more than thirty sickness funds organized on a geographic basis that administer health insurance

Dutch Health Care at a Glance As of 1988

Coverage for hospital and physician services

Sickness fund-sponsored health insurance (ZFW)

- Compulsory for employees below certain income level
- Mainly income-related premiums
- Covers 62 percent of the population

Private insurance

- Optional for persons above certain income level
- Fixed premiums and out-of-pocket payments
- Covers 32 percent of the population

Insurance for persons in public service

- Statutory requirement for civil servants employed by provincial and municipal governments
- Mainly income-related premiums
- Covers 6 percent of the population

Coverage for nursing home and other long-term and institutional care

Exceptional Medical Expenses Act (AWBZ)

- compulsory for entire population
- income-related premiums

Source: Ministry of Welfare, Health and Cultural Affairs, the Netherlands, September 1988.

coverage. Insurers must cover everyone; they cannot deny coverage to individuals nor to certain employers (such as small businesses or employers in high-risk industries). Medical underwriting is not allowed, and insurers cannot exclude preexisting conditions. Premiums are income-related and are a set percentage of salary regardless of an individual's risk category (whether one is healthy or ill, young or old). In this way, the costs and risks of insurance are spread across a broad segment of society. Unlike in Germany, however, single employers cannot set up separate sickness funds for employees covered under the statutory plan (Kirkman-Liff 1991).

The package of benefits covered by the funds is set by the Sickness Funds Council. The council is similar to Germany's Concerted Action in that it consists of representatives of all the major health care players: physicians, hospitals, sickness funds, employers, labor unions, and the government. The council is not a government agency but does have the legal authority to regulate the sickness funds (Kirkman-Liff 1991).

A small percentage of the population (6 percent) is covered under employment-specific statutory insurance plans. These plans cover civil servants employed by provincial and municipal governments and are financed through income-related premiums (Ministry of Welfare, Health and Cultural Affairs 1988).

The remainder of the population (32 percent)—individuals who earn more than the income ceiling for compulsory insurance—are covered by private insurance. Unlike in Germany, where such individuals have the option of coverage under the compulsory plan, higher-income individuals in the Netherlands are not eligible for the compulsory insurance program. If they choose to be insured, they must purchase private insurance from one of the more than forty private insurance companies.

Approximately one-third of all private insurance is group insurance, similar to employer-sponsored plans in the United States. As in the United States, large companies may self-insure by setting up a separate private health insurance company for their higher-income employees (Kirkman-Liff 1991).

The final pillar of the Dutch health care system is a mandatory national catastrophic medical program for the entire population. The Exceptional Medical Expenses Act (AWBZ) is designed to cover all Dutch residents against the cost of catastrophic care. The insurance covers the cost of long-term care and nursing home care, as well as care for the physically disabled and mentally retarded. The national catastrophic health plan is administered at the local level by the sickness funds (Kirkman-Liff 1991).

Health Care Financing

Health care is financed by income-based premiums paid by employers, employees, retirement funds, and unemployment funds. In this way, all residents, including the unemployed, the poor, and the elderly, have health insurance coverage. In 1989, employer/employee premiums for sickness fund coverage represented slightly more than 8 percent of gross wages, with employers contributing 4.95 percent of wages and employees contributing 3.15 percent of salary, plus a small monthly premium. Employers contribute the same amount to the cost of private insurance for their high-income employees as they do for the employees covered under sickness fund-administered insurance plans. The catastrophic medical plan is also financed by income-related premiums that amounted to 5.4 percent of an employee's salary in 1989 (Horkitz 1990; Kirkman-Liff 1991; Ministry of Welfare, Health and Cultural Affairs 1989; Naaborg 1991).

Physician Payment

Physician reimbursement methods in the Netherlands vary depending on whether the physician is a general practitioner or a specialist. General practitioners are paid on a fee-for-service basis for private insurance patients, but are paid on a capitation (per person) basis for patients enrolled in sickness funds. Most physicians treat both sickness-fund insured patients and privately insured patients. General practitioners serve an important role as gatekeepers because patients must have a referral from a general practitioner before seeing a specialist (Kirkman-Liff 1989). Almost all specialists are hospital-based and are paid on a fee-for-service basis for patients under both the private and sickness fund plans (Kirkman-Liff 1991).

The majority of physicians belong to the subsidiary organizations of the Dutch Medical Association. These organizations are critical because they represent physicians in negotiations with both the sickness funds and private insurers to determine physician fee levels and capitation rates (Kirkman-Liff 1989). Physician payment levels for general practitioners contracting with sickness funds are calculated according to a formula that takes into account three factors: the "norm income," the "norm patient-list size," and the "norm practice costs" for physicians. The norm income is not an average or median income, but an income range negotiated between physicians and the government. The norm patient-list size is not an average or median size either, but rather a standard, negotiated practice size (for example, the norm practice size was set at 2,350 patients in 1988). The norm practice cost figure reflects the costs of all elements of a physician's practice, including office space, labor costs of medical and office assistants, and medical equipment. The cost of cars and gasoline is also factored in, as Dutch physicians are expected to make house calls. To calculate physician payment, the norm income is added to the norm practice cost figure. The sum of these two numbers is then divided by the norm practice size to arrive at a monthly capitation rate. This is the per-person rate that the sickness fund will pay the general practitioner (Kirkman-Liff 1989). General practitioners who contract with private insurers, on the other hand, are paid according to a fee schedule that has a fixed price for services such as routine office visits, telephone consultations, and home visits.

Specialists are paid according to a separate fee schedule, and at one time the sickness funds attempted to monitor specialists' incomes. The total amount billed by each specialist was to be added up every year and compared against the norm income for specialists. Any specialist who had exceeded the norm income was to pay back one-third of the first $15,000 above the norm income level. Any specialist earning more than $15,000 above the norm income was to pay back two-thirds of the excess. The practice was intended to discourage specialists from overservicing to increase their incomes (Kirkman-Liff 1989), but was abandoned because the sickness funds were unable to collect the necessary information to make the system work (Abel-Smith 1992).

One factor affecting physician expenditures in the Netherlands has been a rapid increase in the supply of physicians. Between 1976 and 1986, the number of general practitioners increased 27 percent and the number of specialists 37 percent, even though the population grew by only 6 percent during that period. Increased physician supply has served to keep the income levels of individual physicians from escalating rapidly. But physicians compensate for lower fees by providing more services. Increasing numbers of physicians providing increasing numbers of services raises the overall level of health care expenditures. In order to control the volume of services provided, there must be limits on the number of medical professionals providing those services. Clearly, effective cost control requires that limits be set on all three elements of health care expenditures—prices, volume, and physician supply (Kirkman-Liff 1989).

Hospital Financing

All hospitals in the Netherlands are not-for-profit institutions. The Dutch system of hospital reimbursement resembles that of Germany, and hinges on two factors that enable the Netherlands to control costs. First, a prospective budgeting system for hospitals that was implemented in 1983 requires hospitals to operate within the confines of a fixed, predetermined budget that is negotiated with the sickness funds and private insurers. Second, costs are controlled through a planning process. The central government is able to limit hospital supply and technology purchases through its licensing authority. Hospitals need the government's permission to expand facilities or purchase new medical technologies (Lapre 1988). These two procedures—global budgets for hospital services and a strict planning system for the hospital sector—are critical elements of cost control in the Netherlands (Jonsson 1990).

Health Care Reform in the Netherlands

The Dutch government introduced an economy-wide privatization program in 1982. While the health care sector was not immediately affected by this program, a reassessment of the role of government in the health care sector crystallized in 1987 with the publication of the report of the Committee on the Structure and Financing of the Health Care System (Janssen and van der Made 1990). The Dekker Committee was chaired by Dr. W. Dekker, former managing director of the electronics giant Philips N. V., and included experienced individuals who did not have a vested interest in the current system (Lapre 1988). The committee's report, "Readiness for Change," spelled out specific plans for the complete restructuring of the Dutch health care system.

The Dekker Committee concluded that the increased government involvement in the health care sector that was introduced in the mid-1970s did not address the underlying weaknesses in the system, most notably the absence of incentives for improved efficiency. Moreover, better coordination of health services was needed. This included the substitution of more cost-effective treatments, such as the use of ambulatory care rather than in-patient care wherever possible.

The committee's proposals had a decidedly market flair: The emphasis would be shifted from government regulation to market regulation and competitive forces would be introduced to make the system more efficient. Health care consumers, providers, and payers would all be expected to increase their responsibility for health care cost control. The committee stated, however, that increased competition would not come at the expense of health care quality and equity (Ministry of Welfare, Health and Cultural Affairs 1988).

The committee determined that it was necessary to eliminate the public-private system that had developed. This public-private split had resulted in public plans covering the high-risk individuals and private plans covering the low-risk individuals. The health care reform program, known as the Dekker Plan, was designed to eliminate the distinction between public and private insurance plans (Ministry of Welfare, Health and Cultural Affairs 1988).

Single Insurance Plan for All

The Dekker Plan would telescope the four-part system into a dual-track program (see Figure 5-2). A new compulsory public plan, the Basisverzekering (BV), would be established to cover the basic and catastrophic health expenses of the entire population. The basic benefits to be covered under the BV plan would be set by law. Optional

Figure 5-2   Dutch Health Care Reform

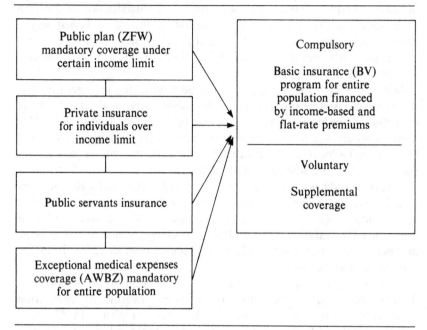

Source: The Wyatt Company, 1991.

supplemental insurance would be available to cover such services as some prescription drugs, private hospital rooms, plastic surgery, and so on. The Dekker Plan would essentially take the current system, which provided comprehensive insurance for two-thirds of the population, and transform it into a program of basic, but limited coverage for the entire population. Private insurance companies and sickness funds would no longer be distinguishable; they would all have to compete for consumers in the same market and to provide a basic package of benefits (van Etten 1990).

All Dutch residents would be charged income-based premiums for basic insurance coverage. These premiums would be set by the government and would cover 75 percent of the financing of the program. The remaining 25 percent would come from a flat-rate premium (not based on income). Insurers would not be able to charge different premium rates (based on risk-related factors), but the flat-rate premiums, which were designed to encourage competition between the insurance companies, would vary. Insurers that negotiate the most cost-effective arrangements with providers would be able to offer lower flat-rate premium rates, and would therefore attract the most clients as individuals will choose insurers for basic insurance based on the cost of the flat-rate premium charged by the insurer. The introduction of flat-rate premiums was also based on the assumption that the insured would become more aware of the cost of health care if they had to bear some of the burden themselves (Ministry of Welfare, Health and Cultural Affairs 1989).

While the flat-rate premiums would be paid to the insurers directly, the income-based premiums would be collected through standard tax collection channels and put into one central fund (see Figure 5-3). This account would act as a central paymaster and would make capitated (per person) allocations to insurers based on the makeup (age, sex, and health risk) of the insured population.

Insurers could. not refuse to cover high-risk individuals. But insurers would not have to focus on selecting the good risks because the central fund would make payments based on the age and risk composition of the insured population (Lapre 1988). Insurers who covered a large number of high-risk individuals would receive compensation from the central fund (Greenberg 1990).

The principle guiding the reforms is "regulation by incentive." This marks a dramatic shift away from government regulation to market regulation (Ministry of Welfare, Health and Cultural Affairs 1988, 16). The reforms aim to create what one analyst characterized as a "social system in a market-oriented setting" (van Etten 1990).

A Reform Plan by Any Other Name

In 1990, as a result of a change in government, the center-right coalition was replaced with a center-left governing coalition. The new government modified the Dekker Plan to expand its scope of coverage. The new plan, named Plan Simons, is, like its predecessor, designed to cover the basic and catastrophic health expenses of the entire Dutch population. The basic benefits to be covered under the plan would be set by law and are expected to cover 97 percent of average health care expenses. Plan Simons will be funded by payroll taxes, the majority of which will be income-related (82 percent) and the remainder (18 percent) will be flat-rate premiums.

As under the Dekker Plan, insurers will compete to provide basic health benefits, and will negotiate prices with competing health care providers. Supplemental private insurance will be available to cover the remaining 3 percent of health care expenses.

Figure 5-3   Financing the Dutch Basic Insurance Plan

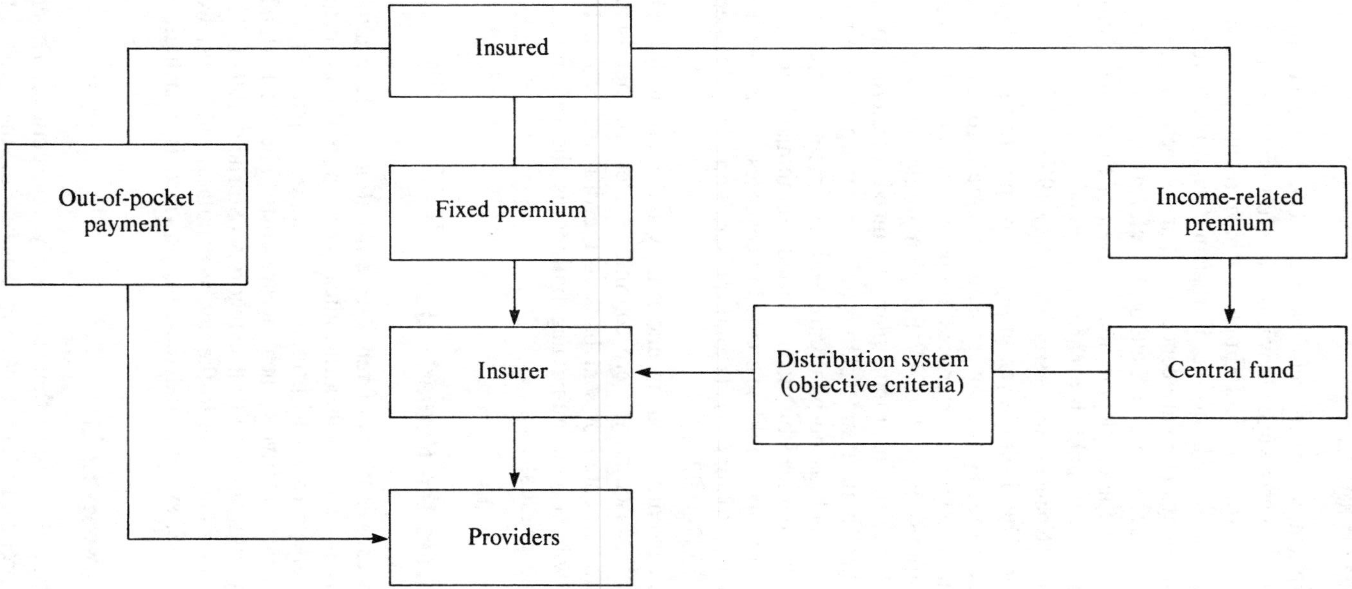

Source: Ministry of Welfare, Health and Cultural Affairs, the Netherlands, 1988.

Uncertain Fate for Reforms

The government's health reforms have been delayed by financing concerns and protests waged by various interest groups including employers and health care providers. Employers have requested a review of Plan Simons by the branch of the European Community responsible for competition policy. They are concerned that competition among insurers might actually decrease as a result of the reforms. Certain actions to date seem to support the employers' fears: Seven of the largest Dutch health insurers agreed to establish a partnership, and two other large insurers have merged (Spencer and Associates 1989-1992).

Two large Dutch employer groups have put forth a proposal that would further modify the government's program to reform the health care system. The employer groups' proposal would create three distinct health programs. First, the AWBZ plan would retain its role as the government health insurance plan, financed through tax revenues. Second, a health insurance plan would be set up to cover expensive medical costs such as hospital care and treatment by specialists. This plan would be financed by income-based premiums. Third, a system of voluntary insurance would be created to cover less expensive health care costs such as doctors' visits and prescription drugs (Spencer and Associates 1989-1992).

There is currently an air of uncertainty surrounding the reforms. As of early 1993, discussions were continuing over whether Plan Simons would be implemented or sent back to the drawing board. It appears that there will be continuing negotiations as the reforms are implemented on a gradual basis.

Lessons from the Netherlands

The health care systems of ten Western nations were evaluated in a recent study in terms of health indicators such as life expectancy and infant mortality, access to primary care, and the public's satisfaction with health care relative to health care costs. The Netherlands scored consistently high marks in all categories (Starfield 1991). The Dutch system provides coverage to the entire population at a cost well below that of the U.S. system, and the care provided is of a high quality.

Basic Health Coverage for All

Certain analysts believe that the newly restructured Dutch health insurance program may hold the answer to the problem of the uninsured in the United States, as the entire population would be covered by basic insurance that is not tied to employment. Insurers are obligated to offer coverage to everyone, without excluding preexisting conditions, medical underwriting, or singling out certain employer groups (Kirkman-Liff 1991). The Dutch health care reforms are designed to compensate those insurers that assume high-risk individuals so there will be no need to avoid them, a practice that has become increasingly common in the U.S. According to one health analyst, the Dutch system may provide "the dose of efficiency and equity that the current health care system in the United States so desperately needs" (Greenberg 1990).

Cost Control

The Netherlands has successfully kept health care costs to slightly more than 8 percent of GDP through several budgeting strategies. First, physicians' incomes have been regulated through negotiations between the payers (insurance associations) and the providers (physicians' associations). As a result, Dutch physicians earn considerably less than their American counterparts. According to salary figures from the American Medical Association and the Dutch Association for General Practitioners, the average Dutch general practitioner's salary was half that of a general practitioner in the United States in 1988 (Frieden 1992).

Second, the Netherlands imposes a global budget on the most costly sector in the health care system: hospital services. Most specialist care is provided in hospitals that must operate within the confines of a fixed budget. The government exerts its control over planning in the hospital sector and can use its licensing power to limit expansion of facilities and purchase of medical technology (Jonssen 1990).

Third, the cost control factor is a consequence of the particular structure of health care financing in the Netherlands. Health care premium payments are based on income and shared between employers and employees. Because of this shared burden, cost control efforts are supported by labor unions and corporate management alike (Kirkman-Liff 1991).

Private System, Public Regulation

The Netherlands has taken big steps away from governmental control over the health care sector that predominated during the 1970s. However, the government remains an influential presence even though health care is privately provided. The government fixes the income-related component of the premiums for basic insurance and legislates the scope of basic insurance coverage, while allowing insurers to compete with one another for patients. Thus in the Netherlands, as in Germany, even though the private sector is a strong force in the health care system, the government maintains an important regulatory role in the system. Both the German and Dutch systems feature key roles for multiple private insurers, negotiated fees and budgets, and income-based premiums rather than general taxes. These particular charac-teristics make the German and Dutch systems more palatable than a government-run system to many U.S. health care reformers (Kirkman-Liff 1991).

Convergence

The Dutch health care system is undergoing a gradual transformation. The new structure will continue to evolve over the next few years as several insurance plans are telescoped into a comprehensive health plan for the entire population. The Dutch health insurance system will be modified to encompass a system of regulated competition among insurers, modeled in large part on American ideas.

The Dutch have taken the managed competition concepts developed by Alain Enthoven in the United States and used them to consolidate the patchwork of insurance plans in the Netherlands. This is another example of the convergence of systems, as the reform of the Dutch health care system is being guided by ideas developed in the United States. The United States needs to observe closely the challenges of importing an essentially American-grown idea into another country. At the same time, the Dutch experience will be important for other European nations because it will provide a " 'demonstration project' to watch closer to home" than the U.S. experience (Enthoven 1990, 68). This is particularly true as the United Kingdom continues to implement reform of the National Health Service, based on Enthoven's concepts of managed competition (see Chapter 7).

It will be interesting to observe how the Netherlands negotiates the choppy waters of health care reform, and what the effect will be on equity and effectiveness in that health care system. If the Dutch master their health care dilemma, the Netherlands may provide the model for reform the United States is seeking.

Made in Japan: Universal Health Insurance

Introduction

Health care analysts in the United States are aided in their efforts to unravel the complex web of organization, financing, and delivery systems in other nations by existing research materials in English. The German health care system, for example, has been fairly well documented, and a plethora of books and articles is available on Canadian health care.

The health care system of Japan is another story. Although Americans are quite familiar with most products of Japan, Japanese-style health care remains a relative mystery. Long fascinated with and frustrated by Japanese expertise in the manufacturing and management arenas, Americans have yet to delve deeply into Japanese experience and performance in the health care sector.

Americans are becoming increasingly interested in all aspects of Japanese society, however, as witnessed by a number of books on the subject that have become best sellers in the United States.[1] Indeed, the health care system of one of our major economic competitors should be a topic of interest to Americans, particularly as U.S. executives continue to cite increasing health care costs as their top concern (Wyatt Company 1990).

The Japanese system is not as different as one might assume. Like

---

[1] A particularly good example is Karel van Wolferen's comprehensive study, *The Enigma of Japanese Power* (New York: Alfred Knopf, 1989).

the United States, Japan has an employment-based, multipayer health care system in which patients have their choice of physician, and health care services are delivered through private channels. The important difference is the strict governmental regulation in the Japanese system that requires all employers to provide health insurance coverage to their employees and dependents, either by financing an independent health insurance plan or by contributing to insurance plans managed by the government. Thus, similar to one of the alternatives under consideration for U.S. health care reform, the Japanese health insurance system embodies an employer-mandate approach to health insurance coverage.

This chapter begins with an overview of Japanese health care, followed by a section that traces the roots of Japan's complex health care system and identifies the cultural influences that have shaped its development. Further sections detail the organization and financing of health care in Japan, as well as the potential lessons for the United States.

The Japanese Advantage

Health care expenses alone do not determine whether a company is competitive or not, but they do constitute a significant portion of a company's total labor costs. Frustration with what many executives view as Japan's unfair advantage in this area is evident in one U.S. corporate executive's complaint that U.S. companies pay as much as "$3,500 a year per employee and the Japanese are paying virtually nothing" (*Wall Street Journal* 1990). While this statement is not entirely accurate—Japanese firms do contribute to their employees' health care costs—it reflects a commonly held belief that high U.S. health care costs put American companies at a cost disadvantage when competing with Japanese firms.

On a broader level, health care expenditures in the United States absorbed more than 12 percent of GDP in 1990 and are steadily increasing. Education, research and development, and other activities critical to remaining competitive in the global arena must therefore vie for shares of a shrinking pool of available resources (Maher 1990; Mitchell 1990; Reinhardt 1989, 1990; Schramm 1990). By contrast, Japanese health care expenditures consumed 6.5 percent of GDP in 1990—slightly more than half of the U.S. share devoted to health care, and significantly less than the health care expenditures of Germany and Canada. The United States spent more than twice as much as Japan on health care on a per capita basis in 1990 (see Figure 6-1).

Thus Japan provides health insurance coverage for its entire population while devoting far fewer financial resources to health care than the United States. Japan's universal coverage rate is a relatively recent

Figure 6-1   Total Health Expenditures As a Percentage of Gross Domestic Product, Japan and the United States, 1970-1990

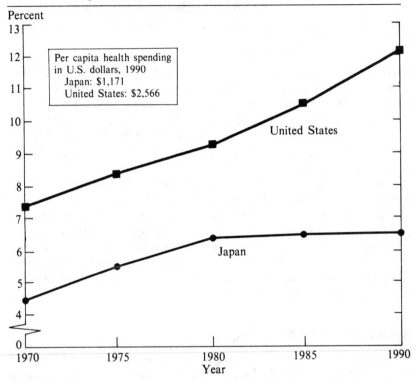

Source: Schieber, George, Jean-Pierre Poullier, and Leslie M. Greenwald. "U.S. Health Expenditure Performance: An International Comparison and Data Update." *Health Care Financing Review* 13, 4:(1-15). HCFA Pub. no. 03331. Office of Research and Demonstrations. Health Care Financing Administration. Washington, D.C.: U.S. Government Printing Office, September 1992.

achievement. In fact, Japan has successfully made the transition from a nation considered to be a "welfare-laggard" to one with a system of universal health insurance (Steslicke 1982).

Japan leads the world in terms of life expectancy at birth (75.6 years for men and 81.4 years for women)—an impressive achievement given that four decades ago life expectancy rates in Japan were only 50 years for men and 53.9 years for women. Japan also boasts infant mortality rates that are among the world's lowest. It would seem that Japan has achieved a "health miracle" comparable to its success in the economic and business spheres (Steslicke 1989, 104). But it is important to remember that such statistics must not be interpreted in isolation because the relationship between these health care outcome measures and the way the health care system is organized and financed is not clear. Other factors such as diet, health prevention, income level of population, and prevalence of disease and violent crime may have more to do with health outcomes.

Japan is to Asia what Germany was to Europe: the first nation to introduce a comprehensive social insurance program. In fact, Bismarck's program served as a model for the Japanese version of social insurance. While Japan, like Germany, is a market economy that provides a wide safety net for its citizens, Japan devotes far less to social programs such as social security and health care than most OECD countries. For example, while Germany devoted approximately 33 percent of its GNP to social security plus health care in 1983, Japan's corresponding share was only 14 percent of GNP. The United States devoted 21 and Canada devoted 20 percent (Simanis 1990).

The Japanese health insurance scheme features a prominent role for the private sector, and employers and employees contribute to the financing of the system, similar to the German system. A national health insurance program covers all those not covered by employer plans. Given this public/private mix, Japan occupies the middle ground along the health care continuum.

Confluence of East and West

It is often noted that the Japanese, located at the confluence of East and West, exhibit a remarkable ability to absorb the best of other systems and tailor them to their own environment (Hashimoto 1984, 335). This is certainly true in the health care domain; the major influences on the development of the Japanese health care system include Chinese, Dutch, and German medicine.

The Chinese influence was the earliest. Traditional Chinese medicine made its debut in Japan during the sixth century A.D., with treatment based primarily on the use of acupuncture and herbal medicines. It was a thousand years before Japan felt the influence of Western medical practices, brought by the Portuguese missionary programs. Japan subsequently underwent an extended isolationist period (1600 to 1867) during which its borders were essentially closed. Chinese and Dutch traders were exempt from the ban on foreigners, however. It was through this route that Japan was introduced to Dutch medical care practices, which had a profound impact on the shape of Japan's health care system (Iglehart 1988a).

Japan was torn by a civil war in 1867, known as the Meiji Restoration, which witnessed the elimination of the feudal system by "an alliance of powerful landowners, young samurai and mercantile capitalists." The subsequent period—the Meiji Era (1868 to 1912)—was one of the more important periods in the evolution of Japanese society, as an industrialized nation was born within the relatively short time span of a few decades (Hashimoto 1984, 336).

Japan became increasingly open to Western influences during this period, as the nation's leaders looked to other countries for ideas that were compatible with their drive toward modernization. Japanese leaders believed that Japan's industrialization was perfectly timed because Japan could not only learn from mistakes already made by Western industrialized nations, but would also be forewarned of potential problems related to industrialization (Steslicke 1982). The major influences during this period include the British Navy and Merchant Marines, the Prussian Army, and even American business.

Japan's leaders were particularly attracted to Germany's health care system, which was considered to be the best in Europe at that time (Hashimoto 1984). Even the underlying political and economic conditions in Japan in the early-twentieth century resembled those in Germany in the mid-1800s: The onset of industrialization and the development of organized labor groups had stirred up public demands for social welfare programs. In the words of historian Kenneth Pyle, the Japanese version of German social policy was based on the concept of "a monarch and a neutral bureaucracy standing above narrow class interests, regulating economic conditions, reconciling opposing social forces, and seeking to advance the interests of the whole by intervening in the economy to protect and integrate the lower classes into the nation" (Steslicke 1982, 202).

The Japanese government of this era, similar to that of Bismarck's Germany, wanted simultaneously to ensure a steady supply of healthy workers to drive economic growth and to maintain control over the workers. The Bismarckian mixture of repression and social legislation was adapted and applied in Japan (Steslicke 1982). German health care remained a primary influence on the development of Japanese health care through the end of World War II (Hashimoto 1984).

Legislating Health Insurance Coverage

The cornerstone of the present day Japanese health insurance system was laid in 1922, following enactment of a series of employment-related social welfare laws that began with the Relief Regulations of 1874 (precursor to the present Japanese social security system), and included the Factory Law of 1911, the Popular Life Insurance Law of 1916, and the Military Relief Law of 1917. The Health Insurance Law of 1922, which built on the previous legislation, was designed to provide health insurance coverage to such major occupational groups as factory workers and miners. Excluded from the law were employers with less than five workers, the self-employed such as agricultural workers, and those involved in fishing and forestry (Steslicke 1982).

The new employment-based health insurance law created two general categories of insurers. Companies with more than 700 employees were to form health insurance societies that would provide medical facilities for employees, or cover the cost of care at a medical facility. The other insurer was to be the government; it would manage health insurance programs for employees of smaller firms not covered by insurance societies (Steslicke 1982).

The progression toward codification of social policy continued with the enactment of the National Health Insurance Law in 1938. This law required local governments to extend health insurance coverage to those not covered by the 1922 law, such as individuals involved in farming, fishing, and forestry.

Driven by simultaneous desires to foster economic growth and to prevent a widening income gap from causing social instability, the Japanese government revised the 1938 law in 1958 with the aim of making health insurance coverage universal (Steslicke 1982). The 1958 revision of the law was designed to provide insurance coverage to those not covered by previous legislation, a group that represented approximately 30 percent of the population (Steslicke 1989). The new law was based on residence, whereas previous laws were organized around employment. Every jurisdiction—city, town, or village—was required to implement a health insurance program by 1961.

Thus the health insurance system in Japan, as in Germany, developed gradually, incorporating larger portions of the population over time. By the mid-1960s, virtually the entire population was covered by a health insurance plan—either one offered by employers, or a plan administered by local governments or trade associations.

Health Care Delivery

The Japanese health care delivery system has certain characteristics in common with the U.S. system. For example, Japanese patients have free choice of physician, and health care services are provided by private physicians in both private and public hospitals. Despite these similarities, there are some important differences. First, Japanese law prohibits investor-owned for-profit hospitals. More than 80 percent of all hospitals are privately owned, with one-third of all hospitals owned by individuals. Second, clinics also provide in-patient care. A clinic is a medical facility with less than twenty in-patient beds. Clinics are essentially extensions of a private physician's solo practice. These clinics are numerous in Japan. In 1986 there were almost 80,000 clinics, most of which were owned by physicians. Third, Japanese law requires that all chief executive officers (medical directors) of private hospitals and clinics be physicians. These physician-executives have administrative as well as medical responsibilities, but many lack the necessary background and formal training in hospital administration and management. As of the late 1980s, approximately 40 percent of all physicians owned hospitals or clinics (Iglehart 1988b; Ikegami 1991; Levin, Wolfson, and Akiyama 1987; Murdo 1989; Powell and Anesaki 1990).

Although private hospitals are prohibited by law from operating strictly for profit, the law does allow profits to be earned for the purpose of reinvestment; profits may be used, for example, to expand a hospital's services. So, although private hospitals are nonprofit institutions to the extent that they are not financially accountable to stockholders, physicians who own and operate their own hospitals are clearly interested in their financial sustainability. Since clinics compete with hospitals for patients, there tends to be much duplication of equipment as both facilities invest in the latest medical technology to attract patients (Abe 1985; Iglehart 1988b; Murdo 1989; Powell and Anesaki 1990).

Physicians in Japan are divided into two groups, as in Germany: private ambulatory physicians and hospital-based physicians. As in Germany, doctors not on staff of a hospital (such as clinic-based physicians) cannot follow their patients once they are referred to a hospital for treatment. Approximately one-third of all physicians are private practitioners (generally solo practitioners) and are paid on a fee-for-service basis. Hospital physicians, on the other hand, are full-time, salaried employees for the hospital (except for those physicians who own private hospitals). Physicians in private practice earn significantly more than physicians employed by hospitals. In 1987, for example, the income of private practitioners in Japan was 6.8 times the average wage, while hospital physicians earned 2.4 times the average wage (Ikegami 1991; Marmor 1992).

Health Insurance in Japan: Organized Complexity

Japan's network of interrelated programs and plans through which health insurance coverage is provided may appear complex on the surface, but in operation the system is quite straightforward. Every

Table 6-1   Health Insurance Coverage in Japan (as of March 31, 1991)

Insurance plan	Percent of population covered
Government-managed	29.5
Society-managed (employer-sponsored)	25.8
Seamen's	0.3
Day laborer's	0.1
Mutual aid associations	9.6
National health insurance	34.7
Total	100.0

Source: National Federation of Health Insurance Societies. *Health Insurance and Health Insurance Societies in Japan 1992,* p. 66.

Japanese citizen must be a member of a health insurance plan either through their employer or their local government or trade association. These plans provide a comprehensive package of benefits that is set by law. Covered services range from physician and hospital services, to long-term care, dental care, and prescription drugs. Since the coverage provided under the plans is comprehensive, the role for private insurers is limited to offering supplemental benefits to cover such amenities as private hospital rooms (Ikegami 1991).

The Japanese health care system is organized around two major insurance programs: insurance for employees and their dependents, and national health insurance for those not covered under employment-based plans. Slightly more than 65 percent of Japan's population is covered under insurance plans for employees and their dependents. The remainder of the population (self-employed, unemployed, and the elderly) is covered under the National Health Insurance program (see Table 6-1).

Employee Health Insurance

Health insurance programs for employees and their dependents are managed either by health insurance societies, the government, or mutual aid associations.

Health Insurance Societies.   Large companies (generally those with more than 700 employees) can set up their own independent health insurance plans for their employees. These plans, known as health insurance societies, can also be formed by two or more businesses together employing 3,000 employees or more. The societies, although private, are unlike private insurance groups in the United States, as they are only allowed to function as an alternative to the government-managed plan and are subject to governmental oversight and regulation through the national Ministry of Health and Welfare (Horkitz 1990).

The health insurance societies that run the plans, called *kempo kumias,* serve as financial go-betweens for companies providing insurance benefits for their employees and their dependents (Iglehart 1988a). But the importance of these groups is not limited to providing health insurance, as noted by Wolfson and Levin:

> One of the mottos of Japanese companies ... 'the company is people'—recognizes the value of each employee as a company asset. A healthy, well-informed employee is seen as the most important investment a company can have. The kempos are the principal social and economic vehicles for helping to make this happen (1986, 39).

These insurance societies numbered 1,822 as of 1991 (National Federation of Health Insurance Societies 1992).

Government-Managed Health Insurance.   Employees of small and medium-sized businesses (and their dependents) are covered by insurance plans managed by the government. The government acts as a financial intermediary, and the costs are shared between employer and employee. The insurance organization for government-managed health insurance is the Social Insurance Agency, which administers insurance plans through a network of almost 300 local offices.

Three features distinguish the two major plans for employees and their dependents. First, as noted earlier, is the size of the firm. Larger businesses organize health insurance societies for their employees, leaving the government to manage insurance plans for medium and small-scale businesses. Second, insurance premiums for government-managed insurance are a fixed rate set by law, while insurance societies have much broader latitude to set contribution rates, as described in following sections. Third, government-managed insurance covers only those benefits specified by law, whereas health insurance societies tend to provide additional benefits, such as reimbursement of patient co-payments and supplemental cash benefits in the event of illness (National Federation of Health Insurance Societies 1992).

Other Insurance Groups.   Mutual aid associations provide coverage for national and local government employees, as well as teachers and other school personnel. A small specialized group of people who work on crews of ships are covered by Seamen's Insurance, and workers hired by the day, such as construction workers, are covered by Day Laborer's Insurance.

National Health Insurance

The Japanese National Health Insurance program provides coverage for individuals not covered by any of the types of employees' insurance described above, such as the self-employed, the unemployed, and retirees. National Health Insurance covers a large number of the elderly and low-income earners, and almost one-fifth of all those covered by National Health Insurance are in households without incomes (National Federation of Health Insurance Societies 1992). The National Health Insurance scheme is administered either through local governments (cities, towns, and villages) or trade associations that insure specific professional groups such as carpenters or barbers (Ikegami 1991; Powell and Anesaki 1990).

Health Care for the Elderly

A law enacted in 1972 entitled all Japanese citizens over the age of seventy (age sixty-five if bedridden) to free medical care through the health insurance system. The cost of this free care was to be shared by the different insurance schemes, but because of demographic factors, the National Health Insurance scheme had a disproportionate share of elderly members and therefore carried most of the financial burden. This burden became impossible to maintain as National Health Insurance's share of costs for the elderly increased from 20.8 percent in 1973 to more than 32 percent in 1981 (Steslicke 1989).

These financial pressures culminated in the 1982 Health and Medical Services for the Aged law. This law created a separate insurance plan for retirees. Unlike Germany, where retirees remain in the same fund as when they were employed, retirees in Japan switch from their employee fund to a retiree health plan within the National Health Insurance program (Ikegami 1991).

Health Care Financing

Health insurance in Japan, as in Germany, is financed through employee-employer contributions in the form of a payroll tax. Insurance contribution rates vary according to the particular insurance plan to which an individual belongs (see Table 6-2). Contributions for govern-ment-managed insurance are income-based premiums whose rate is

Table 6-2   Financing Health Insurance in Japan (as of March 31, 1992)

Insurance plan	Premiums	
	Employee	Employer
Government-managed insurance	4.1[a]	4.1
Society-managed insurance (average)	3.6	4.7
Seamen's	4.4	4.4
Mutual aid associations (average range)	4.1 to 4.5	4.1 to 4.5

Source: National Federation of Health Insurance Societies. *Health Insurance and Health Insurance Societies in Japan 1992,* p. 12, and Charles D. Spencer & Associates, *International Benefits Information Service,* 1992.

[a] As of May 1992.

fixed by law. As of May 1992, employers and employees each contributed 4.1 percent of salary toward health insurance.

Premiums for society-managed insurance, on the other hand, are not fixed by law; societies can use their discretion to set premium levels, which range from 3 to 9.5 percent of payroll. In addition, the insurance societies can determine how the premiums will be divided between employers and employees. The employer share under society-managed plans tends to be higher than the employee share.

Individuals covered under the National Health Insurance scheme pay premiums based on income and the size of their household. These premiums are collected as general tax revenue. There is a ceiling on the amount of annual premiums paid per household, which was approximately $3,120 in 1988 (Murdo 1989).

Health care for the elderly is financed by a number of sources. The national government provides 20 percent of the financing of health care for the elderly, local governments provide 10 percent, and employee insurance groups pay the rest. The law also requires cost-sharing by the elderly, but the cost-sharing is so limited (the equivalent of $6 per month for outpatient care and $3 per day for hospital care) that it has served neither as a method of cost control nor as a method of limiting utilization (Fujii and Reich 1988).

Government Funding

The government-managed health insurance scheme for individuals employed by small and medium-sized companies receives a government subsidy that represents 16 percent of total expenditures. The National Health Insurance scheme receives government financial support in the amount of one-half the plan's total costs. And, as noted earlier, the government contributes 30 percent of the financing of health care for the elderly. By contributing to the various plans (with the notable exception of society-managed health insurance, for which a subsidy is considered unnecessary), the government levels the playing field between the different insurance plans and ensures that coverage is available to all (Ikegami 1991). Moreover, the government pays the administrative costs of all of the health plans.

Patient Cost-Sharing

A law enacted in 1984 reduced coverage of 100 percent of costs under the health insurance plans. Employees insured by employer-sponsored plans now pay 10 percent of covered health care costs, while their dependents pay 20 percent of the total cost of in-patient services and 30 percent of outpatient services. Individuals insured under the National Health Insurance plan pay 30 percent of in-patient and outpatient costs.

There are no deductibles under any of the plans. Although there is a significant level of patient cost-sharing, Japan limits the amount of monthly co-payments for medical expenses to $400 per month per person (or $200 for low-income earners). Out-of-pocket expenses for co-payments represent approximately 12 percent of the total of all health care expenditures under the health insurance plans (Ikegami 1991).

Controlling Health Care Costs: Nationwide Fee Schedule

The Japanese government sets targets for total health care spending increases. These targets are linked to growth in Japan's GDP. One means of achieving health care cost control is through the use of a fee schedule, as in Germany and Canada. The fee schedule that operates in Japan is slightly different, however, in that one uniform, nationwide fee schedule determines payment for outpatient and in-patient medical care. All health care providers are reimbursed according to a procedure-based fee schedule (similar to Medicare's resource-based relative value scale), known as the point-fee system. The point-fee system reimburses hospitals according to a standard per-diem rate. All payers pay the same fee for the same service, regardless of whether it was performed in an urban hospital or rural clinic, and regardless of what type of physician performed it. Physicians must accept the fee as payment in full; billing beyond the fixed price is not allowed (Iglehart 1988b; Ikegami 1991; Powell and Anesaki 1990). Cost-shifting among payers is not a problem in Japan, unlike in the U.S. health care system, because covered benefits are set by law and all payers receive the same payment for the same service.

The fee schedule is set through negotiations between the Ministry of Health and Welfare and the Central Social Insurance Medical Council. The council includes representatives of health care providers, payers (insurers, management, and labor), and consumers (lawyers and economists to represent the public interest) (Ikegami 1991), and bears a distinct resemblance to Germany's Concerted Action.

Total health care expenditures in Japan rose steadily from 2.9 percent of GDP in 1960 to 4.4 percent in 1970 to 5.5 percent in 1975 (Schieber and Poullier 1989). Support for increasing amounts of resources devoted to health care came from an economy that was growing at an impressive rate of 10 percent a year through the 1960s and part of the 1970s. This economic growth enabled Japan to survive the worldwide oil shocks and global recession of the mid-1970s, and to undertake a progressive increase in health spending in the absence of major societal upheaval (Iglehart 1988a).

But the worldwide economic slowdown of the mid-1970s gradually took its toll on the Japanese economy, and the impressive growth rate slowed later in the decade. Health care expenditures continued to increase, however, outpacing increases in the national income. Medical costs for the elderly escalated dramatically during this period and several insurance plans began to accumulate serious budget deficits.

As noted earlier, the Japanese government responded to rising health care costs with a 1984 amendment to the health insurance law that introduced cost-sharing requirements and set up the separate health insurance plan for the elderly under National Health Insurance. These measures were designed to control costs by focusing on the demand side of health care, but a second amendment was passed in 1985 to address the supply side of health care by regulating hospital capacity. Such limits were necessary because Japan has the highest number of hospital beds per population among industrialized nations (Schieber, Poullier, and Greenwald 1991).

The Sun Also Sets on Japanese Health Care

Japanese health care expenditures as a percentage of GDP have remained relatively constant, staying below 7 percent throughout the 1980s and into the 1990s. Such stability in health care expenditures has been maintained as the Japanese economy has been expanding and income levels have been rising. But economic factors, such as a slowing economy, and demographic factors, such as the aging of the population, will certainly increase the financial pressures on the Japanese health care system in years to come.

The ability of the Japanese health care system to respond to these challenges, however, will be constrained by certain cultural characteristics. The current health system is well entrenched within Japanese society—often referred to as "a dynamic society without change" (Hashimoto 1984, 335)—and any reform efforts face the considerable influence of the medical profession. Such resistance to change will make it difficult to address some of the system's underlying weaknesses.

Areas for Reform

A poll conducted by Robert Blendon that surveyed the level of satisfaction with health care in ten nations revealed that 47 percent of the Japanese polled believed their health care system needed fundamental reform (Blendon, Leitman, Morrison, and Donelan 1990). We will discuss some of the more significant problems facing Japan's health care system.

Quality of Care. There are no formal quality control programs within the Japanese system. Some observers trace quality problems to the fee-schedule-based reimbursement method. Since all providers are paid the same fee for the same service, regardless of quality, no incentives exist to guarantee or improve the quality of care (Ikegami 1991). Indeed, there is no direct relationship between a physician's training and salary level. As noted earlier, salaried hospital physicians (who are often better trained) earn significantly less than private practitioners. There are also gaps in the distribution of physicians. Although the supply of physicians has been increasing steadily, many rural areas remain underserved (Marmor 1992; Powell and Anesaki 1990).

As a consequence of binding limits on physicians' fees, many physicians "game the system" by increasing the volume of services, or by keeping consultations brief so as to necessitate repeated office visits. Physicians also compensate for fee controls on their office visits by prescribing more medicines or ordering more tests that carry a higher point value (Abe 1985; Ikegami 1991; Murdo 1989). Moreover, the "dual role of the individual practitioner—doctor and businessman— gives rise to some dubious medical practices and conflicts of interest" (Powell and Anesaki 1990, 234).

Physicians as Pharmacists. One particularly unique feature of the Japanese health care system is that physicians serve the dual role of prescriber and dispenser of prescription drugs. This feature may account for Japan's high rate of consumption of prescription drugs: Japan leads the world in per-capita prescription drug consumption. Pharmaceuticals represented 18.4 percent of total health expenditures in Japan in 1988, compared to 8.3 percent in the United States (Schieber, Poullier, and Greenwald 1991).

A significant portion of a physician's income is derived from dispensing drugs, so it is clearly in the physician's interest to continue the prescriber/dispenser arrangement. Official drug prices are set by the Ministry of Health and Welfare, but doctors negotiate with drug companies and purchase prescription drugs at discounted rates. Doctors are reimbursed the full official price from the insurers, however, and keep the difference—known as the "doctor's margin." This margin is substantial; in 1991 it amounted to 25 percent (Eisenstodt 1992; Powell and Anesaki 1990). Dutch journalist Karel van Wolferen, writing in his influential and controversial book, *The Enigma of Japanese Power,* notes that this practice has led to "corrupt relations with the pharmaceutical industry, to an alarming degree of over-medication, and to some very rich doctors" (1989, 54). Indeed, the practice of over-prescription of drugs is so widespread in Japan that it has given rise to its own phrase: *kusuri zuke,* literally translated as "pickling with drugs" (Powell and Anesaki 1990, 174). The government is working to address this situation by taking steps to prevent drug manufacturers from negotiating discounted prices with doctors (Eisenstodt 1992).

Prolonged Hospital Stays. Hospitals in Japan differ from those in the United States and other Western nations in that chronically ill patients who would normally be put in nursing homes in other countries are treated as in-patients in Japanese hospitals. This practice of keeping geriatric, long-term patients in hospitals is reflected in average length of hospital stay, which at 52.1 days is more than five times longer than the average hospital stay in the United States and considerably longer than that of other nations (Schieber, Poullier, and Greenwald 1991).

The practice of "social hospitalization" is a result of the slow development of nursing homes in Japan, which stems from cultural factors including a strong sense of responsibility to one's family (Hashimoto 1984). A social stigma is attached to institutionalization, which is often compared with the ancient practice of *obasuteyama,* or leaving one's family member on the mountain to die (EBRI 1989; Murdo 1989).

Limited Referral System. Since the majority of Japanese hospitals and clinics are privately run and many are physician-owned, physicians clearly have little interest in referring patients to their competitors or allowing physicians who are not salaried employees of the hospital to have admitting privileges in their hospitals. Keeping the system closed precludes any organized system of patient referral and ensures much duplication of tests, procedures, and equipment. This is particularly the case as physicians own much of the medical equipment in Japan, so there is a powerful financial incentive to order more tests and procedures. Indeed, in the absence of any limits on acquisition of technology there has been a proliferation of highly advanced medical equipment in Japan. Consider the case of computerized tomography (CT) scanners. In 1982, Japan had 18.5 CT scanners per million people, compared to 10.7 in the United States, 2.1 in West Germany, 3.1 in Canada, and 5.7 in the Netherlands. Whereas there was a total of 664 whole body CT scanners in Japan in 1981, this number increased five-fold by 1987 (Abe 1985; Marmor 1992; Murdo 1991; Powell and Anesaki 1990).

Lessons from Japan

It has been suggested that Americans "take advantage of their position as 'health insurance laggards' to study and reflect critically on the experience of Japan" (Steslicke 1982, 197). Japan, like Germany, gradually phased in insurance coverage, which is now provided to the entire population. And in Japan, as in Germany and Canada, universal coverage coexists with health care cost-control mechanisms.

Any attempts to apply lessons drawn from the Japanese health care experience to the U.S. health care system must first take into account differences in the composition of Japanese and American societies. While it is often noted that poverty and other social ills in Japan, as well as the existence of minority groups, are kept well hidden from foreigners, Japanese society is nonetheless far more homogeneous than American society. Health care analyst Masami Hashimoto writes: In Japan "the people are ethnically homogeneous and speak one language. Illiteracy presents no problem" (1984, 335). There is less disparity in income levels, and lower unemployment rates than in the United States. In contrast, the U.S. population is one of the more heterogeneous in the world, and includes a sizable long-term poor population. The stresses, demands, and pressures on the U.S. system, therefore, are not comparable with those on the Japanese system.

Despite these differences, there are lessons to be learned. Indeed, one area in which the Japanese experience could prove beneficial to U.S. health care reform efforts is that of cost-control practices.

The message that emerges from this overview of Japanese health care is consistent with that of the previous chapters on the Canadian and German health care systems: Health care costs are controlled through governmental oversight of a system in which care is essentially privately financed and delivered. In Japan, both employers and employees contribute toward the cost of health insurance, and government subsidizes a significant portion of insurance costs. All parties, therefore, have a shared interest in cost containment (Murdo 1989). In Japan, as in Germany, Canada, and other nations, binding fee schedules govern physician reimbursement (as well as hospital fees in Japan). While physician and hospital payment levels are set by the government, there is significant input from payers and providers.

Japan has also benefited from administrative cost savings. The health care claims processing system is simplified by mandatory coverage and uniform fees, which preclude any haggling over what is or is not covered. Moreover, because health care consumers have no real choice of insurance plan, there are no high marketing costs for insurers (Ikegami 1991).

Another area in which Japan could potentially provide lessons for the United States is that of health-related policies for the aging. Japan's population is one of the oldest in the world; slightly more than 10 percent of Japan's citizens are over the age of 65, but this share is expected to reach 25 percent of the population by 2025. The United States and Japan are facing the same pressures of how to distribute the financial burden of health care for a growing elderly population.

Health policy analyst John Iglehart notes that Japan, by shifting the cost of insuring the elderly to employment-based plans, has shown that it is "more willing than the United States to impose policies on employers that are deemed to reflect their legitimate social obligation—in Japan's case, requiring employers and employees to shoulder a greater proportion of the cost of care for the elderly" (Iglehart 1988a, 812). This serves as a contrast to current trends in the United States toward reduction of retiree health care benefits.

In an effort to confront the challenge of its aging population, the Japanese government unveiled a new program—the so-called Golden Plan—a ten-year strategy aimed at shifting the elderly from long-term institutional care in hospitals and the limited number of nursing homes to home care programs. It is expected that the plan will cost more than $40 billion to implement over a ten-year period. Income-adjusted fees for home care support are expected to contribute toward some of the cost of the program (Butler and Osako 1990; Spencer 1990).

Convergence

Mitsuru Fujii and Michael Reich identify several broad patterns in Japanese health policy that are similar to trends within the health care systems of other nations. The first observation is that the 1980s witnessed an increase in government regulation in the health care arena. This trend is clear in Japan where government regulation and oversight of health insurers is a critical feature of the system. Although the Japanese system does not rely on expenditure targets as in Germany or Canada, the influence of the government in negotiating provider fees is significant (Horkitz 1990).

The government's role can be expected to remain strong, and even get an added boost by the ebbing influence of the Japan Medical Association (JMA). As the total number of clinic-based physicians— the JMA's core constituency—continues to lose ground to hospital-based physicians, the power of the JMA will decrease commensurately (Yoshikawa 1992).

Parallel with this development is a new accent on cost control that takes precedence over such health care goals as improving quality and access to care. This shift in priority is evident in the United States as well as other nations that look to stem the growth in health care expenditures. In a related observation, Fujii and Reich note that medical services policy has taken a back seat to health insurance policy, which is in turn driven by economic factors. The introduction of increased patient cost-sharing in many nations, for example, is more a response to fiscal realities than a goal of medical services policy. Health insurance policy in many nations has been essentially reactive in nature. Changes in policy occur as a result of socio-economic developments and political pressures, and are not based on long-range planning toward some desired medical goal. Budget deficits in many nations, for example, have guided the development of health care reforms (Fujii and Reich 1988).

Thus, as the health care systems of different nations experience the same pressures and face similar problems, it is likely that there will be further signs of convergence toward common ground—such as increased governmental regulation over privately based systems that will call increasingly on health care consumers to shoulder more of the burden of health care costs.

C H A P T E R 7

Reforming the British National Health Service: More Like U.S.?

Introduction

Previous chapters have examined the health care systems of Canada, Germany, the Netherlands, and Japan. Some of these systems have been considered as potential models for reform of the U.S. health care system. Britain's National Health Service (NHS), on the other hand, is often presented in the United States as an example of the negative consequences of government ownership and control of health care. For example, a *Wall Street Journal* editorial on U.S. health care reform efforts likened U.S. proposals on national health insurance to "nationalized health, that great solution that nearly bankrupted England and brought health-care rationing, in the form of long waits for needed attention, to that sceptered isle" (*Wall Street Journal* 1989).

The "specter" of British health care is raised repeatedly in the U.S. literature. Descriptions of the British NHS are usually accompanied by accounts of rationing "designed to evoke horror and revulsion," and to underscore the unacceptability of a British-style system for the United States (Marmor and Klein 1986, 20).

Such views beg the question of why one should bother to study the British system at all. While it is not likely that the United States would ever adopt the British model of health care, there are several very good reasons why the British system merits U.S. attention. First, the NHS was the pioneer of national health care. Whereas Bismarck's social insurance program blazed new trails in the field of legislating coverage for workers, the NHS set a precedent as the first comprehensive, nationalized system of health care.

Second, the NHS is the largest, most centralized, public health care system in Europe, and with more than one million workers, it is Europe's largest employer. The system treats over 30 million patients annually, and had a budget of approximately $50 billion in 1992. Private insurance covers approximately 12 percent of the population, but provides coverage for only a limited range of treatment. As such it is a supplement rather than a replacement for NHS treatment. Thus, the entire British population depends on the NHS for most of its health care needs.

Third, it is important to examine a system that represents for many Americans the epitome of "socialized medicine," and provides fuel for discussions supporting or opposing nationalized health care. To proponents of nationalized health care, the NHS represents an equitable and cost-effective approach to providing health care. Critics of the NHS model, on the other hand, focus on its weaknesses, particularly the system's funding problems, lack of responsiveness to consumers, and "organizational inertia" (Day and Klein 1989, 1; 1991).

The profound differences between the way the United States and Britain finance and provide health care for their populations reflect significant political, cultural, and economic differences between the two nations. While the United States and Britain share a common language, commitment to democratic ideals, and similar medical education systems (Aaron and Schwartz 1990), Britain is "a relatively poor industrial nation, with a unified parliamentary regime, a class structure far more rigid than that of the United States, and a spectrum of political ideologies far wider than America's" (Marmor and Klein 1986, 21). In the health care arena, the differences between Britain and the United States are perhaps most apparent in the wide disparity in health care expenditure levels (see Figure 7-1).

Finally, and most importantly, the United Kingdom has undertaken a comprehensive health care reform program that will result in the most significant changes to the venerable NHS since its creation more than forty years ago. The reform program, similar in some respects to that of the Netherlands, also draws its inspiration from Stanford University professor Alain Enthoven's concepts of managed competition. In the context of the British health care system, such reform will entail infusing competition and consumer choice—or in Enthoven's terms, the creation of an internal market—into the NHS. The ways in which such similar competition-driven reforms play out in Britain and the Netherlands—two very different health care systems and societies—will clearly have important implications for comparative health care analysis.

The reform program, officially launched in April 1991, is the product of a conservative government, yet it is quite radical in nature. The

Figure 7-1   Total Health Expenditures As a Percentage of Gross Domestic Product, the United Kingdom and the United States, 1970-1990

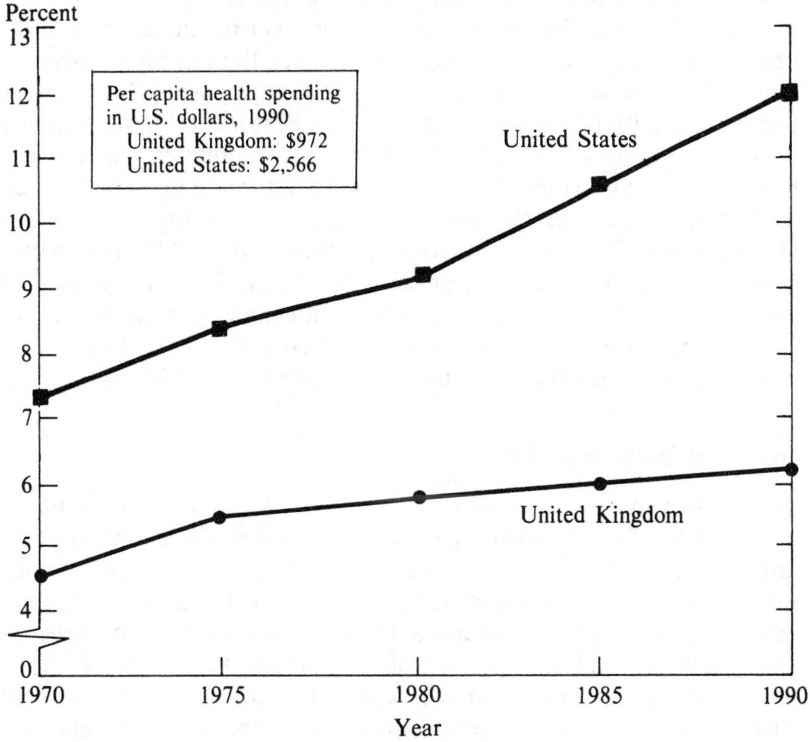

Percent

Per capita health spending
in U.S. dollars, 1990
United Kingdom: $972
United States: $2,566

United States

United Kingdom

Year

Source: Schieber, George, Jean-Pierre Poullier, and Leslie M. Greenwald. "U.S. Health Expenditure Performance: An International Comparison and Data Update." *Health Care Financing Review* 13, 4:(1-15). HCFA Pub. no. 03331. Office of Research and Demonstrations. Health Care Financing Administration. Washington, D.C.: U.S. Government Printing Office, September 1992.

reforms are "a design for health care delivery in the twenty-first century which would marry old-style British ideals of social justice with new-style American ideas about competition" (Day and Klein 1989, 1). If implemented fully, the reform program would create an entirely new approach to health care, untried in the United Kingdom. As one British analyst pointed out prior to the implementation of the reform program, Britain is "lurching into a massive, uncontrolled experiment which will doubtless be fascinating for you all to monitor from the safe distance of this side of the Atlantic, if less exhilaratingly so for us who are going to live with it" (Culyer 1989). How the new conservative radicalism transforms the NHS and whether it creates "a new hybrid model of health care delivery," therefore, should be of interest to the United States (Charny, Klein, Lewis, and Tipping 1990).

The United Kingdom is located on the market-minimized pole of the health care continuum (Anderson 1989), since the central government plays a key role in health care planning and setting expenditure limits, and the majority of the population receives health care services from a wholly government-run and publicly financed entity. It would seem, however, that both poles of the continuum are turning in on each other, as Britain has modeled the most significant restructuring in the history of the popular NHS on the core concepts that drive the U.S. health care system. Many observers question why the United States has been used as a model when there is scant evidence that competition has helped the U.S. health care system to address problems of overall health care quality, costs, and access (Light, 1990a, 1990b, 1991b).

Overview of British Health Care

The British health care system stands out as the most centrally managed and financed health care system in the world. In the words of health care analyst Odin Anderson, the NHS is "an anomaly" among western industrialized nations (Anderson 1989, 42). The NHS was once viewed as one of the best systems in the world; comprehensive cradle-to-grave care is provided, regardless of one's ability to pay and is free to the patient at the point of service. Admiration for the system has been on the wane, however, as long waiting lists, shortages of technology, decaying facilities, and underfunding have cast a pall over the NHS. Despite its flaws, the NHS has retained its popular support for more than four decades.

Viewing U.K. health care expenditures from an international perspective reveals that Britain dedicates far less to health care than all other nations examined in this study. Per capita spending on health care in Britain in 1990 was $972. Per capita spending on health care in the United States was more than two-and-a-half times that amount in 1990. The United Kingdom devoted 6.2 percent of GDP to health care in 1990, slightly more than one-half the amount that the United States spent that year (Schieber, Poullier, and Greenwald 1992).

While Britain spends half as much on health care as the United States, health status indicators such as infant mortality and life expectancy reveal that the British and U.S. systems have similar statistics. Reliance on such statistics may lead one to believe that since Britain's nationalized health care system appears to provide similar care at lower cost, it is more efficient than the U.S. system. But there are other factors to consider that would change one's perception, particularly if the health system was judged also by the amount of time a patient must spend waiting for care and the patients' level of satisfaction with the care provided (Pfaff 1990).

Britain's Sacred Cow: The National Health Service

The 1911 National Health Insurance Act mandated limited medical coverage for low-income workers. But unlike the social insurance systems in Germany and Japan, the U.K. health insurance plan covered only general practitioners' services and excluded workers' dependents (Anderson 1989). From the 1920s through the 1940s, dissatisfaction with the insurance system grew, especially with respect to services provided during the war (Maynard 1990).

The combination of postwar hardships and sense of solidarity in difficult times facilitated the creation of a comprehensive, national health service for the entire population (Anderson 1989). A report published in 1942 by the economist Lord Beveridge proposed reforming the social insurance system and laid out a blueprint for a national health service. The health service was to be predicated on four principles: health services were to be (1) universal; (2) comprehensive; (3) free to the patient; and (4) financed by general tax revenues (Anderson 1989, 28). The report reflected the environment of wartime shortages and rationing and demands for social welfare support from the government (Day and Klein 1989; Maynard 1990).

The enabling legislation to launch the NHS made its way through Parliament in 1946 without the support of the British Medical Association. Indeed, a poll taken that year revealed that more than half of all physicians surveyed opposed the NHS. Even two years later, just months before the official inauguration of the NHS, physician opposition was still very high (Rogaly 1989). To secure physician support for the nationalized health care system, Minister of Health Aneurin Bevan got to the physicians through their wallets—"lined their teeth with gold," in his words. Physicians were offered the right to hold part-time hospital positions and to have a private practice if they so chose. With the assurance that they would not have to become salaried civil servants, physicians went along with the new system. While some physicians left the country, the majority joined the new system (Anderson 1989).

The postwar Labour government had set in motion an extensive program of state ownership of major industries; nationalization of the health care system was one aspect of this strategy (Aaron and Schwartz

1984). Thus, some 2,000 hospitals were nationalized (200 hospitals kept their private sector status). There was a cost-control objective to this strategy, as it would allow the government to "gain some control over both the hospital-based specialists and the nonhospital-based general practitioners to limit the use of hospital services" (Potter and Porter 1989, 345).

The world's first comprehensive national health care system, the National Health Service, formally came into being in 1948. The NHS, the cornerstone of the British welfare state, was created in the nation that was at the forefront of the industrial revolution, a strong proponent of laissez-faire economics, and an ardent supporter of limited government. The "planned economy for health" deviated from these positions (Anderson 1989).

Structure of the NHS

The NHS is divided into three distinct components for hospital care, primary care, and community/social services and long-term care. In the hospital sector, there are twelve Regional Health Authorities (RHAs) each of which is responsible for four to five million people. Every RHA is divided into approximately fifteen District Health Authorities (DHAs). Each of the almost 200 DHAs is responsible for four to five hospitals.

The primary care sector (general practitioners, dentists, pharmacists, opticians) is managed by Family Practitioner Committees (FPCs). The FPCs cover several DHA areas and receive their funding directly from the Department of Health.

Each British citizen enrolls with a general practitioner, typically one close to their home. The general practitioners (GPs) are the patient's first point of contact with the system; they make the initial diagnosis and determine when a patient will see a specialist (Day and Klein 1989). Should the GP determine that a patient needs to see a specialist, called a consultant, the GP describes the patient's condition in writing, specifies whether it is urgent or not, and requests that the specialist see the patient (Potter and Porter 1989).

The third component of the NHS is the personal social services (PSS) category. Local government provides services to patients in the community. These community-based services include nursing homes, home care for the elderly, and other support services (Maynard 1990).

NHS Financing

The British National Health Service is distinct from the private and social insurance programs discussed in earlier chapters in many facets, not least of all the financing aspect. Britain's NHS is financed mainly from general tax revenues. Eighty-four percent of total health expenditure is public; out-of-pocket payments represent approximately 4 percent of all health spending (Schieber, Poullier, and Greenwald 1992). There are patient charges for eyeglasses, dentures, and prescription drugs (the elderly are exempt). Charges are also paid by non-nationals, by individuals purchasing private care in NHS facilities, and by individuals wishing to upgrade their accommodation in NHS facilities. The NHS budget is fixed every year, based on the previous year's budget, and is adjusted according to estimates for inflation. Funds are allocated to the four regions of the United Kingdom (England, Wales, Scotland, and Northern Ireland) (Maynard 1990).

The three NHS components just described have different budgetary considerations. The hospital sector has a cash-limited budget that is allocated to the RHAs according to a formula that takes into account the age and mortality rates of the particular population it is to cover. Because the hospital sector must operate within the constraints of a limited budget, it often "seeks to push patients out into the community to meet demand for care" (Maynard 1990, 8).

The Family Practitioner component is not subject to any such budgetary constraints. Family Practitioner Committees have an open-ended budget for two main reasons. First, family practitioners such as GPs, dentists, pharmacists, and opticians are not government employees but work on contract to the NHS. Second, a very large portion of the FPC budget goes to prescription drugs. The central government, through the Pharmaceutical Price Regulation Scheme, controls the prices and profits of both domestic and foreign drug companies. The government guarantees the companies a return on capital of approximately 19 percent (*The Economist* 1989g; Maynard 1990). The FPC budget is open-ended then, because it is determined by demand: One component of the budget depends on the number of NHS contractors and the amount of services provided, and the other component is based on the drug industry's rate of return (Maynard 1990).

The third component of NHS services, local government-sponsored social services, is financed primarily with central government funds. The central government has been cutting back on these funds in recent years, however, limiting the resources available (Maynard 1990).

Physician Reimbursement

Different payment practices exist for physicians. General practitioners are independent entrepreneurs who contract with the NHS to provide health care services. Their salaries consist of three separate components.

A base salary covers the fixed costs of operating a practice. Another portion of the salary depends on the number of patients on a physician's list; this capitation rate accounts for approximately one-half of a physician's income. The third component consists of income received from services for which a fee is charged, including certain vaccinations, tests, and so forth (Maynard 1990; Potter and Porter 1989).

In general, GP salaries in the United Kingdom are lower than those in other nations. Yet, GP salaries were three times that of the national average wage in the United Kingdom in 1985 (Sandier 1990).

Hospital consultants (specialists) have the choice of taking a full-time position with the NHS or a part-time position. If they choose the latter, they are allowed to perform as many private sector services as they like. If they are full-timers, however, their private practice must be limited to 10 percent of their NHS salary (Maynard 1990).

Budgetary Constraints

While the U.S. health care system is characterized by its relatively open-ended approach to spending, Britain puts a cap on health care expenditures. The central government sets the health budget prospectively each year and then allocates amounts to the regional and district health authorities. This top-down budgetary process means that the "British government essentially decides how much health care the British people should consume every year" (Willets 1989, 66).

Limits on health budgets have collided head-on with a growing demand for health services by the population. The U.K. health care system faces the same pressures as the U.S. system, including an aging population, the high cost of advanced technology, and the spread of serious diseases such as AIDS and cancer. The widening gap between available resources and demand for care has brought the existence of rationing to the forefront (Maynard 1990, 10-11).

Perhaps the most frequently cited examples of rationing of health services in the United Kingdom are in the area of kidney disease. Aaron and Schwartz's controversial 1984 study on the availability of various medical procedures in the United Kingdom, *The Painful Prescription,* compared the rate of hemodialysis (among other procedures) in the United States and the United Kingdom. Aaron and Schwartz argue that "in imposing ... [expenditure] limits, the British have encountered problems and made choices that the U.S. will face if it should undertake to sharply limit medical expenditures" (1984, 6). The study revealed that the overall rate of kidney dialysis treatment in Britain was approximately one-third that of other Western European countries and the United States. The age of the patient was seen to be a limiting factor, as British dialysis rates for patients under age forty-five were equal to that of patients in the United States and Western Europe, but the rates declined as the patient's age increased. Kidney dialysis treatment for patients age sixty-five, for example, was performed at a rate approximately one-tenth that of other nations (Aaron and Schwartz 1984). While Britain does not have a formal, explicit age limit for dialysis treatment, it is clear that certain "policy decisions are implicitly made based on budget allocations" (Potter and Porter 1989, 351).

Critics have taken issue with Aaron and Schwartz, arguing that the study neglects the higher rate of home treatment and transplantation for kidney disease in Britain (Potter and Porter 1989). Moreover, critics contend that the underlying assumptions of the study—that the U.S. system is the baseline standard against which Britain should be measured—may be flawed due to evidence that overprovision of services may occur in the United States (Marmor and Klein 1986).

Finally, others have argued that the United States focuses on rationing in Britain to mask the deficiencies in our own health care system, particularly the existence of more than 35 million people who lack insurance—or the existence, in other words, of rationing by ability to pay. It appears that rationing is in the eyes of the beholder: To the British, the necessity of insurance benefits to attain access to care in the United States would be considered rationing (Potter and Porter 1989).

The Role of the Private Sector

Tight budgetary constraints have led to waiting lists for particular types of nonemergency surgery in Britain. Waiting lists have been a persistent feature of the NHS since its inception; the NHS was created in an environment of postwar rationing of all goods and services. Yet public willingness to wait for certain surgical procedures has steadily declined as the "democracy of the till [became] more attractive than the equity of the queue" (Day and Klein 1989, 27; Willets 1989). It is estimated that there are currently more than 900,000 people on waiting lists for such procedures as hernia repair, treatment of varicose veins, hip replacements, and cataract removal, according to the U.K. Health Department (Whitney 1992). A safety valve exists for certain procedures, however, in the form of private sector care.

There has been a significant increase in the prevalence of private medical coverage in Britain over the past two decades (see Figure 7-2). Less than 4 percent of the population was covered by private insurance in 1971, and by 1980 private coverage rates had only increased to 5 percent. As of 1989, however, approximately 11 percent of the popula-

Figure 7-2   Private Health Insurance Coverage in the United Kingdom, 1970-1992

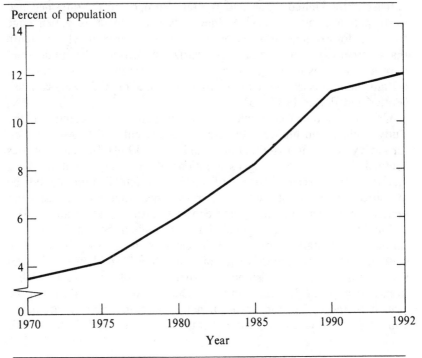

Percent of population

Source: Joseph, Bryan. "Cured in Comfort?" *Pensions World* (May 1990). Reprinted with kind permission of *Pensions World*.

tion was covered by private insurance (Joseph 1990). Between 1978 and 1988, the number of beds in private hospitals increased 50 percent (Day and Klein 1989). By 1991 12 percent of the population was covered by private insurance (Pike 1992).

The creation of the NHS did not entail the outlawing of private insurance for those benefits covered by the national plan, as the Canadian system did. And unlike Germany, where citizens can opt out of the public plan if their incomes are high enough, British citizens cannot opt out of the plan by not paying taxes (Anderson 1989). Thus, they move back and forth between the NHS and private plans. Private insurance plans allow patients to seek care in private hospitals or even in NHS hospitals that have beds for private patients—known as "pay beds." The private sector route enables patients to get around long waiting times for elective surgery. As one policy study noted: "The private patient pays to avoid waiting, the NHS patient waits to avoid paying" (Aaron and Schwartz 1984, 23).

The increased prevalence of private insurance coverage in Britain can be traced to several factors. First, there is a widespread belief that the NHS provides second-class care, due largely to the existence of waiting lists for some procedures. Private coverage allows those covered, among other things, to choose where they would like to have a particular medical procedure performed, by which specialist, and at a time that is convenient for them (Joseph 1990).

The growth of the private sector indicates there are insufficient services within the NHS causing patients to look elsewhere for care, but private sector care is specialized and limited to such elective (nonemergency) surgical procedures as hernias and varicose vein surgery (Marmor and Klein 1986). Almost 20 percent of all elective surgery is performed in the private sector, and 6 percent of acute hospital beds are private beds (Pike 1989b). It is important to note, however, that the private sector in Britain "offers treatment to improve the quality of life for people of working age rather than coping with life-threatening conditions for the population as a whole" (Day and Klein 1989, 14).

The growth of the private sector does not appear to have come at the expense of the popularity of the NHS, which despite long waiting lists for some procedures maintains a high level of public support. Increasing rates of private insurance coverage certainly reflect frustration over having to wait for certain medical procedures. But increased private coverage is also the result of patients' desires for control over such specific aspects as the timing of an operation, the particular surgeon to perform the operation, and the particular hospital in which the procedure is performed (Day and Klein 1989).

The second major factor fueling the growth of private insurance coverage is the increase in employer-provided private insurance that became popular in the 1960s and 1970s. During this period of wage freezes, employers offered private insurance benefits to augment pay packages (Potter and Porter 1989). In the 1980s, private medical coverage, once viewed as a perk reserved for executives, began to be offered to greater numbers of employees (Joseph 1990). Yet this broadening process appears to be a slow one. According to the 1988 General Household Survey, 23 percent of professionals under the age of forty-four had private medical insurance, while only 4 percent of skilled manual workers in the same age group had private coverage (*The Economist* 1989a). At any rate, U.K. employers are increasingly compelled to provide private coverage to attract and retain qualified staff members. Private insurance is also popular because coverage for an employee's family is provided as well (Joseph 1990).

Approximately 70 percent of private coverage is provided by employers. Employer-provided health insurance is a taxable benefit to the employee; the employer pays the premium (which is a tax-deductible business expense) and the employee pays taxes on the premium paid on his or her behalf. Private group insurance plans are either employer-paid plans in which the employer pays all or part of the cost of coverage, or employer-sponsored plans in which the employer sets up a group plan that provides rates lower than those of individual plans. The employer does not pay the cost of the latter for the employee. This type of coverage is not very prevalent; approximately 75 percent of voluntary plans had a participation rate of less than 5 percent according to a 1990 survey by the Wyatt Company (Joseph 1990).

Three large commercial insurers cover 90 percent of those covered by private health insurance. British United Provident Association (BUPA) is the largest private health insurer, with approximately 60 percent of the market of private insurance customers (Maynard 1990). BUPA's premiums have risen dramatically over the past decade; between 1980 and 1987 premiums rose 186 percent, while the retail price index rose only 53 percent (Day and Klein 1989). Private insurers have begun to look to their American counterparts for cost-containment strategies.

Private Sector Expands

The private sector has made very strong inroads into the hospital and nursing home sector. Nursing and residential homes for the elderly are big business for private firms, as only 20 percent of the elderly are cared for in NHS geriatric wards. The majority of the aged who are institutionalized are cared for either in public community homes or in private nursing homes (EBRI 1990). Whereas in the acute sector, private providers represent a small portion of total health care services, they have virtually taken over the institutional long-stay elderly care sector (Day and Klein 1989).

Currently only 5 percent of the British elderly (between the ages of sixty-five and seventy-four) are covered by private medical insurance for acute care coverage. A new law took effect in April 1990 that allows those over age 65 to claim private insurance premiums for acute care coverage as an income tax deduction. If a family member pays for private health insurance for a relative, the individual who pays may deduct it from his or her income tax. There has not been any indication, however, that such favorable tax treatment has increased the prevalence of private insurance among the elderly.

There may be other growth areas for private insurance coverage, simply as a consequence of increasing affluence in British society. Kenneth Clarke, minister of health under former prime minister Margaret Thatcher, predicted an expansion in private sector coverage based on "the sort of society we are." Clarke noted that "disposable incomes are rising and people with more disposable incomes are now beginning to want personalized choice in health care, in just the same way as they are accustomed to choosing their car and choosing their house" (Pike 1989a, 2).

Another factor that will affect the growth of the private sector is the reform program designed to transform the NHS into a more efficient, cost-effective health service. It is not yet clear whether the NHS reforms will benefit or harm the U.K. private insurance sector.

NHS Reforms: The White Paper

During the 1980s, the cracks in the NHS system became increasingly evident: Concerns over declining quality, the closing of hospital wards due to lack of funds, long waiting lists for certain surgical procedures, nurses' strikes, and pervasive morale problems were just a few signs of an overloaded system (Day and Klein 1989). The number of patients on waiting lists continued to increase even as more funds were being pumped into the system.

Periodic attempts to restructure the NHS in the early 1980s were shelved. Indeed, there was always a significant risk attached to any effort to reshape the NHS. The system was popular despite its obvious weaknesses, provided cradle-to-grave services, and thus touched the lives of every British citizen. It was assumed that "politicians tamper with the NHS at their peril" (Pike 1990f).

Former prime minister Thatcher was certainly never one to shy from controversy, however, and at her request, a review of the NHS was conducted in 1988. Many NHS reform proposals were considered, focusing either on the creation of an insurance-based health care system to replace the tax-financed NHS, or ways to make best use of the existing resources within the NHS through structural modifications (Day and Klein 1989).

The Thatcher government's review of the NHS culminated in a White Paper (precursor to legislation) published in January 1989, which contained the broad strokes of significant NHS reforms. The reforms focus on structural and organizational changes; market forces would be relied on to increase competition and efficiency in the health care system. The funding basis of the NHS was left completely unchanged, however, as the system was to remain tax-financed.

The White Paper set off a firestorm of protest, as doctors and other medical professionals, as well as the public, opposed the government's proposed reforms. Thatcher effectively ignored calls from the medical profession for increased funding to solve NHS problems, countering that lack of management and competition were the real source of the system's ills. Polls indicated that the public believed the controversial reforms would result in cuts in services, and heralded the end of public sector health care. Many believed the reforms represented the thin edge of the privatization wedge, and were merely a continuation of the selling spree of such state-run entities to the private sector as British Airways, British Steel, and Rolls Royce (Blendon and Donelan 1989).

The health reforms were seen as the third pillar of Thatcher's social revolution, which included the poll tax, education reforms, and NHS restructuring (Melcher and Maremont 1989; Rule 1990). Thatcher's popularity plummeted as a result of the controversial poll tax and many believe that the health reforms were yet another factor that led to her downfall.

The NHS reforms are an unlikely combination of conservatism and radicalism (Day and Klein 1989), but do not change the four original principles that created the NHS—that care be universal, comprehensive, free at the point of service, and financed by taxes. Yet the reforms do envision fundamental structural changes that will radically alter the NHS. The proposals are conservative because they do not depart from the policy positions expressed during the 1980s calling for tighter management control over the NHS. But at the same time, the proposals are quite radical because they aim to reshape the NHS through heightened competition and patient choice (Day and Klein 1989). It is interesting to note the reform program envisioned infusing "the Thatcherite principles of free markets and competition" into a publicly financed health service that provides care in public institutions (Willets 1989, 65).

Another paradoxical feature of the health reforms is that they are coming out of an environment of relative frugality in terms of health care expenditures, particularly compared to other nations such as the United States and Canada. While the United States is developing health care reform proposals in an effort to stem escalating health care expenditures, U.K. expenditures are among the lowest in the industrialized world and have increased less dramatically than other nations. For example, during the period from 1980 to 1987, when U.S. health care expenditures as a percentage of GDP increased from 9.2 to 11.2 percent, and those of Canada from 7.4 to 8.6 percent, U.K. expenditures remained fairly flat, increasing only from 5.8 to 6.1 percent of GDP (Blendon and Donelan 1989; Schieber and Poullier 1989).

Experimental Surgery or Cure-All?

The reforms contained in the White Paper were enshrined in the National Health Service and Community Care Act approved on June 29, 1990. The reforms were slated to take effect in April 1991. The main objectives of the NHS reforms were:

- to separate supply from demand—create two distinct entities, one responsible for the purchasing of health care and the other for provision;
- to create an internal market within the NHS that would make the NHS more efficient and cost-effective through competition among health care providers; and
- to empower patients to act more like consumers.

Two major changes are at the heart of the reform program. First, in the hospital sector, certain NHS hospitals (generally those with more than 250 beds) will be transformed into what will be known as NHS self-governing trusts. Second, in the primary care sector, certain general practitioners (generally those with large practices) will be given their own budgets with which to purchase care for their patients. The two reforms are described in the following sections.

Hospital Sector.   Certain large hospitals will have the opportunity to apply for status as NHS self-governing trusts. Such trusts would be independent of the district health authorities (DHA) to which all NHS hospitals previously reported. These self-governing trusts will not be privatized. They will still be part of the NHS, but will have much more freedom over their operations, and will be able to do things other hospitals cannot. For example, self-governing trusts will be able to raise their own capital and will have more control over their own finances. Moreover, they will be able to set the pay levels for their staff, which will free them from the highly centralized pay agreements that are currently fixed on a national basis (Day and Klein 1989).

The self-governing trusts will contract with district health authorities, and other self-governing hospitals, as well as private insurers to provide their services. As of April 1992, 156 hospitals had become self-governing trusts; that number is expected to double by April 1993 (Willman 1992).

The reforms would also change the status of the DHAs. In the pre-reform arrangements, DHAs, as purchasers and providers of care, were caught between the demands of both health care providers and consumers. The reforms aim to move the DHAs away from the provision of care. Instead, they will be directly responsible for negotiating contracts with health care providers. DHAs will purchase care from either NHS hospitals, private sector hospitals, or newly formed NHS self-governing trusts (Prowse 1989b, 1990b), depending on which offers the best price and quality of health care services.

Primary Care Sector.   In the primary care sector, general practitioners with large practices (generally more than 9,000 patients) will have their own budgets, which would be set according to the makeup of their patient list. GPs will use these budgets to purchase such health care services for their patients as diagnostic services, elective surgery, and outpatient care, operating in effect, like small-scale HMOs. They will shop around for the best hospital services for their patients that they can purchase from either public or private hospitals. Both public and private hospitals will compete for GPs, and thus for patients, and "money will follow patients" to the most efficient providers of care (Culyer 1989; Day and Klein 1989, 1991).

General practitioners will also be encouraged to compete for patients. The current physician reimbursement scheme allows approximately one-half of a GP's income to come from a capitation payment. This share will be increased to 60 percent to provide GPs an incentive to attract more patients. Finally, GPs will be able to keep any budget surplus they may have and use it to improve their practices (Day and Klein 1991).

The establishment of budget-holding GP practices is a radical change for the NHS. Competition among GPs for patients is expected to make them more efficient health care providers and establish linkage between the primary and secondary care sectors, as GPs coordinate the services provided to patients. In addition, it is expected that GPs, having shed their bureaucratic shackles, will be able to be much more innovative (Weiner and Ferriss 1990).

Community Care Sector.   In addition to reforms in the hospital and primary care sectors, the NHS reforms also target the community care sector, particularly the care provided to elderly, chronically ill, and mentally handicapped individuals. Chronic and long-term care services are a significant component of the NHS, and the importance of these services will increase as demographic pressures mount. It has been estimated that the number of persons age eighty-five and over, for example, will increase 65 percent over the period from 1986 to 2001.

The NHS reforms aim to promote home care services and to transform the local authorities responsible for community care from providers to purchasers of health care services. To obtain better value for taxpayers' money, legislation has been passed that would require local authorities to use case-management techniques and develop budgetary systems. The government's plan to promote home care services will undoubtedly have an effect on the private nursing home sector (Pike 1991b).

The Once and Future NHS

The Labour Party tried to make the 1991 general election a referendum on the NHS, promising to turn back the reforms and save the NHS from certain destruction at the hands of the conservatives. But the conservatives won the election and although it is still too early to say with any degree of certainty, far from destroying the NHS, the reform program appears to be having positive results. For example, the number of people waiting for an operation for more than two years fell by 16 percent from April to September 1991 (*The Economist* 1992a).

The government's plan to make government more accountable to people—dubbed the Citizen's Charter—includes the goal of making the NHS more customer-friendly. The charter promises all patients fixed appointments and guarantees a maximum amount of time a patient would have to wait for an operation (Pike 1991b). Surveys reveal that the most common reason people take out private insurance is to avoid waiting for an operation. It is not yet clear whether improved NHS service will cut into the private insurance market (Pike 1992).

The new internal market in health care will most likely not be fully up and running for another five or even ten years. Those involved in health care have little experience with competition and free-market principles; it will take time to develop the expertise to run a market-oriented system. Even though the NHS had detailed budgets for health services, there is a serious dearth of information regarding the cost of services in the NHS. In order to set up a competitive market in health care, the specific products to be sold need to be defined, data systems need to be created so that the prices of those products can be determined, and systems need to be developed to evaluate and monitor health contracts and services. The transformation of the "primitive" information system of the NHS into a modern database responsive to the complex demands of a new competitive system will be a very expensive process (Day and Klein 1991, 50; Light 1991a). Moreover, not only do patients lack the knowledge about different health services and are inexperienced in the role of educated consumer, but the district health authorities are not experienced in the purchase of health care services (Charny, Klein, Lewis, and Tipping 1990; *The Economist* 1990).

As one analyst points out, "for every one of the many positive possibilities offered by the White Paper, there is a corresponding down side, and none of us knows how these will work out" (Culyer 1989, 11). One potential problem is that the reforms may actually increase expenditure levels as investment in qualified staff, new management information, and billing systems will be necessary. Health care systems that are based on competition tend to involve higher costs, particularly for administration, as U.S. experience bears out. As the U.K. health care market becomes more competitive, administrative costs will most likely increase (Prowse 1989b, 1989c, 1990b).

Additional cost increases may also arise because the NHS will no longer be the "near-monopoly employer of labor." As a result, hospital staff salaries will likely increase because the self-governing hospitals will be able to negotiate their own pay structures (Pike 1989a).

Many analysts fear that the emphasis on competition and profit-making will supersede concern for patients. While in the past the demand for health care had been limited by fixed budgets, the introduction of budgets for GPs and the self-governing status for some NHS hospitals raises the possibility that health care providers will become captives to the emphasis on attracting more and more business. Budget-holding GPs may be tempted to shun very ill patients as they focus more on keeping any budget surplus that may remain (Prowse 1989b).

The U.S. health care system is cited as an illustration of what ultimately may happen to British health care. Yet, in response to critics who asserted that the former Thatcher government was trying to turn the U.K. health care system into a competitive, free-market system along U.S. lines, the minister of state for health wrote in the *Financial Times* that:

> [T]he U.S. health system is not a model to which anyone in this government aspires.... We are standing by the fundamental principle that the NHS should be mainly financed out of general taxation and free at the point of use. That nationwide financing system means that we avoid the American problems of insurers wanting to cover healthy groups but not risky categories (Mellor 1989).

It is still unclear whether the reforms will breathe new life into the NHS or will be merely a band-aid covering other significant problems. The reforms will not address one of the key imbalances within the system: budgetary limits versus patient demands (Day and Klein 1989). Britain's NHS already provides health services on a cost-effective basis; indeed the real issue is why Britain dedicates far fewer resources to health care than other industrialized nations (Light 1991b). As Brookings Institution economist Henry Aaron pointed out: "[T]he idea that savings from competition are going to bail them out of the dilemma is nonsense. The British have to decide whether or not they are going to spend more of their wealth on modern health care" (Lohr 1988).

Convergence

This chapter began with a brief overview of how the U.K. and U.S. systems differ. The reforms discussed, however, would seem to indicate movement within the U.K. system toward the U.S. system and that of other nations that separate health care financing from health care provision. Similarities will become sharper as the newly restructured NHS continues to evolve. The NHS reforms can be viewed as part of an emerging trend toward relying on management principles and practices to achieve greater health care efficiency and effectiveness (Day and Klein 1989). The new role for GP budget holders, for example, is a modified version of the U.S. practice of managed care through HMOs (Weiner and Ferriss 1990).

Certain parallels can be also drawn to the U.S. Medicare and Medicaid systems, as the U.S. government, like the DHAs, buys health care for the elderly and the poor from private hospitals and physicians. It is precisely this type of arrangement, with the U.K. public sector purchasing health care from competing providers, that is being established within the NHS (Prowse 1989a).

Another key area of convergence between the two systems can be seen in recent U.S. health care reform proposals that focus on the need to set limits on health care spending. Health analyst Rudolf Klein postulates that the "United States may be moving toward adopting a framework of financial regulation within which competition can flourish, just as Britain has introduced an element of competition within the already existing framework of regulation" (Klein 1991, 288-289). Regulation in the U.S. system will not be the same as regulation in Britain and competition in the NHS will not be the same as competition within the U.S. system. But despite these qualifications, one can see convergence in the concepts guiding reform in the two countries (Klein 1991).

These signs of convergence notwithstanding, fundamental differences will remain. In the final analysis, it would appear that cultural distinctions do indeed play a significant role in explaining differences between health care systems. Klein articulates the differences between the U.S. and U.K. health care systems:

I have often argued that Britain is an "original sin" society, where we don't believe that the world can be totally put to rights. We accept problems and are rather fatalistic about our capacity to deal with some of them. In contrast, America is a "perfectibility of man" society, where the view is that if there is a problem, you can solve it (quoted in Potter and Porter 1989, 364).

Such cultural differences between the two societies—such as one's stronger confidence in its problem-solving abilities—are reflected in their approaches to health care and explain British patients' tolerance of waiting lists, as well as American insistence on trying every available medical procedure when someone is ill. These profound differences render the debate over the possibility of creating an NHS in the United States, or of exporting the U.S. system to Britain, an exercise in futility "because it would mean trying to transplant cultural institutions between societies with totally different patterns of cultural values" (Rudolf Klein, quoted in Potter and Porter 1989, 364). While it is clear that the United States and Britain have two very different systems that reflect their different cultures, a shared reliance on management principles within the health care sector transcends these differences. This is reflected in the growing prominence of managed care arrangements in the U.S. system and the "managerial revolution" within the NHS (Day and Klein 1989; Pike 1990d).

Will U.S. Health Care Be Shaped by International Experience?

Introduction

In contrast to some public policy issues, health care is not an abstract concept, but rather an issue that is real and has direct impact on each and every American. The debate over the future of this nation's health care system has caught fire nationwide among corporate executives, labor union representatives, employees, health care workers, and the insurance industry—in short, all the health care payers, consumers, and providers. The consensus among these diverse groups is that this nation's costly and fragmented health care system falls short of the mark.

As a result of this consensus, the 1992 presidential election was the first election in almost three decades in which health care was a prominent issue in policy debates. The debates focused not on whether change was needed in the health care system, but rather on what the scope of that change should be. George Bush advocated incremental change and much tinkering around the edges, while Bill Clinton called for universal coverage through an overhaul of the nation's health care system. President Clinton has pledged to present a legislative proposal for congressional consideration within the first 100 days of his administration. To that end he appointed First Lady Hillary Rodham Clinton to head an interdepartmental health care task force charged with crafting a comprehensive blueprint for reform.

It is clear from the preceding analysis that no ideal health care system exists and that each system examined has its shortcomings. The U.S. health care system is one of the most technically advanced in the world, but increasing costs, declining access, and growing public dissatisfaction indicate that the system is in crisis.

The United States is distinguished from the other nations in this study because of a lack of a single system that provides universal health insurance coverage to the entire population. The U.S. approach to health insurance is a fragmented, uncoordinated patchwork of public and private programs that "underscores society's profound ambivalence about whether medical care for all is a social good, of which the cost should be borne by society," or an employment benefit for workers, with government insurance for nonworkers (Iglehart 1992a, 962). Resolving those ambivalent feelings will be an essential first step in the effort to reform the U.S. health care system.

The adoption of some form of national health insurance has been a policy issue in the United States for more than forty years. Its endurance as an issue in a world of short attention spans is evidence of significant interest (if not strong support) for the concept. If support does reach critical mass, and if a system of national health insurance is considered as a serious option for reform of the U.S. health care system, existing systems will serve as guides for the development of an American national health insurance system. As this study has indicated, different models have been operational around the world for many years and they provide a wealth of experience from which the United States can draw.

Are International Comparisons Valid?

One of the occupational hazards of comparative health analysis is that the analysis is shaped to a large degree by the type of data and information available. For example, statistics on health outcome measures indicate that other nations are getting better health status results than the United States—according to such health quality indicators as infant mortality and life expectancy. The United States spends more money on health care, both on a per person basis and as a share of total national economic output, than any other nation. The United States ranks twentieth in infant mortality, seventeenth in male life expectancy at birth, and sixteenth in female life expectancy at birth among the twenty-four OECD nations (Schieber, Poullier, and Greenwald 1991). Thus, life expectancy or infant mortality—both of which are, at best, proxy indicators of the quality of health care being delivered to the populations of various nations—and the amount of health care expenditures would not appear to be strongly related. Despite the limitations of such aggregate measures of quality, no other immediately available measures can be used for cross-national comparisons.

Some analysts argue that comparisons of infant mortality and life expectancy rates do not reflect the quality of U.S. health care. These analysts point out that the American population is more heterogeneous than those of other countries, and poverty rates among children in the United States are higher than in Japan or Western Europe. They also note that Americans' drug, drinking, and smoking habits, as well as other lifestyle characteristics, may contribute to higher U.S. infant mortality and lower life expectancy figures.

Such demographic and lifestyle factors must be taken into consideration. That the U.S. population differs markedly from those of the other nations examined in this study is undeniable. But these differences should not be used to dismiss the importance of understanding how other nations finance and organize their health care systems. Such factors as crime, drug abuse, teenage pregnancy, and so on, clearly contribute to escalating health care costs in the United States, but we do not yet have a definite sense of how much these factors contribute to the cost differential among countries (Davis 1990; Schieber and Poullier 1991). Moreover, the United States is not alone in experiencing these social problems; other nations must face them as well, albeit on a smaller scale because their populations are not as large or as diverse as that of the United States (Fuchs 1991; Starfield 1991). Clearly, more research is needed to determine how different health spending levels affect the quality of life of a given population (Schieber, Poullier, and Greenwald 1991).

Regardless of the demographic differences between the United States and other nations, the fact remains that the American health care delivery system is not reaching large segments of the population and that costs continue to escalate. Changes in the system are therefore inevitable, and other nations' health care experiences can help the United States assess reforms designed to increase the health care returns from its large financial investment (Schieber and Poullier 1990). Examining the methods of health care organization and finance of other nations is not incompatible with the recognition that the U.S. demographic and social situation is different from other nations and it can help "guard against ethnocentrism in explanation by identifying similarities in different systems" (Klein 1991, 283). All the health care systems analyzed in this study certainly face the shared problems of escalating health care costs and finite health resources.

Any reform of the U.S. health care system, even if based in part on lessons learned from other nations' systems, will certainly be shaped by the cultural, political, and economic factors that are unique to the United States. We consequently return to the question posed at the beginning of this study: What are the "politically feasible incremental changes ... that have a reasonably good chance of making things better?" (Enthoven 1990, 58). To answer this question, we must first recognize how the U.S. health care system differs from that of other industrialized nations.

The United States Stands Alone

This study has revealed the broad range of approaches to health care organization and finance in industrialized nations. The spectrum stretches from the globally budgeted, centrally run British National Health Service to the open-ended private voluntary system in the United States, and includes the provincial government-administered Canadian national health insurance system and the public/private mix of government-mandated health insurance systems in Germany, Japan, and the Netherlands. The United States emerges as one of a kind due to a number of characteristics particular to American health care.

Nature of Insurance Coverage

Health care coverage in the United States is neither universal nor comprehensive. More than 35 million Americans lack health insurance coverage, and many millions more do not have adequate coverage against the high costs of health care. Nations that provide universal coverage to their populations have accomplished this through a com-bination of compulsion and subsidization; individuals are required to have health insurance, insurers are required to cover everyone, and cross-subsidization across risk groups allows the entire population to have health insurance coverage (Fuchs 1991).

The United States has not yet reached this point because it does not accept compulsion and subsidization—the two basic premises of social insurance. Ideological factors come into play, as national health insurance is denounced by many Americans as a form of socialism. Ironically, national health insurance was introduced in Germany and Japan as an antidote to the spread of socialism (Ikegami 1991; Starr 1992).

The majority of the U.S. nonelderly population receives health insurance through private health plans tied to employment. Employers' share of health care costs continues to increase rapidly, and many corporate leaders argue that this is having a deleterious effect on the bottom line. Employees are also feeling the impact of escalating health care cost, through loss of coverage, reduction in health benefits, and the absorption of these costs through smaller wage increases. Moreover, employees are faced with a phenomenon known as "job lock": the inability to change jobs for fear of losing one's health coverage. This is not the case in other nations—even those such as Germany, Japan, and the Netherlands that have employment-based health systems—because mandated coverage ensures that an individual always has health insurance.

Role of Government

The government is a much more active participant in the health care systems in other nations. Governments are directly involved in financing health care, as well as setting overall funding levels, and establishing uniform fee schedules for physicians and annual budgets for hospitals. While one expects this to be the case in the systems of the United Kingdom and Canada, it is also true in the predominantly private systems of Germany, the Netherlands, and Japan. In these latter countries, the government serves an important role in guaranteeing universal coverage, as well as exerting a powerful influence on cost-control processes. Moreover, by setting up a payment process whereby everyone pays the same price for the same service, the problem of cost-shifting, which has become so prevalent in the United States, is nonexistent.

Government regulation of the health sector in other nations has effectively held costs in check. Moreover, as health analyst Brian Abel-Smith points out: "It is acceptable for government to do the regulating ... [and] there is no question of the regulated taking over the regulators" (Abel-Smith 1992, 415). Given the powerful interest groups supporting the U.S. health care status quo, the diffusion of power among the different U.S. governmental bodies, and Americans' inherent mistrust of government, it is not clear whether such an arrangement could be successful in the United States (Abel-Smith 1992).

Health Care Financing

All the other health care systems considered in this study are financed by tax revenues to a greater extent than the U.S. system, and, in this way, the burden of health care costs is shared by the entire society. Health premiums are based on income, and not risk status, so both the costs and risks of insurance are spread across the entire population. U.S. tax rates are low compared with other industrialized nations, which use their higher tax rates to fund social programs such as health care for their populations. For example, U.S. tax revenues, as a percentage of gross domestic product, were 30 percent in 1990, compared to 34 percent in Canada, and 37 percent in Germany and the United Kingdom (Schieber, Poullier, and Greenwald 1991). The strong anti-

Table 8-1   Health Care Cost-Containment Strategies

Target	Micromanagement	Macromanagement
Supply-side strategies	Encouragement of efficiency in the production of medical treatments through economic incentives, for example, diagnosis-related groups or capitation. Legal constraints on the ownership of health care facilities.	Regional planning designed to limit physical capacity of the health system and to ensure its desired distribution among regions and social classes.
Demand-side strategies	Conversion of patients to consumers through cost-sharing. Hands-on supervision of doctors and their patients (managed care).	Predetermined global budgets for hospitals and expenditure caps for physicians.
Strategies aimed at the market as a whole		Price controls.

Source: Reinhardt, Uwe, in *Health Care Systems in Transition: The Search for Efficiency,* p. 107. Paris: OECD, 1990.

tax climate in this country dims the chances that a health care financing approach that relies more heavily on tax revenues will be adopted in the United States in the near term.

Health Care Expenditure Limits

Perhaps the most common thread that ties the different systems examined in this study together is what can be termed "a philosophy of limits" (Levey and Hill 1989, 1752). This manifests itself in several ways, one of which is the willingness and capability on the part of payers to exert enough leverage to impose and enforce restraints to keep health costs in check. Such restraints are evident throughout the health care system, including the reimbursement methods for health care providers, the physician specialty mix, the way decisions are made regarding allocation of medical technology, and capital investment in health care facilities and equipment (Fuchs 1991).

Cost-control methods can be designed to target either the supply side or the demand side of the health care economy, through macromanagement or micromanagement of the health care sector (see Table 8-1). While the United States has focused on micromanagement strategies, most of the countries examined apply macromanagement techniques—regional planning on the supply side, coupled with fee controls and prospective global budgets on the demand side of the health care equation (Reinhardt 1990a, 106).

In other nations, powerful groups act as intermediaries to negotiate between health care providers and payers (as the sickness funds in the Netherlands and Germany), or a single body acts as the central paymaster (as the provincial governments in Canada). This is not the case in the U.S. system, for, as one analyst notes, "No other country gives doctors and hospitals so much freedom to increase their incomes through higher fees and increased use of services. No other country has a system in which the payers (government and employers) exercise so little control over spending" (Taylor 1990).

The ratio of general practitioners to specialists also sets the United States apart from other nations. In the United Kingdom and the Netherlands general practitioners serve as the health care system's gatekeepers and provide the majority of health care services. The U.S. system, in contrast, is noted for its emphasis on highly technical and specialized care. Whereas the ratio of primary care physicians to specialists in many other nations tends to be equal, only 32 percent of all physicians in the United States are trained in primary care. Such a concentration of high-cost specialists contributes to escalating health care costs (Kosterlitz 1992a).

Negotiations over physician fee levels occur in the Netherlands, Canada, Japan, and Germany, and physicians must accept the price set by the fee schedule as payment in full. Physician expenditure caps are applied in several Canadian provinces, and, until recently, in Germany. These regulations serve to control a major component of health care expenditures—providers' incomes. In contrast, "only in America have providers succeeded in commanding an ever-growing share of national economic resources" (Evans and Barer 1990, 80).

Other nations control the allocation of medical technology and capital investment for medical facilities and equipment. We have seen that the government has strict control over planning in the hospital sector in Germany and the Netherlands. In both Canada and Germany, high-cost, high-technology medical equipment is concentrated in teaching hospitals. There is no such control in the U.S. system.

Convergence among Systems

There is no one health care system that is either a completely freemarket, competitive system or a wholly regulatory system; rather, a combination of both features exists in all systems (Meyer 1990). The United States, whose system is closest to the freemarket pole of the continuum, is considering options that would increase governmental regulation throughout the health care system. The country at the market-minimized pole, the United Kingdom, has introduced significant market-based reforms into its health care system; the Netherlands has undertaken a health care reform program to introduce competition and patient choice into a system that was previously heavily regulated. These two countries have shaped their health care reforms based on the concept of managed competition, an arrangement that seems to have the flexibility to work within such different health care environments as the predominately private insurance market in the United States, the national social insurance program in the Netherlands, and the globally budgeted National Health Service in the United Kingdom (Hurst 1990).

Thus we see signs of convergence among health care systems, but it is a convergence of ideas such as managed competition that shapes specific health care institutions rather than convergence among the health care institutions themselves (Klein 1991, 289). For example, even though the Netherlands and the United Kingdom have undertaken fairly radical health care reform programs, they have kept intact their nations' health care systems (Iglehart 1992c).

Increased Regulation of the U.S. System

Increased regulation of the U.S. health care system could take several forms—from guaranteed universal access to health care through an employer mandate program, to the application of Medicare's physician fee limits for private insurance, or government regulation of insurers. According to a survey by Louis Harris and Associates for Metropolitan Life, the majority of respondents indicated that the most appropriate role for the government in the health care sector would be as a "rulemaker setting the rules for the private sector, rather than as manager and administrator" (Harris and Associates 1990, 4). Almost 80 percent of all respondents believe that government initiatives are needed to address the current health care crisis, although an overwhelming majority believe that there should continue to be a mix of public and private forces in the health care system (Harris and Associates 1990).

A 1991 study prepared by the Congressional Budget Office (CBO) noted that the experience of other nations suggests that the United States could restrain its health care costs by implementing a number of cost-control measures including: setting uniform payment levels for all health care payers (in other words, a fixed schedule of charges for physicians and hospitals coupled with a ban on billing beyond the set fee); annual limits on spending on either a regional or national basis; or expenditure targets for specific types of health care services, as in Canada's binding physician fee schedules and global hospital budgets or Germany's expenditure cap for physician services (Congressional Budget Office 1991).

The CBO recommendations are drawn from, and supported by, the experience of the nations examined in this study. Moreover, such measures would seem to be acceptable to health care leaders in the United States. Louis Harris and Associates polled the major actors in the health care system and asked what they would be willing to give up (if all other health care actors had to compromise as well). According to the survey, a majority of physician leaders would accept being paid (on the current fee-for-service basis) from a fixed budget with an expenditure cap. Moreover, a majority (albeit small—53 percent) of hospital CEOs surveyed said they were willing to accept having to operate within predetermined global budgets and to operate under a system of uniform payment levels for all health plans, both public and private (Harris and Associates 1990).

Many believe it will not be long before limits imposed on physician fees under the Medicare system will be adopted by private payers. According to a study prepared by two consumers' groups, the United States could save approximately $250 billion per year by the year 2000 if private payers were to adopt fee schedules similar to Medicare's reimbursement controls (Families USA/Citizen Action 1990).

Should the United States decide to broaden the role of regulation in the health care sector it can follow the Canadian model of government-administered insurance or the private but regulated system found in Germany. The Canadian system may entail too many sacrifices to be a realistic model for the United States. But Americans may look more seriously at the German system, given that coverage is comprehensive and universal. Health services are delivered through private channels; patients have free choice of provider and the system is employment-based. Moreover, health care is financed through contributions made by employers and employees, and doctors and hospitals have a responsibility to control health care costs. Princeton University professor Uwe Reinhardt's prediction that the U.S. system may gradually evolve toward a system similar to Germany's may prove prescient (Reinhardt 1990b).

Even Dr. James Todd, the executive vice president of the American Medical Association (AMA), is looking at the German system. Dr. Todd believes that American physicians can only hope to exert more influence on future U.S. health policy directions by securing a role for the AMA that is akin to physicians' organizations in Germany: a government-mandated role in negotiating all aspects of health policy, from cost control to access to care (Iglehart 1992b). However, the AMA is currently prevented by federal antitrust laws from collectively bargaining with health care plans. But the AMA has been working to change such laws by petitioning the Federal Trade Commission and lobbying members of Congress. If the AMA succeeds in changing the laws, the process of physician payment negotiation in the United States may start to resemble that of other nations such as Germany and Canada (Kosterlitz 1992c). These potential legal changes notwithstanding, it is important to note that the willingness of the German medical profession to self-regulate and implement cost-control policies is critical to Germany's success in controlling health care costs. It is not clear whether this arrangement would work in the American system (Klein 1991).

The Future Shape of U.S. Health Care

The national debate over reform of the ailing U.S. health care system continues to focus on the roles of the private and public sectors in the health care arena. Should health care be treated like any other good or service and be competitively bought and sold, or should it be treated as a public good guaranteed and regulated by the government? The precise organization and financing arrangements of the reformed U.S. health care system will be determined to a large degree by the balance struck between free-market competition and government regulation.

President Clinton's proposals for health care reform, while still short on specifics, generally embrace an approach known as managed competition. This approach has received strong support from a wide variety of backers. Despite this support, it is still unclear exactly what this approach will entail. In the words of one analyst, managed competition "seems to have as many definitions as it has adherents" (Kosterlitz 1993a, 99; Stout 1992a).

The three architects of managed competition are economist Alain Enthoven; Dr. Paul Ellwood, a nonpracticing pediatrician and neurologist; and Lynn Etheredger, an independent health care consultant. Their approach relies on a blend of free-market competition and government regulation to control health care costs. Under managed competition, employers would be required by law to provide a standard package of benefits for their employees. The centerpiece of the system is a network of what Enthoven calls collective purchasing agents, or health insurance purchasing cooperatives. These cooperatives would shop around for the best health plan for individuals and small employers, and would use their size to force health care providers to compete for their business based on price and quality of care. The unemployed would join health insurance purchasing cooperatives as well, but they would receive government subsidies to pay for coverage. Providers, for their part, would join together in managed care-type organizations to offer the highest quality services at the lowest cost (Enthoven 1993; Stout 1992a).

A controversial element of the managed competition proposal is a limit on the tax deductibility of employee benefits. The goal is to use the tax code to make health care consumers more cost conscious. This could be accomplished by setting a limit on the amount of benefits an employee is allowed to receive tax free; an employee would have to pay tax on any benefits above the standard limit. Advocates argue that this would give employees the financial incentive to choose the most cost-effective health plan. Another approach would be to put a cap on tax deductions that businesses are allowed to claim for health care expenses. President Clinton has not endorsed any such limits, but it is an option that is likely to receive serious consideration (Priest 1993; Stout 1992b).

Clinton's proposals diverge from the original managed competition model by the inclusion of expanded federal regulation in the form of a national health board with independence and stature similar to the U.S. Federal Reserve Board. This board would determine the basic package of benefits that employers must provide, set the maximum cost of the benefits package, and, most importantly, set limits on national health spending. Comprised of representatives of health care payers, providers, and consumers, the board would resemble Germany's Concerted Action.

Clinton's proposals thus provide for a combination of competition and regulation. Health care would continue to be provided by private doctors and hospitals, but there would be increased government regulation to ensure universal coverage and control costs. Whether this approach will provide the "best of both worlds" remains to be seen (Thorpe 1992). More importantly, serious questions remain as to how the new system would be organized and financed. The major issues to be resolved include, but are certainly not limited to: how universal coverage will be financed; how managed competition will coexist with spending limits; how the quality of health care services will be monitored; what benefits will be included in the standard benefits package; how the tax deductibility of employee health benefits will be limited; and how managed competition would work in rural areas where there are not sufficient numbers of competing providers.

Traditional Opposition to Reform on the Wane

Two powerful opponents of reform in the past—the medical community in the form of the AMA, and the insurance industry under the auspices of the HIAA—have adopted conciliatory stances that indicate that they are more open to reform than at any time in the past. Both organizations have developed their own health care reform proposals to ensure universal coverage.

The AMA endorsed Clinton's proposal for managed competition as the route to reform. The support of the AMA is surprising given the proposal's reliance on the health maintenance organizations and other managed care arrangements that have traditionally been viewed by the AMA as a threat to physician autonomy. But despite its support of managed competition, the AMA did restate its strong objection to one element of Clinton's plan: caps on health care spending. The HIAA, in dramatic reversal, endorsed certain components of President Clinton's health care reform proposals, including a requirement that all employers provide a standard package of health benefits for their employees, and limits on the tax deductibility of employer-sponsored health benefits. The HIAA also expressed willingness to accept greater government involvement in setting standard rates for hospitals and physicians (Kosterlitz 1992c; 1993a; Pear 1992).

Such a reversal of position seems to indicate acceptance on the part of these key groups of the near-term inevitability of health care reform. For the insurers, a governmentally imposed mandate on employers to provide insurance for their employees is certainly preferable to a government takeover of the insurance industry. The AMA is also being pragmatic, trying to enact changes its members will find least offensive (Kosterlitz 1992c; 1993a).

Employers have joined the insurance industry and the medical community in offering certain concessions. One large group representing employers, the Association of Private Pension and Welfare Plans, dropped its long-held opposition to mandating employer-sponsored health benefits and expressed willingness to consider some new taxes on employee health plans.

All these groups will play key roles in the national health care reform debate. But the American public is a powerful potential obstacle to reform that cannot be overlooked, since the proposed health care reforms will demand sacrifices that the public is not necessarily willing to accept. Although polls indicate that the public is in favor of health care reform, there is a dangerous mixture of confusion and apathy concerning the specifics of health care reform. Americans profess to support wholesale reform, but once they are presented with the tradeoffs and sacrifices such reform would inevitably entail—such as higher out-of-pocket costs, limits on what benefits are covered, or limits on patients' choice of physician—support quickly fades (Kosterlitz 1993b).

Gap in Perceptions

One of the more serious factors inhibiting consensus on health care reform is the "perception gap" between the public on the one hand, and political, business, and health care leaders on the other. Research conducted by the Public Agenda Foundation, in association with the Employee Benefit Research Institute and the Gallup Organization, reveals an alarming split between what the public views as the specific health care problems and potential solutions for these problems and what leaders in the fields of politics, business, and health care think about those same issues. The perception gap covers a wide array of issues ranging from how much the United States spends on health care and what the public views as its share of health care costs, to who is covered and who is not and the public's belief that the high cost of health care is merely a result of providers' greed and the waste inherent in the system (Immerwahr 1992).

The researchers concluded that the public needs a "healthy dose of realism." The public's misperceptions pose very serious obstacles to reform of the U.S. health care system because a solution to the health care crisis will never be found without a shared understanding of, and strong agreement on, precisely what ails the U.S. health care system (Immerwahr 1992). The passage and subsequent repeal of Medicare catastrophic legislation in 1989 serves as a powerful reminder of the importance of strong public support for legislation.

Do the Right Thing

Dr. Uwe Reinhardt cites a comment made by Winston Churchill during World War II and applies it to the U.S. search for health care reform alternatives: "In the long run, Americans will always do the right thing, after exploring all other alternatives" (Reinhardt 1989, 138). Compelling evidence from Europe, Japan, and Canada indicates that it is possible to maintain a system of universal health insurance, in which premiums are related to a person's income and not his or her risk status, and that costs can be controlled by one or several powerful health care purchasers—be they governmental, such as provincial governments in Canada, or nongovernmental, such as sickness funds in Germany.

The U.S. health care system will only be what we make of it. As Rosemary Stevens points out in her book on the U.S. hospital system, "the quality of American medical care is, indeed, an index of American civilization" (1989, 365). Even if the United States applies lessons learned from the experience of other nations, we will continue to have a uniquely American system reflective of our cultural preferences.

References

Chapter 1

Anderson, Odin. 1989. *The Health Services Continuum in Democratic States*. Ann Arbor, Mich.: Health Administration Press.

Blank, Robert. 1988. *Rationing Medicine*. New York: Columbia University Press.

Davis, Karen. 1990. Response to Bengt Jonsson's article in *Health Care Systems in Transition*. Paris: OECD.

Enthoven, Alain. 1990. "What Can Europeans Learn from Americans?" in *Health Care Systems in Transition*. Paris: OECD.

Evans, Robert G. 1986. "The Spurious Dilemma: Reconciling Medical Progress and Cost Control." *Health Matrix* 4, no. 1.

Evans, Robert G., and Morris L. Barer. 1990. "The American Predicament," in *Health Care Systems in Transition*. Paris: OECD.

Henke, Klaus-Dirk. 1990. Response to Bengt Jonsson's article in *Health Care Systems in Transition*. Paris: OECD.

Iglehart, John. 1989. "American Business Looks Abroad." *Health Affairs* 8, no. 4.

_____. 1990. "How Green Is Your Grass?" (Paper delivered to the Ontario Medical Association, Toronto, Canada, June 7-8).

Jonsson, Bengt. 1990. "What Can Americans Learn from Europeans?" in *Health Care Systems in Transition*. Paris: OECD.

Kirkman-Liff, Bradford. 1989. "Cost Containment and Physician Payment Methods in the Netherlands." *Inquiry* 26.

Klein, Rudolf. 1991. "Risks and Benefits of Comparative Studies: Notes from Another Shore." *Milbank Quarterly* 69, no 2.

Meyer, Jack. 1990. Response to Bengt Jonsson's article in *Health Care Systems in Transition*. Paris: OECD.

Morone, James. 1990. "American Political Culture and the Search for Lessons from Abroad." *Journal of Health Politics, Policy and Law* 15, no. 1.

Organization for Economic Cooperation and Development. 1987. Social Policy Studies No. 4. *Financing and Delivering Health Care*. Paris: OECD.

Pfaff, Martin. 1990. "Differences in Health Care Spending across Countries: Statistical Evidence." *Journal of Health Politics, Policy and Law* 15, no. 1.

Poullier, Jean-Pierre. 1986. "Levels and Trends in the Public-Private Mix of the Industrialized Countries' Health Care Systems," in ed., A. J. Culyer and Bengt Jonsson, *Public and Private Health Services.* Oxford: Basil Blackwell.

Reinhardt, Uwe. 1990. Response to Bengt Jonsson's article in *Health Care Systems in Transition.* Paris: OECD.

Chapter 2

American Management Association. 1988. "Managing Health Care Costs." *AMA Research Report.*

Andreopoulous, Spyros, ed. 1975. *National Health Insurance: Can We Learn from Canada?* New York: John Wiley and Sons.

Arnett, Elsa. 1989. "Survey: Workers Paying More for Health Care." *Washington Post,* June 22.

Ashby, John Jr. 1992. "The Burden of Uncompensated Care Grows." *Healthcare Financial Management* (April).

Bacon, Kenneth. 1989. "Business and Labor Reach a Consensus." *Wall Street Journal,* November 1.

_____. 1990. "Plan to Provide Health Insurance to All Is Being Completed by Panel in Congress." *Wall Street Journal,* March 1.

Blank, Robert. 1988. *Rationing Medicine.* New York: Columbia University Press.

Blendon, Robert. 1989. "Three Systems: A Comparative Survey." *Health Management Quarterly* 11 (First Quarter).

Blendon, Robert, and Karen Donelan. 1989. "Public Opinion and the Future of Health Benefits." *Compensation and Benefits Management* (Autumn).

Blendon, Robert, Robert Leitman, Ian Morrison, and Karen Donelan. 1990. "Satisfaction with Health Systems in Ten Nations." *Health Affairs* 9, no. 2.

Blendon, Robert, and Humphrey Taylor. 1989. "Views of Health Care: Public Opinion in Three Nations." *Health Affairs* 8, no. 1.

Blumenthal, David, and Robert Berenson. 1989. "Health Care Issues in Presidential Campaigns." *New England Journal of Medicine* 321, no. 13.

Brown, Kenneth. 1989. "What We Can Learn from the Canadian Health Care System," in EBRI's *Business, Work and Benefits: Adjusting to Change.* Washington, D.C.: Employee Benefits Research Institute.

Buckley, Patricia A., and Kenneth McLennan. 1989. "Crisis in the U.S. Health Care System: How Should Government and Industry Respond?" *MAPI Policy Review* (May).

Bureau of National Affairs. 1986. "Health Care Costs: Where's the Bottom Line?" *A BNA Special Report.* Washington, D.C.

Business and Health. "The 1990 National Executive Poll on Health Care Costs and Benefits." *Business and Health* (April).

Califano, Joseph A. 1986. *America's Health Care Revolution.* New York: Simon and Schuster.

_____. 1989. "Billions Blown on Health." *New York Times,* April 12.

Carnevale, Mary Lu. 1989. "Union Workers Begin Strike at Nynex, Bell Atlantic and Pacific Telesis Group." *Wall Street Journal,* August 7.

Chaconas, Judy. 1992. "Providers See Danger in Broadening Use of Medicare Rates." *Trustee* (May).

Clark, Stephen. 1990. "Is Business Up to the Health Care Challenge?" *Institutional Investor* (May).

Coddington, Dean, David J. Keen, Keith D. Moore, and Richard L. Clarke. 1990. *The Crisis in Health Care: Costs, Choices and Strategies.* San Francisco: Jossey-Bass.

The Conference Board. 1988. "A Harder Look at Health Care Costs." *Conference Board Research Report,* no. 910. New York, N.Y.

_____. 1989. *The Conference Board's Management Briefing: Human Resources* 5, no. 4 (April).

Congressional Budget Office. 1992. *Economic Implications of Rising Health Care Costs* (October).

Congressional Research Service. 1988a. "Health Care Expenditures and Prices." *CRS Issue Brief* (December).

_____. 1988b. "Health Care." *CRS Issue Brief* (December).

Crenshaw, Albert. 1989a. "Red Ink Forces Massachusetts to Rethink Health Insurance Program." *Washington Post,* August 7.

_____. 1989b. "Health Care: The New Labor Battleground." *Washington Post,* August 8.

Cronin, Carol. 1989. "How Congress Views a National Health Plan." *Business and Health* (July).

Culyer, A. J., and Bengt Jonsson, eds. 1986. *Public and Private Health Services.* Oxford: Basil Blackwell.

Davis, Jennifer. 1991. "Retiree Health Benefits: Issues of Structure, Financing and Coverage." *Issue Brief,* no. 112 (March). Employee Benefit Research Institute. Washington, D.C.

Davis, Karen. 1990. Response to Bengt Johnson's article in *Health Care Systems in Transition.* Paris: OECD.

Dobson, Allen, and Richard Clarke. 1992. "Shifting No Solution to Problem of Increasing Costs." *Healthcare Financial Management* (July).

The Economist. 1989. "Pay Now, Pay Later." (June 24).

_____. 1989. "Health Insurance: Who Pays?" (October 7).

Employee Benefit Research Institute. 1989a. "Managing Health Care Costs and Quality." *EBRI Issue Brief,* no. 87 (February).

_____. 1989b. "Canada's Health Care System: Lessons for the U.S." *EBRI Issue Brief,* no. 90 (May).

Enthoven, Alain, and Richard Kronick. 1989. "A Consumer-Choice Health Plan for the 1990s." *New England Journal of Medicine* (two-part series) 320, nos. 2 and 15.

Evans, Robert G. 1975. "Beyond the Medical Marketplace: Expenditure, Utilization and Pricing of Insured Health in Canada," in *National Health Insurance,* ed. Spyros Andreopoulous. New York: Wiley.

_____. 1986a. "The Spurious Dilemma: Reconciling Medical Progress and Cost Control." *Health Matrix* 4, no. 1.

_____. 1986b. "Finding the Levers, Finding the Courage: Lessons on Cost Containment in North America." *Journal of Health Politics, Policy and Law* 11, no. 4.

_____. 1987. "Hang Together or Hang Separately: The Viability of a Universal Health Care System in an Aging Society." *Canadian Public Policy* 13, no. 2.

_____. 1988. "Split Vision: Interpreting Cross-Border Differences in Health Spending." *Health Affairs* 7, no. 4.

_____. 1989. "Controlling Health Expenditures—the Canadian Reality." *New England Journal of Medicine* 320, no. 9.

_____. 1990. "Tension, Compression and Shear: Directions, Stresses and Outcomes of Health Care Cost Control." *Journal of Health Politics, Policy and Law* 15, no. 1.

_____. 1993. "Characteristics of Health Insurance and Characteristics of the Uninsured." EBRI *Issue Brief*, no. 133 (January).

Evans, Robert G., and G. L. Stoddart, eds. 1986. *Medicare at Maturity: Achievements, Lessons and Challenges.* Calgary: University of Calgary Press.

Farnham, Alan. 1989. "No More Health Care on the House." *Fortune* (February 27).

Foley, Jill. 1993. "Sources of Health Insurance and Characteristics of the Uninsured, Analysis of the March 1992 Current Population Survey." EBRI *Issue Brief*, no. 133 (January).

Freitag, Michael. 1989. "The Battle over Medical Costs." *New York Times*, August 17.

Freudenheim, Milt. 1989a. "A Health Care Taboo Is Broken." *New York Times*, May 8.

_____. 1989b. "Calling for a Bigger U.S. Health Role." *New York Times*, May 30.

_____. 1989c. "Debating Canadian Health 'Model.' " *New York Times*, June 29.

_____. 1989d. "Efforts to Reduce Retiree Costs." *New York Times*, August 15.

_____. 1989e. "Volleyball on Health Care Costs." *New York Times*, December 7.

_____. 1990. "Insurers Seek Help for Uninsured." *New York Times*, January 11.

Frieden, Joyce. 1990. "Pepper Commission Report Released." *Business and Health* (April).

Gabel, Jon, Howard Cohen, and Stephen Fink. 1989. "Americans' Views on Health Care." *Health Affairs* 8, no. 1.

Garland, Susan, and Barbara Buell. 1989. "Health Care for All or an Excuse for Cutbacks?" *Business Week* (June 26).

Geisel, Jerry. 1989. "Senate Committee Approves Revised Health Plan Mandate." *Business Insurance* (July 17).

Ginzberg, Eli. 1990. "Health Care Reform—Why So Slow?" *New England Journal of Medicine* 322, no. 20.

Gladwell, Malcolm. 1991. "Uninsured Get Less Care." *Washington Post*, January 16.

Glaser, William A. 1978. *Health Insurance Bargaining: Foreign Lessons for Americans.* New York: Gardner Press.

Gold, Allan. 1989. "The Struggle to Make Do without Health Insurance." *New York Times*, July 30.

Ham, Faith. 1989. "Who Will Pay for Health Benefits?" *Business and Health* (August).

Hamilton, Joan. 1989. "The Prognosis on Health Care: Critical—And Getting Worse." *Business Week* (January 9).

Hamilton, Joan, Emily T. Smith, and Susan Garland. 1989. "High Tech Health Care: New Medical Technologies Can Save Lives—At a Price." *Business Week* (February 6).

Harris, Louis. 1989. "Calling for Reform." *Health Management Quarterly* (Fourth Quarter).

Hayes, Donald M. 1989. "The Needs, Desires and Demands of Employers and Employees for Cost-Conscious Medical Service," in *The Medical Cost-Containment Crisis,* ed. Jack McCue. Ann Arbor: Health Administration Press.

Hilts, Philip. 1989. "Major Changes for Health System Seen in Wake of the AIDS Finding." *New York Times,* August 19.

Himmelstein, David U., and Steffie Woolhandler. 1989. "A National Health Program for the United States: A Physicians' Proposal." *New England Journal of Medicine* 320, no. 2.

Hunt, John. 1989. "Health Costs Threaten Profits in U.S." *Financial Times* (May 27).

Iglehart, John. 1989. "American Business Looks Abroad." *Health Affairs* 8, no. 4.

———. 1990. "The New Law on Medicare's Payments to Physicians." *New England Journal of Medicine* 322, no. 17.

Jasinowski, Jerry, and Sharon Canner. 1989. *Meeting the Health Care Crisis.* National Association of Manufacturers (May).

Jencks, Stephen, and George J. Schieber. 1991. "Containing U.S. Health Care Costs: What Bullet to Bite?" *Health Care Financing Review* (1991 Annual Supplement).

Kaletsky, Anatole. 1989. "Why Every Chrysler Has a $700 Health Care Bill." *Financial Times* (September 1).

Karr, Albert, and Mary Lu Carnevale. 1989. "Facing Off over Health-Care Benefits." *Wall Street Journal,* August 11.

Kinzer, David. 1988. "The Decline and Fall of Deregulation." *New England Journal of Medicine* 318, no. 2.

———. 1990. "Universal Entitlement to Health Care: Can We Get There From Here?" *New England Journal of Medicine* 322, no. 7.

Kosterlitz, Julie. 1989a. "But Not for Us?" *National Journal* (July 22).

———. 1989b. "Bottom Line Pain." *National Journal* (September 9).

———. 1989c. "The Year of Commissions." *National Journal* (October 28).

———. 1990a. "Sick about Health." *National Journal* (February 3).

———. 1990b. "Seeking the Cure." *National Journal* (March 24).

———. 1991. "The Growth Industry." *National Journal* (November 30).

———. 1992. "A Sick System." *National Journal* (February 15).

Kramon, Glen. 1989. "Small Business Is Overwhelmed by Health Costs." *New York Times,* October 1.

———. 1990. "Four Health Care Vigilantes." *New York Times,* September 24.

Lamm, Richard D. 1989. "Saving a Few, Sacrificing Many—at Great Cost." *New York Times,* August 2.

Levey, Samuel, and James Hill. 1989. "National Health Insurance—The Triumph of Equivocation." *New England Journal of Medicine* 321, no. 25.

Levit, Katharine R., and Cathy A. Cowan. 1991. "Business, Households, and Governments: Health Care Costs, 1990." *Health Care Financing Review* 13, no. 2.

Levit, Katharine R., Mark S. Freeland, and Daniel R. Waldo. 1989. "Health Spending and Ability to Pay: Business, Individuals and Government." *Health Care Financing Review* 10, no. 3 (Spring).

Levit, Katharine R., Helen Lazenby, Cathy A. Cowan, and Suzanne Letsch. 1991. "National Health Expenditures, 1990." *Health Care Financing Review* 13, no. 1.

Lyall, Sarah. 1989. "Phone Workers Strike in 15 States; Delays Expected in Assisted Calls." *New York Times,* August 7.

MacKenzie, Colin. 1989. "National Health Plan Becoming U.S. Option." *Globe and Mail* (Toronto), May 23.

MacNabb, Richard. 1988. "Health Care Costs and Cost Containment—Getting Specific." *MAPI Economic Report* (June).

Maher, Walter B. 1989. "Reform Medicare: The Rest Will Follow." *New York Times,* July 9.

Marmor, Theodore, and Rudolf Klein. 1986. "Cost vs. Care: America's Health Care Dilemma Wrongly Considered." *Health Matrix* 4, no. 1 (Spring).

McCue, Jack, ed. 1989. *The Medical Cost-Containment Crisis.* Ann Arbor, Mich.: Health Administration Press Perspectives.

Meyer, Jack, Sean Sullivan, and Nancy S. Bagby. 1986. *Health Care Today: Issues, Trends, and Developments in Cost Management.* Washington, D.C.: National Chamber Foundation.

Mitchell, Samuel. 1988. "Defending the U.S. Approach to Health Spending." *Health Affairs* 7, no. 4.

Morone, James. 1990. "American Political Culture and the Search for Lessons from Abroad." *Journal of Health Politics, Policy and Law* 15, no. 1.

O'Keefe, Janet. 1992. "Health Care Financing: How Much Reform Is Needed?" *Issues in Science and Technology* VIII, no. 3.

Organization for Economic Cooperation and Development. 1985. *Measuring Health Care 1960-1983.* Social Policy Studies, no. 2. Paris: OECD.

_____. 1987. *Financing and Delivering Health Care.* Social Policy Studies, no. 4. Paris: OECD.

_____. 1989. *OECD in Figures: Statistics on the Member Countries.* Supplement to the OECD *Observer,* no. 158 (June-July).

Pear, Robert. 1993. "Health Care Costs Up Sharply Again, Posing New Threat." *New York Times,* January 5.

Pfaff, Martin. 1990. "Differences in Health Care Spending across Countries: Statistical Evidence." *Journal of Health Politics, Policy and Law* 15, no. 1.

Poullier, Jean-Pierre. 1986. "Levels and Trends in the Public-Private Mix of the Industrialized Countries' Health Care Systems," in *Public and Private Health Services,* ed. A. J. Culyer and Bengt Jonsson. Oxford: Basil Blackwell.

Prowse, Michael. 1990a. "The Not So Great Society." *Financial Times* (April 20).

_____. 1990b. "Casualty of the Markets." *Financial Times* (April 27).

Reinhardt, Uwe. 1987. "Health Insurance for the Nation's Poor." *Health Affairs* 6, no. 1.

_____. 1989a. "Toward a Fail-Safe Health Insurance System." *Wall Street Journal,* January 11.

_____. 1989b. "Health Care Spending and American Competitiveness." *Health Affairs* 8, no. 4.

Relman, Arnold. 1988. "Assessment and Accountability: The Third Revolution in Medical Care." *New England Journal of Medicine* 319, no. 18.

_____. 1989a. "Universal Health Insurance: Its Time Has Come." *New England Journal of Medicine* 320, no. 2.

_____. 1989b. "The National Leadership Commission's Health Care Plan." *New England Journal of Medicine* 320, no. 5.

_____. 1989c. "American Medicine at the Crossroads: Signs from Canada." *New England Journal of Medicine* 320, no. 9.

_____. 1991. "Where Does All That Money Go?" *Health Management Quarterly* (Fourth Quarter).

Rich, Spencer. 1987. "U.S. Health Costs Continue Steep Rise." *Washington Post,* October 11.

_____. 1989. "Restructuring the Nation's Health System." *Washington Post,* August 10.

Rodwin, Victor G. 1987. "American Exceptionalism in the Health Sector: The Advantages of Backwardness in Learning from Abroad." *Medical Care Review* 44, no. 1.

Samuelson, Robert. 1989. "The Cost of Chaos in Health Care." *Washington Post,* September 27.

Schieber, George, and Jean-Pierre Poullier. 1988. "International Health Care Expenditure Trends: 1986." *Health Affairs* 7, no. 3.

_____. 1989. "International Health Care Expenditure Trends: 1987." *Health Affairs* 8, no. 3.

_____. 1991. "International Health Spending: Issues and Trends." *Health Affairs* 10, no. 1.

Schieber, George, Jean-Pierre Poullier, and Leslie Greenwald. 1991. "Health Care Systems in Twenty-four Countries." *Health Affairs* 10, no. 3.

_____. 1992. "U.S. Health Expenditure Performance: An International Comparison and Data Update." *Health Care Financing Review* 13, no. 4.

Service Employees International Union. 1990. *Labor and Management: On a Collision Course over Health Care.* Department of Public Policy, AFL-CIO (February).

Short, P., A. Monheit, and K. Beauregard. 1989. *A Profile of Uninsured Americans.* DHHS Publication No. (PHS) 89-3443 (September).

Smith, Mark D., Drew E. Altman, Robert Leitman, Thomas Moloney, and Humphrey Taylor. 1992. "Taking the Pulse on Health System Reform." *Health Affairs* 11, no. 2.

Snider, Sarah. 1992. "Features of Employer-Sponsored Health Plans." *EBRI Issue Brief,* no. 128 (August).

Sonnefeld, Sally T., Daniel R. Waldo, Jeffrey A. Lemieux, and David R. McKusick. 1991. "Projections of National Health Expenditures through the Year 2000." *Health Care Financing Review* 13, no. 1.

Specter, Michael. 1990. "Health Care Woes Apparent, Cure Isn't." *Washington Post,* June 15.

Starr, Paul. 1982. *The Social Transformation of American Medicine.* New York: Basic Books.

Stevens, Carol. 1989. "Why Business Is Rushing to Support NHI." *Medical Economics* (August 21).

Stout, Hilary. 1989. "Private Industry Labor Costs Rose by 4.9% in 1988." *Wall Street Journal,* January 25.

Sullivan, Louis. 1989. "How to Curb Physician Payments." *Washington Post,* July 11.

Swoboda, Frank. 1990a. "Major Firms, Unions Join in National Health Insurance Bid." *Washington Post,* March 14.

_____. 1990b. "Corporate Leaders Oppose National Health Insurance." *Washington Post,* March 27.

Swoboda, Frank, and Albert B. Crenshaw. 1989. "Pushing for National Health." *Washington Post,* September 3.

Taylor, Humphrey. 1990. "U.S. Health Care: Built for Waste." *New York Times,* April 17.

Taylor, Roger, and Bonnie Newton. 1991. "Can Managed Care Reduce Employers' Retiree Medical Liability?" *Benefits Quarterly* 7, no. 4.

Thompson, Roger. 1989. "Curbing the High Cost of Health Care." *Nation's Business* (September).

Todd, James S. 1989. "It Is Time for Universal Access, Not Universal Insurance." *New England Journal of Medicine* 321, no. 1.

Tolchin, Martin. 1989. "Sudden Support for National Health Care." *New York Times,* September 24.

U.S. Chamber of Commerce. 1990. Employee Benefits: Survey Data from Benefit Year 1989. U.S. Chamber Research Center.

U.S. Department of Commerce. 1986. *The National Insurance and Product Accounts of the United States, 1929-1982.* Washington, D.C.: Bureau of Economic Analysis (September).

———. 1990. *Survey of Current Business, Revised NIPA Estimates.* Washington, D.C.

Uchitelle, Louis. 1989. "They Are in Growing Demand, but Workers Are Settling for Less." *New York Times,* August 10.

Verhovek, Sam. 1989. "New York Health Chief Proposes Medical Insurance for All in State." *New York Times,* September 7.

Victor, Kirk. 1990. "Gut Issue." *National Journal* (March 24).

Waldo, Daniel R., Sally T. Sonnefeld, Jeffrey A. Lemieux, and David R. McKusick. 1991. "Health Spending through 2030: Three Scenarios." *Health Affairs* 10, no. 4.

Welles, Chris, and Christopher Farrell. 1989. "Insurers under Seige." *Business Week* (August 21).

Wilensky, Gail. 1988. "Filling the Gaps in Health Insurance: Impact on Competition." *Health Affairs* 7, no. 2.

Woolsey, Christine. "Canadian Health Plan." 1990. *Business Insurance* (January 22).

The Wyatt Company. *1988 Group Benefits Survey: A Survey of Health and Welfare Plans Covering Salaried Employees of U.S. Employers.* Washington, D.C.: The Wyatt Company

———. 1990a. *Management USA—Leading a Changing Work Force.* Washington, D.C.: The Wyatt Company

———. 1990b. *Medical Benefits for Active and Retired Employees.* Washington, D.C.: The Wyatt Company.

———. 1991. "Employer-Sponsored Health Benefits Programs: A Chronic Affliction or a Growing Malignancy?" Washington, D.C.: The Wyatt Company.

———. 1992. "Financing Reform: Who Will Pay the Price for America's Health Care?" *Minnesota Medicine* 75 (March). Washington, D.C.: The Wyatt Company.

Chapter 3

Anderson, Odin W. 1989. *The Health Services Continuum in Democratic States: An Inquiry into Solvable Problems.* Ann Arbor, Mich.: Health Administration Press.

Andreopoulous, Spyros, ed. 1975. *National Health Insurance: Can We Learn from Canada?* New York: John Wiley and Sons.

Barber, John. 1989. "Sick to Death." *Maclean's* (February 13).

Barer, Morris. 1988. "Regulating Physician Supply: The Evolution of British Columbia's Bill 41." *Journal of Health Politics, Policy and Law* 13, no. 1.

Barer, Morris, and Robert G. Evans. 1986. "Riding North on a South-Bound Horse? Expenditures, Prices, Utilization and Incomes in the Canadian Health Care System." In *Medicare at Maturity,* ed. Robert G. Evans and Greg L. Stoddart. Calgary: University of Calgary Press.

Barer, Morris, Robert G. Evans, and Roberta J. Labelle. 1988. "Fee Controls As Cost Control: Tales from the Frozen North." *Milbank Quarterly* 66, no. 1.

Barer, Morris L., W. Pete Welch, and Laurie Antioch. 1991. "Canadian/U.S. Health Care: Reflections on the HIAA's Analysis." *Health Affairs* 10, no. 3.

Barkin, Martin. 1988. "Cost, Quality Concern Canada, Too." *Health Management Quarterly* (Second Quarter).

Blendon, Robert. 1989a. "Three Systems: A Comparative Survey." *Health Management Quarterly* (First Quarter).

_____. 1989b. "The Public's View of Health Care and the Implications for Corporations." In *A Bottom Line Perspective on Health Care Costs.* New York: The Conference Board Research Report, no. 939.

Blendon, Robert, and Karen Donelan. 1990. "The Public and the Emerging Debate over National Health Insurance." *New England Journal of Medicine* 323, no. 3.

Blendon, Robert, and Humphrey Taylor. 1989. "Views of Health Care: Public Opinion in Three Nations." *Health Affairs* 8, no. 1.

Blendon, Robert, Robert Leitman, Ian Morrison, and Karen Donelan. 1990. "Satisfaction with Health Systems in Ten Nations." *Health Affairs* 9, no 2.

Breckenridge, Joan. 1988. "Fee System Fails to Curb Health Costs in Ontario, U.S. College Study Finds." *Globe and Mail* (Toronto), July 23.

_____. 1989. "Rationing of Health Services Attributed to Government Moves." *Globe and Mail* (Toronto), June 2.

Brown, Barry. 1989. "How Canada's Health System Works." *Business and Health* (July).

Brown, Kenneth. 1989. "What We Can Learn from the Canadian Health Care System," in EBRI's *Business, Work and Benefits: Adjusting to Change.* Washington, D.C.: Employee Benefits Research Institute.

Business and Health. 1989. "Protection from the Health Cost Storm: Is the Answer in Canada?" Special Report (July).

Chambliss, Lauren. 1990. "Just Say Aah!" *Financial World* (November 27).

Chollet, Deborah. 1990. "Update Americans without Health Insurance" EBRI *Issue Brief,* no. 104.

Claiborne, William. 1990. "Canadian Tax Revolt Intensifies." *Washington Post,* April 13.

Consumer Reports. 1990. "The Crisis in Health Insurance." (September).

Coyte, Peter C., Donald N. Dewees, and Michael Trebilock. 1991. "Medical Malpractice—The Canadian Experience." *New England Journal of Medicine* 324, no. 2.

Culyer, A. J. 1988. *Health Care Expenditures in Canada: Myth and Reality; Past and Future.* Toronto: Canadian Tax Foundation.

Culyer, A. J., and Bengt Jonsson, eds. 1986. *Public and Private Health Services.* Oxford: Basil Blackwell.

Cu-Uy-Gam, Miriam. 1989. "Cost of Keeping Canadians Healthy Soars." *Financial Post* (Toronto), (June 19).

Detsky, Allan, Howard B. Abrams, Laila Ladha, and Sidney R. Stacey. 1986. "Global Budgeting and the Teaching Hospital in Ontario." *Medical Care* 24, no. 1.

Doherty, Kathleen. 1989. "Is the Canadian System As Good As It Looks for Employers?" *Business and Health* (July).

Dougherty, N. R., and H. L. Price. 1987. "The United States and Canada: Different Approaches to Health Care." *New England Journal of Medicine* 317, no. 5.

Ellwood, Paul. 1989. "Managed Care: How Applicable for Canada?" *Financial Post* Conference (June).

Employee Benefits Research Institute. 1989. "Canada's Health Care System: Lessons for the U.S." *EBRI Issue Brief,* no. 90 (May).

Evans, Robert G. 1975. "Beyond the Medical Marketplace: Expenditure, Utilization and Pricing of Insured Health in Canada." In *National Health Insurance,* Spryos Andreopoulous, ed. New York: Wiley.

———. 1984. *Strained Mercy: The Economics of Canadian Health Care.* Toronto: Butterworths.

———. 1986a. "Finding the Levers, Finding the Courage: Lessons on Cost Containment in North America." *Journal of Health Politics, Policy and Law* 11, no. 4.

———. 1986b. "The Spurious Dilemma: Reconciling Medical Progress and Cost Control." *Health Matrix* 4, no. 1.

———. 1987. "Hang Together or Hang Separately: The Viability of a Universal Health Care System in an Aging Society." *Canadian Public Policy* 12, no. 2.

———. 1988a. "We'll Take Care of It for You: Health Care in the Canadian Community." *Daedalus* (Fall).

———. 1988b. "Split Vision: Interpreting Cross-Border Differences in Health Spending." *Health Affairs* 7, no. 4.

———. 1990. "Tension, Compression, and Shear: Directions, Stresses and Outcomes of Health Care Cost Control." *Journal of Health Politics, Policy and Law* 15, no. 1.

Evans, Robert G., Jonathan Lomas, Morris Barer, Roberta Labelle, Catherine Fooks, Gregory Stoddart, Geoffrey Anderson, David Feeny, Amiran Gafni, George Torrance, and William Tholl. 1989. "Controlling Health Expenditures— The Canadian Reality." *New England Journal of Medicine* 320, no. 9.

Evans, Robert G., and G. L. Stoddart, eds. 1986. *Medicare at Maturity: Achievements, Lessons and Challenges.* Calgary: University of Calgary Press.

Ferguson, Derek. 1990. "Patients Should Pay User Fee, Tory Says." *Toronto Star,* April 22.

Ferguson, Tim. 1990. "AMA Sounding a Clear Note, But Its Tune Has Changed." *Wall Street Journal,* April 10.

Financial Post. 1989. "Canadian Medicare Delivers Well." (April 13).

Financial Post Conference. 1989. "Health Care in Canada: Cost-Control and the Rationing of Care." Toronto (June).

Foster, Les. 1989. "Technology and Access." *Financial Post* Conference (June).

Freudenheim, Milt. 1989a. "A Health-Care Taboo Is Broken." *New York Times,* May 8.

———. 1989b. "Debating Canadian Health 'Model.'" *New York Times,* June 29.

Fuchs, Victor. 1988. "Learning from the Canadian Experience." *Health Affairs* 7, no. 4.

Fuchs, Victor, and James S. Hahn. 1990. "How Does Canada Do It? A Comparison of Expenditures for Physicians' Services in the United States and Canada." *New England Journal of Medicine* 323, no. 13.

Gabel, Jon, Howard Cohen, and Stephen Fink. 1989. "Americans' Views on Health Care." *Health Affairs* 8, no. 1.

Geddes, John. 1990. "Health Care Control Should Shift: Official." *Financial Post* (Toronto), May 14.

Ginzberg, Eli. 1990. "Health Care Reform—Why So Slow?" *New England Journal of Medicine* 322, no. 20.

Glaser, William A. 1978. *Health Insurance Bargaining: Foreign Lessons for Americans.* New York: Gardner Press.

Green, Carolyn. 1989. "Health-Care Sectors Seek Greater Cost Efficiency." *Financial Post* (June 2).

Ham, Faith. 1989. "Why Americans Like Canada's Health System." *Business and Health* (July).

Harrietha, Paul. 1989. "Dispensing with the 35-Cent Cure." *Benefits Canada* (March).

Hastings, John, and Eugene Vayda. 1986. "Health Services Organization and Delivery: Promise and Reality." In *Medicare at Maturity,* Robert G. Evans and Greg L. Stoddart, eds. Calgary: University of Calgary Press.

Health and Welfare Canada. 1989. Speaking Notes for the Honourable Perrin Beatty, P.C., M.P., Minister of National Health and Welfare. Presentation to Families U.S.A. Foundation, Washington, D.C. (October 30).

Iglehart, John K. 1986a. "Canada's Health Care System." *New England Journal of Medicine* (three-part series) 315, no. 3.

———. 1986b. "Canada's Health Care System." *New England Journal of Medicine* 315, no. 12.

———. 1986c. "Canada's Health Care System." *New England Journal of Medicine* 315, no. 25.

———. 1989. "The United States Looks at Canadian Health Care." *New England Journal of Medicine* 321, no. 25.

———. 1990a. "Canada's Health Care System Faces Its Problems." *New England Journal of Medicine* 322, no. 8.

———. 1990b. "The World of Ways and Means: A Conversation with Dan Rostenkowski." *Health Affairs* 9, no. 1.

Kaletsky, Anatole. 1989. "Why Every Chrysler Has a $700 Health Care Bill." *Financial Times* (September 1).

Kane, Rosalie, and Robert Kane. 1985. "The Feasibility of Universal Long-Term Care Benefits: Ideas from Canada." *New England Journal of Medicine* 312, no. 21.

Kosterlitz, Julie. 1989a. "Taking Care of Canada." *National Journal* (July 15).

———. 1989b. "But Not for Us?" *National Journal* (July 22).

———. 1990. "Seeking the Cure." *National Journal* (March 24).

Leader, Shelah, Jack Guildroy, Stephanie Kennan, Eugene Lehrmann, and Eva Skinner. 1988. *The Canadian Health Care System: A Special Report on Quebec and Ontario.* American Association of Retired Persons (July).

Linton, Adam. 1989. "The Ethics of Rationing Care: If We Must, How Can It Be Done Ethically?" *Financial Post* Conference "Health Care in Canada" (Toronto).

———. 1990a. "The Canadian Health Care System: A Canadian Physician's Perspective." *New England Journal of Medicine* 322, no. 3.

_____. 1990b. "Clinical Guidelines." Presentation at the Ontario Medical Association Conference "How Green Is Your Grass?" (Toronto), (June 7-8).

Lomas, Jonathan, Catherine Fooks, Thomas Rice, and Roberta Labelle. 1989. "Paying Physicians in Canada." *Health Affairs* 8, no. 1.

MacKenzie, Colin. 1989. "National Health Plan Becoming U.S. Option." *Globe and Mail* (Canada), May 23.

_____. 1990. "Allure of Canadian Health Care System Spawning Opposition, Criticism, in U.S." *Globe and Mail* (Canada), January 12.

Manga, Pran. 1988. *The Canada-U.S. Free Trade Agreement: Possible Implications on Canada's Health Care Systems.* Discussion Paper no. 348. Economic Council of Ottawa, Canada (May).

Marmor, Theodore. 1982. "Canada's Path, America's Choices: Lessons from the Canadian Experience with National Health Insurance." In *Compulsory Health Insurance: The Continuing American Debate,* Ronald Numbers, ed. Westport, Conn.: Greenwood Press.

Marmor, Theodore, and Jerry Mashaw. 1990. "Canada's Health Insurance and Ours: The Real Lessons, The Big Choices." *American Prospect* (Fall).

Matthiessen, Constance. 1990. "Should the U.S. Copy Canada?" *Washington Post,* November 27.

Meyer, Jack. 1990. Response to Bengt Jonsson's article, "What Can Americans Learn from Europeans?" In *Health Care Systems in Transition.* Paris: OECD.

Micay, Jack. 1988. "Could Free-Trade Deal Lead to Bottom-Line Medicine?" *Globe and Mail* (Canada), December 1.

Mitchell, Samuel. 1988. "Defending the U.S. Approach to Health Spending." *Health Affairs* 7, no. 4.

Morone, James. 1990. "American Political Culture and the Search for Lessons from Abroad." *Journal of Health Politics, Policy and Law* 15, no. 1.

Naylor, David. 1990. "An Overview of the Big Picture." Presentation at the Ontario Medical Association Conference "How Green Is Your Grass?" (Toronto), (June 7-8).

_____. 1991. "A Different View of Queues in Ontario." *Health Affairs* 10, no. 3.

Neuschler, Edward. 1990. *Canadian Health Care: The Implications of Public Health Insurance.* HIAA Research Bulletin (June).

Newhouse, Joseph P., Geoffrey Anderson, and Leslie L. Roos. 1988. "Hospital Spending in the United States and Canada: A Comparison." *Health Affairs* 7, no. 4.

Organization for Economic Cooperation and Development. 1985. *Measuring Health Care 1960-1983.* OECD Social Policy Studies no. 2. Paris: OECD.

_____. 1987. Financing and Delivering Health Care. Social Policy Studies no. 4. Paris: OECD.

_____. 1989. *OECD in Figures: Statistics on the Member Countries.* Supplement to the OECD *Observer* no. 158. Paris: OECD.

_____. 1990. *Health Care Systems in Transition.* Paris: OECD.

Page, Leigh. 1989. "Does Canada Offer Answers for U.S.?" *American Medical News* (April 7).

Poullier, Jean-Pierre. 1986. "Levels and Trends in the Public-Private Mix of the Industrialized Countries' Health Care Systems." In *Public and Private Health Services,* A. J. Culyer and Bengt Jonsson, eds. Oxford: Basil Blackwell.

Priest, Alicia. 1990. "Doctors, Hospital Workers Disappointed by Health-Care Share." *Vancouver Sun,* April 20.

Rachlis, Michael, and Carol Kushner. 1989. *Second Opinion: What's Wrong with Canada's Health Care System and How to Fix It*. Toronto: Collins.

Regush, Nicholas. 1987. *Condition Critical: Canada's Health Care System*. Toronto: Macmillan of Canada.

Reinhardt, Uwe. 1989a. "Toward a Fail-Safe Health Insurance System." *Wall Street Journal*, January 11.

―――. 1989b. "Health Care in Canada." Luncheon Presentation at Financial Post Conference. (June 2).

Relman, Arnold. 1986. "The United States and Canada: Different Approaches to Health Care." *New England Journal of Medicine* 315, no. 25.

―――. 1988. "Assessment and Accountability: The Third Revolution in Medical Care." *New England Journal of Medicine* 319, no. 18.

―――. 1989a. "Universal Health Insurance: Its Time Has Come." *New England Journal of Medicine* 320, no. 2.

―――. 1989b. "The National Leadership Commission's Health Care Plan." *New England Journal of Medicine* 320, no. 5.

―――. 1989c. "American Medicine at the Crossroads: Signs from Canada." *New England Journal of Medicine* 320, no. 9.

Rich, Spencer. 1990. "National Health Insurance Ruled Out." *Washington Post*, July 24.

Robbins, Aldona, and Gary Robbins. 1990. *What a Canadian-Style Health Care System Would Cost U.S. Employers and Employees*. National Center for Health Policy Studies, National Center for Policy Analysis. Dallas, Texas (February).

Rosenthal, Elisabeth. 1991. "In Canada, a Government System that Provides Health Care to All." *New York Times*, April 30.

Rublee, Dale. 1987. "Canada's Extra Billing Controversy Could Signify Implications for the U.S." *Business and Health* (January).

―――. 1989. "Medical Technology in Canada, Germany and the United States." *Health Affairs* 8, no. 3.

Schachner, Michael. 1991. "Canadian Health Care Costs." *Business Insurance* (January 7).

Schieber, George, and Jean-Pierre Poullier. 1988. "International Health Spending and Utilization Trends." *Health Affairs* 7, no. 3.

―――. 1989. "International Health Care Expenditure Trends: 1987." *Health Affairs* 8, no. 3.

Specter, Michael. 1989. "Health Care in Canada: A Model with Limits." *Washington Post*, December 18.

Stevenson, H. Michael, A. Paul Williams, and Eugene Vayda. 1988. "Medical Politics and Canadian Medicare: Professional Response to the Canada Health Act." *Milbank Quarterly* 66, no. 1.

Stoffman, Daniel. 1988. "Losing Patience: Are Hospitals Killing the Taxpayer?" *Canadian Business* (November).

Stout, Hilary. 1992. "Health Care Choices: A Bigger Federal Role or a Market Approach?" *Wall Street Journal*, January 15.

Sullivan, Louis. 1989. "How to Curb Physician Payments." *Washington Post*, July 11.

Sweet, Lois. 1990. "Is There a Bed Crisis?" *Toronto Star*, April 22.

Swoboda, Frank, and Albert B. Crenshaw. 1989. "Pushing for National Health." *Washington Post*, September 3.

Taylor, Humphrey, and Uwe E. Reinhardt. 1991. *Health Management Quarterly* (Third Quarter).

Taylor, Malcolm. 1986. "The Canadian Health Care System 1974-1984." In *Medicare at Maturity*, R. G. Evans and G. L. Stoddart, eds. Calgary: University of Calgary Press.

Thompson, Roger. 1989. "Curbing the High Cost of Health Care." *Nation's Business* (September).

Timbrell, Dennis. 1989. "Entrepreneurship Rediscovers Health Care: Beyond the Public Purse." *Financial Post* Conference.

Todd, James S. 1989. "It Is Time for Universal Access, Not Universal Insurance." *New England Journal of Medicine* 321, no. 1.

Tolchin, Martin. 1989. "Sudden Support for National Health Care." *New York Times*, September 24.

Toughill, Kelly. 1989. "1 in 6 Metro Hospital Beds Shut Down." *Toronto Star*, June 29.

———. 1990. "Our Sick Are Not Stampeding to U.S." *Toronto Star*, March 26.

Tuohy, C. J. 1986. "Conflict and Accommodation in the Canadian Health Care System." In *Medicare at Maturity*, R. G. Evans and G. L. Stoddart, eds. Calgary: University of Calgary Press.

United States Congress. 1989. *Public Health in the Provinces: Canadian National Health Insurance Strategy*. House Wednesday Group. (September 22).

United States Government Accounting Office. 1991. "Canadian Health Insurance: Lessons for the United States." Washington, D.C. (June).

University of Washington, Health Policy Analysis Program, Department of Health Services, School of Public Health and Community Medicine. 1989. *A Tale of Two Systems* (September).

Vladek, Bruce. 1986. "American Perspective: If the War of 1812 Had Turned Out Differently, Would There Now Be PPOs in Manitoba or Global Budgeting in Vermont?" In *Medicare at Maturity*, R. G. Evans and G. L. Stoddart, eds. Calgary: University of Calgary Press.

Vowles, Andrew. 1989. "The Benefits of Choice." *Benefits Canada* (December).

Walker, Michael. 1989. *Why Canada's Health Care System Is No Cure for America's Ills*. Vancouver: Fraser Institute.

Welles, Chris, and Christopher Farrell. 1989. "Insurers under Seige." *Business Week* (August 21).

Wennberg, John E. 1990. "Outcomes Research, Cost Containment, and the Fear of Health Care Rationing." *New England Journal of Medicine* 323, no. 17.

Whitcomb, Michael E., and J. P. Desgroseilliers. 1992. "Primary Care Medicine in Canada." *New England Journal of Medicine* 326, no. 22.

Wilensky, Gail. 1988. "Filling the Gaps in Health Insurance: Impact on Competition." *Health Affairs* 7, no. 2.

Winslow, Ron. 1990. "Care in Canadian Hospitals Is Equal to that in U.S., for Less, Study Says." *Wall Street Journal*, May 9.

Woods, David. 1989. "Health-Care Canadian Style: Americans Beware!" Letters to the Editor. *New York Times*, July 4.

Woolhandler, Steffie, and David U. Himmelstein. 1991. "The Deteriorating Administrative Efficiency of the U.S. Health Care System." *New England Journal of Medicine* 324, no. 18.

Woolsey, Christine. 1990. "Canadian Health Plan." *Business Insurance* (January 22).

Wyatt Company. 1990a. *Survey of Group Benefits Plans Covering Salaried Employees of Canadian Employers.* Washington, D.C.: The Wyatt Company.
_____. 1990b. *Management USA—Leading a Changing Work Force.* Washington, D.C.: The Wyatt Company.

Chapter 4

Abel-Smith, Brian. 1984. *Cost Containment in Health Care: The Experience of Twelve European Countries (1977-1983).* Luxembourg: Office of Official Publications of the European Communities.
_____. 1985. "Who Is the Odd Man Out?: The Experience of Western Europe in Containing the Costs of Health Care." *Milbank Memorial Fund Quarterly/ Health and Society* 63, no. 1.
Abel-Smith, Brian, and Alan Maynard. 1979. *The Organization, Financing and Cost of Health Care in the European Community.* Luxembourg: Office of Official Publications of the European Communities.
Altenstetter, Christa. 1985. "Hospital Policy and Resource Allocation in the Federal Republic of Germany." *In Public Policy across Nations: Social Welfare in Industrial Settings,* A. J. Groth and L. L. Wade, ed., Greenwich, Conn.: JAI Press.
_____. 1986. "German Social Security Programs: An Interpretation of Their Development, 1883-1985." In *Nationalizing Social Security in Europe and America,* D. E. Ashford and W. W. Kelley, ed., Greenwich, Conn.: JAI Press.
_____. 1987. "An End to the Consensus on Health Care in the Federal Republic of Germany?" *Journal of Health Politics, Policy and Law* 12, no. 3.
Anderson, Odin. 1989. *The Health Services Continuum in Democratic States.* Ann Arbor, Mich.: Health Administration Press.
Blanpain, Jan, L. Delesie, and H. Nys, eds. 1978. National Health Insurance and Health Resources: *The European Experience.* Cambridge, Mass.: Harvard University Press.
Blendon, Robert, Robert Leitman, Ian Morrison, and Karen Donelan. 1990. "Satisfaction with Health Systems in Ten Nations." *Health Affairs* 9, no. 2.
Brenner, Gerhard, and Dale A. Rublee. 1991. "The 1987 Revision of Physician Fees in Germany." *Health Affairs* 10, no. 3.
"Country Profile: West Germany." 1990. *IDS European Report* 343 (July).
Culyer, Anthony. 1990. "Cost Containment in Europe." In *Health Care Systems in Transition.* Paris: OECD.
Dahrendorf, Ralf. 1976. *Society and Democracy in Germany.* New York: W. W. Norton.
Davis, Karen. 1990. Response to Bengt Jonsson's article in *Health Care Systems in Transition.* Paris: OECD.
The Economist. 1988. "Europeans Seek the Right Treatment." (July 16).
Eichhorn, Siegfried. 1984. "Health Services in the Federal Republic of Germany." In *Comparative Health Systems: Descriptive Analyses of Fourteen National Health Systems,* Marshall Raffel, ed. University Park: Pennsylvania State University Press.
Evans, Robert G. 1990. "Tension, Compression, and Shear: Directions, Stresses and Outcomes of Health Care Cost Control." *Journal of Health Politics, Policy and Law* 15, no. 1.

"Federal Republic of Germany: Major Reform of the Sickness Insurance Scheme." 1989. *International Social Security Review* (February).

Fisher, Marc. 1992. "Germany's Health System: Model for America or Plan in Crisis?" *Washington Post,* December 28.

"Forum: Is Canada a Better Health Care Model for America Than Germany?" 1992. *Washington Post* (Health Section), March 3.

Glaser, William. 1978. *Health Insurance Bargaining: Lessons for Americans.* New York: Gardner Press.

———. 1983. "Lessons from Germany: Some Reflections Occasioned by Schulenburg's Report." *Journal of Health Politics, Policy and Law* 8, no. 2.

———. 1984. "Hospital Rate Regulation: American and Foreign Comparisons." *Journal of Health Politics, Policy and Law* 8, no. 4.

Godt, Paul. 1987. "Confrontation, Consent and Corporatism: State Strategies and the Medical Profession in France, Great Britain and West Germany." *Journal of Health Politics, Policy and Law* 12, no. 3.

Goebel, Willi. 1989. "Reform of Health Services in the Federal Republic of Germany." *International Social Security Review* (April).

Hamerow, Theodore, ed. 1973. *The Age of Bismarck.* New York: Harper and Row.

Henke, Klaus-Dirk. 1986. "A 'Concerted' Approach to Health Care in Financing in the Federal Republic of Germany." *Health Policy* 6.

———. 1990a. Response to Bengt Jonsson's article in *Health Care Systems in Transition.* Paris: OECD.

———. 1990b. "The Federal Republic of Germany." In *Advances in Health Economics and Health Services Research.* Supplement #1: Comparative Health Care Systems. Greenwich, Conn.: JAI Press.

Henke, Klaus-Dirk, and Cornelia S. Behrens. 1986. "The Economic Cost of Illness in the Federal Republic of Germany in the Year 1980." *Health Policy* 6.

Holborn, Hajo. 1969. *A History of Modern Germany 1840-1945.* Princeton: Princeton University Press.

Horkitz, Karen. 1990. "International Benefits: Part One—Health Care." *EBRI Issue Brief,* no. 106 (September).

Hurst, Jeremy W. 1991. "Reform of Health Care in Germany." *Health Care Financing Review* 12, no. 3.

Iglehart, John K. 1989. "The United States Looks at Canadian Health Care." *New England Journal of Medicine* 321, no. 25.

———. 1990. "The New Law in Medicare's Payments to Physicians." *New England Journal of Medicine* 322, no. 17.

———. 1991a. "Germany's Health Care System." (Part One) *New England Journal of Medicine* 324, no. 7.

———. 1991b. "Germany's Health Care System." (Part Two) *New England Journal of Medicine* 324, no. 24.

Jonsson, Bengt. 1990. "What Can Americans Learn from Europeans?" In *Health Care Systems in Transition.* Paris: OECD.

Kirkman-Liff, Bradford. 1989. "Cost Containment and Physician Payment Methods in the Netherlands." *Inquiry* 26.

———. 1990. "Physician Payment Reform and Cost-Containment Strategies in West Germany: Suggestions for Medicare Reform." *Journal of Health Politics, Policy and Law* 15, no. 1.

Kosterlitz, Julie. 1990. "Bye-Bye Canada; Hi, Germany." *National Journal* (July 21).

Light, Donald W. 1985. "Values and Structure in the German Health Care Systems." *Milbank Memorial Fund Quarterly/Health and Society* 63, no. 4.

Lockhart, Charles. 1981. "Values and Policy Conceptions of Health Policy Elites in the United States, the United Kingdom and the Federal Republic of Germany." *Journal of Health Politics and Law* 6, no. 1.

Marsh, David. 1990a. "A Gamble with Nations at Stake." *Financial Times* (May 21).

_____. 1990b. "Two Germanys Try Their Hand at Unity." *Financial Times* (August 19).

Meyer, Jack. 1990. Response to Bengt Jonsson's article in *Health Care Systems in Transition.* Paris: OECD.

Pfaff, Martin. 1990. "Differences in Health Care Spending across Countries: Statistical Evidence." *Journal of Health Politics, Policy and Law* 15, no. 1.

Reinhardt, Uwe. 1981a. "Health Insurance and Cost Containment Policies: The Experience Abroad." In *A New Approach to the Economics of Health Care,* Mancur Olson, ed. Washington, D.C.: American Enterprise Institute.

_____. 1981b. "Health Insurance and Health Policy in the Federal Republic of Germany." *Health Care Financing* Review 3, no. 2.

_____. 1986. "Resource Allocation in Health Care: The Allocation of Lifestyles to Providers." *Milbank Quarterly* 65, no. 2.

_____. 1990a. Response to Bengt Jonsson's article in *Health Care Systems in Transition.* Paris: OECD.

_____. 1990b. "West Germany's Health Care and Health Insurance System: Combining Universal Access with Cost Control." Report Prepared for the U.S. Bipartisan Commission on Comprehensive Health Care, Washington, D.C. (June 25).

Rich, Spencer. 1990. "National Health Insurance Ruled Out." *Washington Post,* July 24.

Rublee, Dale. 1989. "Medical Technology in Canada, Germany, and the United States." *Health Affairs* 8, no. 3.

_____. 1992. "Health Care Uber Alles: How It Works in Germany." *Health Care Financial Management* (January).

Sandier, Simone. 1990. "Health Services Utilization and Physician Income Trends," in *Health Care Systems in Transition.* Paris: OECD.

Schieber, George, and Jean-Pierre Poullier. 1989. "International Health Care Expenditure Trends: 1987." *Health Affairs* 8, no. 3.

_____. 1991. "International Health Spending: Issues and Trends." *Health Affairs* 10, no. 1.

Schieber, George, Jean-Pierre Poullier, and Leslie M. Greenwald. 1991. "Health Care Systems in Twenty-Four Countries." *Health Affairs* 10, no. 3.

_____. 1992. "U.S. Health Expenditure Performance: An International Comparison and Data Update." *Health Care Financing Review* 13, no. 4.

Schneider, Markus. 1991. "Health Care Cost Containment in the Federal Republic of Germany." *Health Care Financing Review* 12, no. 3.

Shulenburg, J.-Matthias Graf. 1983. "Report from Germany: Current Conditions and Controversies in the Health Care System." *Journal of Health Politics, Policy and Law* 8, no. 2.

Simanis, Joseph G. 1990. "National Expenditures on Social Security and Health in Selected Countries." *Social Security Bulletin* 53, no. 1.

Spencer, Charles D., and Associates, Inc. 1989-1992. *International Benefits Information Service.*

Stevens, Carol. 1992. "Does Germany Hold the Key to U.S. Health Care Reform?" *Medical Economics* (January 6).

Starr, Paul. 1982. *The Social Transformation of American Medicine.* New York: Basic Books.

Stone, Deborah A. 1977. "Professionalism and Accountability: Controlling Health Services in the United States and West Germany." *Journal of Health Politics, Policy and Law* 2, no. 1.

―――. 1979. "Health Care Cost Containment in West Germany." *Journal of Health Politics, Policy and Law* 4, no. 2.

―――. 1980. *The Limits of Professional Power: National Health Care in the Federal Republic of Germany.* Chicago: University of Chicago.

―――. 1991. "German Unification: East Meets West in the Doctor's Office." *Journal of Health Politics, Policy and Law* 16, no. 2.

Swabey, John. 1990. "Social Security in the German Democratic Republic." *Benefits and Compensation International* (June).

United States General Accounting Office. 1991. "Health Care Spending Control: The Experience of France, Germany, and Japan" (November).

Will, Wolfgang. 1989. "Health Reform in the Federal Republic of Germany." *Benefits and Compensation International* (August).

Wysong, Jere A., and Thomas Abel. 1990. "Universal Health Insurance and High-Risk Groups in West Germany: Implications for U.S. Health Policy." *Milbank Quarterly* 68, no. 4.

Zollner, Detlev. 1982. "Germany." In *The Evolution of Social Insurance, 1881-1981,* P. A. Kohler and H. F. Zacher, eds. London: Frances Pinter.

Chapter 5

Abel-Smith, Brian. 1988. "The Rise and Decline of the Early HMOs: Some International Experiences." *Milbank Quarterly* 66, no. 4.

―――. 1992. "Cost Containment and New Priorities in the European Community." *Milbank Quarterly* 70, no. 3.

Blanpain, Jan, Luc Delesie, and Herman Nys. 1978. *National Insurance and Health Resources: The European Experience.* Cambridge, Mass.: Harvard University Press.

Blendon, Robert J., Robert Leitman, Ian Morrison, and Karen Donelan. 1990. "Satisfaction with Health Systems in Ten Nations." *Health Affairs* 9, no. 2.

Enthoven, Alain. 1990. "What Can Europeans Learn from Americans?" In *Health Care Systems in Transition.* Paris: OECD.

Frieden, Joyce. 1992. "Is Dutch Health Care a Model for the U.S. Health Care System?" *Business and Health* (May).

Greenberg, Warren. 1990. "Get Rid of Health Benefits on the Job." *Washington Post,* September 25.

Groot, L. M. J. 1987. "Incentives for Cost-Effective Behavior: A Dutch Experience." *Health Policy* 7.

Horkitz, Karen. 1990. "International Benefits: Part One—Health Care." *EBRI Issue Brief,* no. 106 (September).

IBIS Review. 1990. "Dutch Government Takes New Look at Dekker Plan to Reform Health Insurance." (April).

Janssen, Richard, and Jan van der Made. 1990. "Privatization in Health Care: Concepts, Motives and Policies." *Health Policy* 14.

Jonsson, Bengt. 1990. "What Can Americans Learn from Europeans?" In *Health Care Systems in Transition.* Paris: OECD.

Keijser, Guido, and Bradford Kirkman-Liff. 1992. "Competitive Bidding for Health Insurance Contracts." *Health Policy* 21.

Kirkman-Liff, Bradford. 1989. "Cost Containment and Physician Payment Methods in the Netherlands." *Inquiry* 26.

——. 1991. "Health Insurance Values and Implementation in the Netherlands and the Federal Republic of Germany: An Alternative Path to Universal Coverage." *Journal of the American Medical Association* 265, no. 10 (May 15).

Lapre, Ruud. 1988. "A Change of Direction in the Dutch Health Care System?" *Health Policy* 10.

Lapre, Ruud, and Aad A. de Roo. 1989. "Medical Specialist Manpower Planning in the Netherlands." *Health Policy* 15.

Letts, Laurie. 1989. "Dutch Propose Total Reform of Health Insurance System." *IBIS Review* (March).

Ministry of Welfare, Health and Cultural Affairs. 1988. *Changing Health Care in the Netherlands.* Rijswijk.

——. 1989. *Health Insurance in the Netherlands.* Rijswijk.

Naaborg, Ronald. 1991. "Changing the Health Care System in the Netherlands: The End of a Period of Cost Containment?" *International Social Security Review* 44, no 3.

Reier, Sharon. 1990. "The Dutch Model." *Financial World* (November 27).

Schieber, George, and Jean-Pierre Poullier. 1989. "International Health Care Expenditure Trends: 1987." *Health Affairs* 8, no. 3.

——. 1991. "International Health Spending: Issues and Trends." *Health Affairs* 10, no. 1.

Schieber, George, Jean-Pierre Poullier, and Leslie M. Greenwald. 1992. "U.S. Health Care Expenditure Performance: An International Comparison and Data Update." *Health Care Financing Review* 13, no. 4.

Spencer, Charles D., and Associates. 1989-1992. International Benefits Information Service Briefing Service. Chicago, Ill.

Starfield, Barbara. 1991. Primary Care and Health: A Cross-National Comparison." *Journal of the American Medical Association* 266, no. 16.

van de Krol, Ronald. 1990. "Rosy Picture Starts to Pale." *Financial Times,* Survey of the Netherlands, (December 4).

van de Ven, Wynand. 1987. "The Key Role of Health Insurance in a Cost-Effective Health Care System." *Health Policy* 7.

van Etten, G. M. 1990. "Recent Developments in Health Policy in the Netherlands." Presentation given to World Health Organization seminar on Health Services in Europe in the 1990s. Prague (September 25-27).

Chapter 6

Abe, M. A. 1985. "Hospital Reimbursement Schemes: Japan's Point System and the United States' Diagnosis-Related Groups." *Medical Care* 23, no. 9.

Blendon, Robert, Robert Leitman, Ian Morrison, and Karen Donelan. 1990. "Satisfaction with Health Systems in Ten Nations." *Health Affairs* 9, no. 2.

Brannigan, Michael. 1992. "Medicare and Culture in Japan." Letter to Editor. *Health Affairs* 11, no. 1.

Butler, Robert N., and Masako M. Osako. 1990. "Planning for Old Age: How Japan Is Looking Ahead." *Washington Post,* June 5.

The Economist. 1990. "Japanese Health Care: Keeping Well in Their Own Way" (July 7).

———. 1991. Health Care Survey (July 6).

Eisenstodt, Gale. 1992. "The Doctor's Margin." *Forbes* (November 23).

Employee Benefit Research Institute. 1989. "Japan Copes with Its 'Honorable Elders': Retirement and Health Benefit Systems in Japan." EBRI Issue Brief no. 92 (July).

Evans, Robert G. 1990. "Tension, Compression, and Shear: Directions, Stresses and Outcomes of Health Care Cost Control." *Journal of Health Politics, Policy and Law* 15, no. 1.

Fujii, Mitsuru, and Michael Reich. 1988. "Rising Medical Costs and the Reform of Japan's Health Insurance System." *Health Policy* 9.

Hashimoto, Masami. 1984. "Health Services in Japan." In *Comparative Health Systems,* Marshall Raffel, ed. University Park: Penn State University Press.

Horkitz, Karen. 1990. "International Benefits: Part One—Health Care." *EBRI Issue Brief,* no. 106 (September).

Iglehart, John K. 1988a. "Japan's Medical Care System." (Part I) *New England Journal of Medicine* 319, no. 12.

———. 1988b. "Japan's Medical Care System." (Part II) *New England Journal of Medicine* 319, no. 17.

Ikegami, Naoki. 1991. "Japanese Health Care: Low Cost Through Regulated Fees." *Health Affairs* 10, no. 3.

Levin, Peter J., Jay Wolfson, and Hiroko Akiyama. 1987. "The Role of Management in Japanese Hospitals." *Hospital and Health Services Administration* (May).

Maher, Walter. 1990. "Back to Marketplace Basics." *Health Affairs* 9, no 1.

Marmor, Theodore. 1992. "Japan: A Sobering Lesson." *Health Management Quarterly* (Third Quarter).

McNerney, Walter. 1990. "A Macroeconomic Case for Cost Containment." *Health Affairs* 9, no. 1.

Ministry of Health and Welfare. 1988. "Health and Welfare in Japan." Tokyo, Japan.

Mitchell, Samuel. 1990. "Competitiveness and Excellence: Health Costs and U.S. Business." *Health Affairs* 9, no. 1.

Murdo, Pat. 1989. "Challenges to Japan's Health Insurance System." *Japan Economic Institute Report,* no. 16A (April 21).

———. 1991. "Japanese Health-Care System No Panacea for Ailing U.S. Program." *Japan Economic Institute Report,* no. 25A (July 5).

National Federation of Health Insurance Societies. 1992. *Health Insurance and Health Insurance Societies in Japan 1992.* Tokyo, Japan.

Organization for Economic Cooperation and Development. 1990. *Health Care Systems in Transition.* Paris: OECD.

Powell, Margaret, and Masahira Anesaki. 1990. *Health Care in Japan.* London: Routledge.

Reinhardt, Uwe. 1989. "Health Care Spending and Competitiveness." *Health Affairs* 8, no. 4.

_____. 1990. "Health Care Woes of American Business: Reinhardt Responds." *Health Affairs* 9, no. 1.

Sandier, Simone. 1990. "Health Services Utilization and Physician Income Trends" *in Health Care Systems in Transition*. Paris: OECD.

Schieber, George, and Jean-Pierre Poullier. 1989. "International Health Care Expenditure Trends: 1987." *Health Affairs* 8, no. 3.

_____. 1991. "International Health Spending: Issues and Trends." *Health Affairs* 10, no. 1.

Schieber, George, Jean-Pierre Poullier, and Leslie M. Greenwald. 1991. "Health Care Systems in Twenty-Four Countries." *Health Affairs* 10, no. 3.

_____. 1992. "U.S. Health Expenditure Performance: An International Comparison and Data Update." *Health Care Financing Review* 13, no. 4.

Schramm, Carl. 1990. "Living on the Short Side of the Long Run." *Health Affairs* 9, no. 1.

Simanis, Joseph. 1990. "National Expenditures on Social Security and Health in Selected Countries." *Social Security Bulletin* 53, no. 1.

Social Insurance Agency. 1988. *Outline of Social Insurance in Japan*. Tokyo, Japan.

Social Security in Japan. 1988. "About Japan Series," no. 17. Tokyo, Japan: Foreign Press Center.

Spencer, Charles D., and Associates. 1990. "Japan Plans to Spend 6 Trillion Yen for Elder Care." *IBIS Review* (June).

Steslicke, William E. 1982. "Development of Health Insurance Policy in Japan." *Journal of Health Politics, Policy and Law* 7, no. 1.

_____. 1989. "Health Care and the Japanese State." In *Success and Crisis in National Health Systems*, Mark Field, ed. New York: Routledge.

Tanaka, Shigeru. 1990. "Japan." *Advances in Health Economics and Health Services Research, Supplement 1: Comparative Health Systems*. Greenwich, Conn.: JAI Press.

Toh, Tsuneyoshi. 1986. "Medical Costs to Increase with Aging Population." *Business Japan* (June).

United States General Accounting Office. 1991. "Health Care Spending Control: The Experience of France, Germany, and Japan" (November).

van Wolferen, Karel. 1989. *The Enigma of Japanese Power*. New York: Alfred Knopf.

Wall Street Journal. 1990. "Workplace: Working out Personnel Puzzles of the '90s" (July 6).

Wolfson, Jay, and Peter Levin. 1986. "Health Insurance, Japanese Style." *Business and Health* (May).

The Wyatt Company. 1990. "Management USA—Leading a Changing Work Force." Washington, D.C.: The Wyatt Company.

Yoshikawa, Aki. 1992. "Japan's Changing Health Care Environment." Letter to Editor. *Health Affairs* 11, no. 1.

Chapter 7

Aaron, Henry, and William B. Schwartz. 1984. *The Painful Prescription*. Washington, D.C.: Brookings Institution.

_____. 1990. "Rationing Health Care." In *Across the Board* (July/August).

Abel-Smith, Brian. 1985. "Who Is the Odd Man Out?: The Experience of Western Europe in Containing the Costs of Health Care." *Milbank Memorial Fund Quarterly/Health and Society* 63, no. 1.

———. 1992. "Cost Containment and New Priorities in the European Community," *Milbank Quarterly* 70, no. 3.

Anderson, Odin W. 1989. *The Health Services Continuum in Democratic States: An Inquiry into Solvable Problems.* Ann Arbor, Mich.: Health Administration Press.

Birch, Stephen. 1988. "DRGs U.K. Style: A Comparison of U.K. and U.S. Policies for Hospital Cost Containment and Their Implications for Health Status." *Health Policy* 10.

Blendon, Robert J., and Karen Donelan. 1989. "British Public Opinion on National Health Service Reform." *Health Affairs* 8, no. 4.

Blendon, Robert, Robert Leitman, Ian Morrison, and Karen Donelan. 1990. "Satisfaction with Health Systems in Ten Nations." *Health Affairs* 9, no. 2.

Cairncross, Frances. 1987. "For Better U.K. Health Service, Management, Competition Needed." *Financier* (December).

Caring for People—Community Care in the Next Decade and Beyond. 1989. London: Her Majesty's Stationery Office.

Charny, M., R. Klein, P. A. Lewis, and G. K. Tipping. 1990. "Britain's New Market Model of General Practice: Do Consumers Know Enough to Make it Work?" *Health Policy* 14.

Culyer, Anthony. 1989. Presentation at *Financial Post* conference "Health Care in Canada." (Toronto), (June).

Day, Patricia, and Rudolf Klein. 1989. "The Politics of Modernization: Britain's National Health Service in the 1980s." *Milbank Quarterly* 67, no. 1.

———. 1991. "Britain's Health Care Experiment." *Health Affairs,* 10, no. 3.

The Economist. 1987. "Health: Thinking the Unthinkable." (August 22).

———. 1988a. "A Private Cure?" (February 6).

———. 1988b. "Competing Prescriptions." (February 27).

———. 1988c. "Competitive Cure." (May 7).

———. 1988d. "A Slow Cure for Health." (November 19).

———. 1988e. "Half-Bold on Health." (December 17).

———. 1989a. "No Stopping Her." (February 4).

———. 1989b. "Short on Detail, Long on Questions." (February 25).

———. 1989c. "Creeping Radicalism." (April 15).

———. 1989d. "How the Doctors See It." (May 27).

———. 1989e. "Still in Search of a Cure." (August 19).

———. 1989f. "Dangerous Doctors." (August 19).

———. 1989g. "A Tighter Prescription." (September 30).

———. 1989h. "Fanfare for a Year to Avoid." (November 16).

———. 1990. "Treatment Suspended." (June 16).

———. 1991a. "Watered Down Medicine." (March 30).

———. 1991b. "Health Care Survey." (July 6).

———. 1992a. "Getting a Kick out of Reforms." (January 18).

———. 1992b. "Rolling Back the Private Sector." (June 6).

Egerton, John. 1990. "Here's How Rationing of Care Really Works." *Medical Economics* (November 26).

Employee Benefit Research Institute. 1990. *EBRI Issue Brief* (September).

Enthoven, Alain. 1990. "What Can Europeans Learn from Americans?" In *Health Care Systems in Transition.* Paris: OECD.

_____. 1991. "Internal Market Reform of the British National Health Service." *Health Affairs* 10, no. 3.

Ginsburg, Paul. 1990. Book Review. *Journal of Health Politics, Policy and Law* 15, no. 3.

Ham, Christopher. 1988. "Governing the Health Sector: Power and Policy Making in the English and Swedish Health Services." *Milbank Quarterly* 66, no. 2.

Hurst, Jeremy W. 1991. "Reforming Health Care in Seven European Nations." *Health Affairs* 10, no. 3.

Iglehart, John K. 1989. "From Research to Rationing: A Conversation with William B. Schwartz." *Health Affairs* 8, no. 3.

Jonsson, Bengt. 1990. "What Can Americans Learn from Europeans?" In *Health Care Systems in Transition*. Paris: OECD.

Joseph, Bryan. 1990. "Cured in Comfort?" *Pensions World* (May).

Klein, Rudolf. 1991. "Risks and Benefits of Comparative Studies: Notes from Another Shore." *Milbank Quarterly* 69, no. 2.

Kosterlitz, Julie. 1989. "Random Rationing." *National Journal* (April 22).

Light, Donald W. 1990a. "Learning from Their Mistakes?" *Health Service Journal* 100, no. 5221 (October 4).

_____. 1990b. "Bending the Rules." *Health Service Journal* 100, no. 5222 (October 11).

_____. 1991a. "Perestroika for Britain's NHS." *The Lancet* 337, no. 874 (March 30).

_____. 1991b. "Observations on the NHS Reforms: An American Perspective." *British Medical Journal* 303, no. 6802 (September 7).

Lister, John. 1986. "Shattuck Lecture—The Politics of Medicine in Britain and the United States." *New England Journal of Medicine* 315, no. 3 (July 17).

Lohr, Steve. 1988. "British Health Service Faces a Crisis in Funds and Delays." *New York Times*, August 7.

Lynch, Tom. 1989. "Auditors Claim Inefficiency May Impede NHS Reform." *Financial Times* (August 16).

Marmor, Theodore, and Rudolf Klein. 1986. "Cost vs. Care: America's Health Care Dilemma Wrongly Considered." *Health Matrix* 4, no. 1.

Maynard, Alan. 1990a. "The United Kingdom." In *Advances in Health Economics and Health Services Research, Supplement 1: Comparative Health Systems*. Greenwich, Conn.: JAI Press.

_____. 1990b. "The Case of Britain." *Health Policy* 15.

Mechanic, David. 1985. "Cost Containment and the Quality of Medical Care: Rationing Strategies in an Era of Constrained Resources." *Milbank Memorial Fund Quarterly/Health and Society* 63, no. 3.

Melcher, Richard, and Mark Maremont. 1989. "Thatcher's New Revolution." *Business Week* (May 1).

Mellor, David. 1989. "Why There Is No Choice but Change." *Financial Times* (August 30).

Merrill, Jeffrey, and Alan B. Cohen. 1987. "The Emperor's New Clothes: Unraveling the Myths about Rationing." *Inquiry* 24.

Organization for Economic Cooperation and Development. 1990. *Health Care Systems in Transition*. OECD Social Policy Studies, no. 7. Paris.

Paton, Calum. 1986. "British and American Health Policy: Recent Lessons from One System to the Other." *International Journal of Health Planning and Management* 2.

Pettigrew, Andrew, Lorna McKee, and Ewan Ferlie. 1988. "Understanding Change in the NHS." *Public Administration* 66, no. 3.

Pfaff, Martin. 1990. "Differences in Health Care Spending across Countries: Statistical Evidence." *Journal of Health Politics, Policy and Law* 15, no. 1.

Pike, Alan. 1989a. "Health Care." *Financial Times* Survey (April 11).

———. 1989b. "Doctors Resist the Prescription." *Financial Times* (April 27).

———. 1989c. "Doctors Reject Plans for Health Reform." *Financial Times* (May 4).

———. 1989d. "Doctors Urge Public Outcry against Health Reforms." *Financial Times* (5 July).

———. 1989e. "Waiting Lists at Hospitals Longest for Many Years." *Financial Times* (October 21-22).

———. 1990a. "U.K. Health Care." *Financial Times* Survey (January 29).

———. 1990b. "Financial Incentives to Encourage NHS to Refurbish Older Hospitals." *Financial Times* (February 5).

———. 1990c. "Mood of Emergency on the Wards." *Financial Times* (March 10).

———. 1990d. "An Age of Reform Dawns for Britain's Health Service." *Financial Times* (July 3).

———. 1990e. "Health Managers Put Trust in Consultation." *Financial Times* (October 8).

———. 1990f. "Perilous Path that Leads to NHS Reform." *Financial Times* (November 24).

———. 1990g. "Health Reforms under Attack." *Financial Times* (November 26).

———. 1990h. "State Hospitals Win Right to Control Their Finances." *Financial Times* (December 5).

———. 1991a. "A Delicate Operation." *Financial Times* (March 28).

———. 1991b. "In Need of Care and Attention." *Financial Times* (July 30).

———. 1992. "Stitch-Up Treatment." *Financial Times* (September 13).

Potter, Christopher, and Janet Porter. 1989. "American Perceptions of the British National Health Service: Five Myths." *Journal of Health Politics, Policy and Law* 14, no. 2.

Prowse, Michael. 1989a. "A Healthy Skepticism." *Financial Times* (July 27).

———. 1989b. "Competitors in White Coats." *Financial Times* (August 22).

———. 1989c. "An Explosive Recipe." *Financial Times* (November 27).

———. 1990a. "Rewriting the NHS Rule Book." *Financial Times* (January 19).

———. 1990b. "Buying on Behalf of Patients." *Financial Times* (February 28).

———. 1991. "Be Grateful for the NHS." *Financial Times* (May 20).

Rogaly, Joe. 1989. "The Doctors Carve up the Tories." *Financial Times* (October 20).

Rule, Sheila. 1990. "Quite Enough of Thatcher." *New York Times,* April 8.

Sakala, Carol. 1990. "The Development of National Medical Care Programs in the United Kingdom and Canada: Applicability to Current Conditions in the United States." *Journal of Health Politics, Policy and Law* 15, no. 4.

Sandier, Simone. 1990. "Health Services Utilization and Physician Income Trends." In *Health Care Systems in Transition.* Paris: OECD.

Schieber, George, and Jean-Pierre Poullier. 1989. "International Health Care Expenditure Trends: 1987." *Health Affairs* 8, no. 3.

———. 1990. "Overview of International Comparisons of Health Care Expenditures." In *Health Care Systems in Transition.* Paris: OECD.

———. 1991. "International Health Spending: Issues and Trends." *Health Affairs* 10, no. 1.

Schieber, George, Jean-Pierre Poullier, and Leslie M. Greenwald. 1992. "U.S. Health Expenditure Performance: An International Comparison and Data Update." *Health Care Financing Review* 13, no. 4.

Scott, Doug. 1991. "An Age of Change: The U.K. National Health Service." *Benefits and Compensation International* (April).

Underwood, Lynn. 1989. "Public Indifference to Private Health?" *Director* (September).

Wall Street Journal. 1989. "Drifting to National Health," July 10.

Weiner, Jonathan P., and David M. Ferriss. 1990. "GP Budget Holding in the United Kingdom: Learning from American HMOs." *Health Policy* 16.

Whitney, Craig. 1989a. "After Decade of Thatcherism, Have British Values Altered?" *New York Times,* May 2.

_____. 1989b. "Thatcher's New Health Plan: An Outcry Rises on All Sides." *New York Times,* June 26.

_____. 1991. "British Health Service, Much Beloved But Inadequate, Is Facing Changes." *New York Times,* June 9.

_____. 1992. "Health Care Evolves as Issue in Britain's General Election." *New York Times,* March 28.

Willets, David. 1989. "The British Public and the Debate over the National Health Service." *Health Affairs* 8, no. 4.

Willman, John. 1992. "New Structure Expected to Manage NHS." *Financial Times* (August 21).

Working for Patients. 1989. London: Her Majesty's Stationery Office (January).

Chapter 8

Abel-Smith, Brian. 1985. "Who Is the Odd Man Out?: The Experience of Western Europe in Containing the Costs of Health Care." *Milbank Memorial Fund Quarterly/Health and Society* 63, no. 1.

_____. 1992. "Cost Containment and New Priorities in the European Community." *Milbank Quarterly* 70, no. 3.

Blendon, Robert, Robert Leitman, Ian Morrison, and Karen Donelan. 1990. "Satisfaction with Health Systems in Ten Nations." *Health Affairs* 9, no.2.

Clark, Stephen. 1990. "Is Business Up to the Health Care Challenge?" *Institutional Investor* (May).

Clinton, Bill. 1992. "The Clinton Health Care Plan." *New England Journal of Medicine* 327, no. 11.

Congressional Budget Office. 1991. *Rising Health Care Costs: Causes, Implications and Strategies.* Washington, D.C.: U.S. Congress.

Davis, Karen. 1990. Response to Bengt Jonsson's article in *Health Care Systems in Transition.* Paris: OECD.

Eckholm, Erik. 1991. "Rescuing Health Care." *New York Times,* May 2.

Enthoven, Alain. 1990. "What Can Europeans Learn from Americans?" In *Health Care Systems in Transition.* Paris: OECD.

_____. 1992. "Commentary: Measuring the Candidates on Health Care." *New England Journal of Medicine* 327, no. 11.

_____. 1993. "The History and Principles of Managed Competition." *Health Affairs Supplement* 1993.

Etheredge, Lynn, and Stanley Jones. 1991. "Managing a Pluralist Health System." *Health Affairs* 10, no. 1.

Evans, Robert G., and Morris L. Barer. 1990. "The American Predicament." In *Health Care Systems in Transition.* Paris: OECD.

Families USA Foundation in cooperation with Citizens Action. 1990. *To the Rescue: Toward Solving America's Health Cost Crisis.* Washington, D.C. (November).

Fuchs, Victor R. 1991. "National Health Insurance Revisited." *Health Affairs* 10, no. 4.

Louis Harris and Associates, Inc. 1990. "Trade-Offs and Choices: Health Policy Options for the 1990s." A survey conducted for the Metropolitan Life Insurance Company.

Holoweiko, Mark. 1992. "How Four Health-Care Gurus Would Change American Medicine." *Medical Economics* (February 17).

Hurst, Jeremy. 1990. Response to Enthoven's article in *Health Care Systems in Transition.* Paris: OECD.

Iglehart, John K. 1992a. "The American Health Care System—Introduction." *New England Journal of Medicine* 326, no. 14.

——. 1992b. "The American Health Care System—Private Insurance." *New England Journal of Medicine* 326, no. 25.

——. 1992c. "Desperately Seeking Solutions." *Health Management Quarterly* (Third Quarter).

Ikegami, Naoki. 1991. "Japanese Health Care: Low Cost through Regulated Fees." *Health Affairs* 10, no 3.

Immerwahr, John. 1992. "Faulty Diagnosis: Public Misperceptions about Health Care Reform." A Report from the Public Agenda Foundation. New York, N.Y.

Jencks, Stephen, and George J. Schieber. 1991. "Containing U.S. Health Care Costs: What Bullet to Bite?" *Health Care Financing Review* (Annual Supplement). Jonsson, Bengt. 1990. "What Can Americans Learn from Europeans?" In *Health Care Systems in Transition.* Paris: OECD.

Kane, William. 1992. "Physicians' Role in Containing Costs." *Journal of Health Care Benefits* 2, no. 1 (September/October).

Klein, Rudolf. 1991. "Risks and Benefits of Comparative Studies: Notes from Another Shore." *Milbank Quarterly* 69, no. 2.

Kosterlitz, Julie. 1991a. "Softening Resistance." *National Journal* (January 12).

——. 1991b. "Agenda-Setting ... Again." *National Journal* (January 19).

——. 1991c. "Establishing a Free Market for Health Care." *National Journal* (January 26).

——. 1991d. "Radical Surgeons." *National Journal* (April 27).

——. 1992a. "Wanted: GPs." *National Journal* (September 5).

——. 1992b. "Less-Radical Surgery." *National Journal* (September 19).

——. 1992c. "Survival Tactics." *National Journal* (October 24).

——. 1993a. "Excess Baggage." *National Journal* (February 9).

——. 1993b. "Dangerous Diagnosis." *National Journal* (January 16).

Levey, Samuel, and James Hill. 1989. "National Health Insurance—The Triumph of Equivocation." *New England Journal of Medicine* 321, no. 25.

Meyer, Jack. 1990. Response to Bengt Jonsson's article in *Health Care Systems in Transition.* Paris: OECD.

Murray, Alan. 1992. "Candidates Fall Short on Health Care Reform with Proposals Marked by Gaps, Equivocation." *Wall Street Journal,* October 15.

Office of National Cost Estimates. 1990. "National Health Expenditures, 1988." *Health Care Financing Review* 11, no. 4.

Pear, Robert. 1992. "In Shift, Insurers Ask U.S. to Require Coverage for All." *New York Times,* December 3.

Pope, Gregory C., and John E. Schneider. 1992. "Trends in Physician Income." *Health Affairs* 11, no. 1.

Priest, Dana. 1992. "Differing Prescriptions for Nation's Ailing System." *Washington Post,* October 13.

———. 1993. "Draft CBO Report Backs Tax on Some Employee Health Benefits." *Washington Post,* January 7.

Prowse, Michael. 1991. "The Malaise in U.S. Health Care." *Financial Times* February 4.

Reinhardt, Uwe. 1989. "Health Care in Canada: Cost Control and the Rationing of Care." Luncheon Address at *Financial Post* conference. June 1-2, 1989. Toronto, Canada.

———. 1990a. Response to Bengt Jonsson's article in *Health Care Systems in Transition.* Paris: OECD.

———. 1990b. "West Germany's Health-Care and Health-Insurance System: Combining Universal Access with Cost Control." Paper prepared for the U.S. Bipartisan Commission on Comprehensive Health Care. Washington, D.C. (August 30, 1989, Revised June 25, 1990).

———. 1992a. "Pricing Health Care: Hotels and Airlines Do It, Why Not Hospitals?" *Wall Street Journal,* January 14.

———. 1992b. "Neither Is the Free Market." *Washington Post,* March 22.

———. 1992c. "Commentary: Politics and the Health Care System." *New England Journal of Medicine* 327, no. 11.

Rich, Spencer. 1991a. " 'MediPlan': Coverage for Rest of U.S." *Washington Post,* January 28.

———. 1991b. "National Health Insurance Proposed." *Washington Post,* March 7.

Schieber, George, and Jean-Pierre Poullier. 1990. "Overview of International Comparisons of Health Care Expenditures." In *Health Care Systems in Transition.* Paris: OECD.

———. 1991. "International Health Spending: Issues and Trends." *Health Affairs* 10, no. 1.

Schieber, George, Jean-Pierre Poullier, and Leslie Greenwald. 1991. "Health Care Systems in Twenty-Four Countries." *Health Affairs* 10, no. 4.

Schieber, Sylvester. 1990. *Benefits Bargain: Why We Should Not Tax Employee Benefits.* Washington, D.C.: Association of Private Pension and Welfare Plans.

Siler, Julia Flynn, and Susan B. Garland. 1991. "Let's Play 'Shuffle the Costs.' " *Business Week* (January 14).

Starfield, Barbara. 1991. "Primary Care and Health: A Cross-National Comparison." *Journal of the American Medical Association* 266, no. 16.

Starr, Paul. 1992. "The Ideological War over Health Care." *New York Times,* February 4.

Stevens, Rosemary. 1989. *In Sickness and in Wealth: American Hospitals in the Twentieth Century.* New York: Basic Books.

Stout, Hilary. 1991. "Health Care Choices: A Bigger Federal Role or a Market Approach?" *Wall Street Journal,* January 15.

———. 1992a. "Idea of Managed Competition Gains Support." *Wall Street Journal,* November 2.

_____. 1992b. "Benefits-Taxation Idea Returns to White House under Clinton after Failing as a Bush Proposal." *Wall Street Journal,* December 30.

Sullivan, Louis. 1992. "The Bush Administration's Health Care Plan." *New England Journal of Medicine* 327, no. 11.

Taylor, Humphrey. 1990. "U.S. Health Care: Built for Waste." *New York Times,* April 17.

Thorpe, Kenneth. 1992. "The Best of Both Worlds: Merging Competition and Regulation." *Journal of American Health Policy* (July/August).

Whitcomb, Michael E., and J. P. Desgroseilliers. 1992. "Primary Care Medicine in Canada." *New England Journal of Medicine* 326, no. 22.

Winslow, Ron. 1991. "Some Companies Try 'Managed Care' in Bid to Curb Health Costs." *Wall Street Journal,* February 1.

The Wyatt Company. 1990. *Management USA—Leading a Changing Workforce.* Washington, D.C.: The Wyatt Company.

Index